# The River and the Gauntlet

# The RIVER and the GAUNTLET

*Defeat of the Eighth Army by the Chinese Communist Forces, November, 1950, in the Battle of the Chongchon River, Korea*

*by*

S. L. A. MARSHALL

Consultant, Operations Research Office, Johns Hopkins University;
Infantry Operations Analyst, ORO, G3, Eighth Army, Korea;
Chief Historian, European Theater of Operations

GREENWOOD PRESS, PUBLISHERS
WESTPORT, CONNECTICUT

*Maps and Drawings by* H. GARVER MILLER

The Library of Congress cataloged this book as follows:

Marshall, Samuel Lyman Atwood, 1900–
    The river and the gauntlet; defeat of the Eighth Army
by the Chinese Communist forces, November, 1950, in the
Battle of the Chongchon River, Korea, by S. L. A. Marshall. Westport, Conn., Greenwood Press [1970, °1953]

    x, 385 p. illus., maps. 23 cm.


    1. Ch'ŏngch'ŏn-gang, Battle of, 1950. 2. U. S. Army. Eighth
Army. 3. Korean War, 1950–1953 —Regimental histories — U. S. —
Eighth Army. I. Title.

DS918.2.C4M3   1970      951.9'042        74–100239
SBN 8371–3011–5                                    MARC

Library of Congress         70 [4]

To the Staff of the Eighth Army,
resolute men of a breed whose usual portion is
hard work. sacrifice. and brickbats.

# CONTENTS

# FIELD MAPS

# The River and the Gauntlet

# 1

# Between Fog and Dark

On THANKSGIVING NIGHT, 1950, TWO ARMIES CON-
fronted each other along the valley of the Chongchon River,
a broad but shallow stream which flows southwestward to the
Yellow Sea through northwestern Korea.

Both armies were poised to attack on the morrow.

There the likeness in their situations ended. Deployed in
line to the south of the river, the United States Eighth Army
was an open book. Its battle objective and hour of movement
had been published to the world; war correspondents had described in intimate detail the strength and location of its
forces. Concentrated in a tight maneuver mass, guarded by
an entrenched screen, north of the river, the Chinese Communist Army was a phantom which cast no shadow. Its every
main secret—its strength, its position, and its intention—had
been kept to perfection, and thereby it was doubly armed.

From these ingredients came inevitable surprise, as complete as any ever put upon an army. There resulted one of the
major decisive battles of the present century followed by the
longest retreat in American history. No course other than the
long withdrawal would have saved the defeated host and preserved its cause.

In the hour of its defeat the Eighth Army was a wholly
modern force technologically, sprung from a nation which
prides itself on being as well informed as any of earth's
people.

The Chinese Communist Army was a peasant body composed in the main of illiterates. Much of its means for getting

1

the word around were highly primitive. In recent centuries, its people had displayed no great skill and less hardihood in war. But they matured their battle plan and became victors on the field of the Chongchon because they had a decisive superiority in information.

Men ask why it happened. Though the battle's course has remained a mystery and the modern world knows less of it than of actions fought near the dawn of history, public curiosity about how the surprise was accomplished runs ahead of public interest in what came of it.

It may seem pointless to protest this lack of perspective. The explanation of how the Eighth Army was deceived by its enemy is hardly separable from the story of its reaction to the unexpected situation. But in my judgment, there is no doubt about the main theme. All Americans had some share in the mistakes which precipitated the winter battle with the Chinese; from the record of error lessons may be drawn in time to our possible profit. On the other hand, it fell to but a few of our countrymen to redeem with their sweat, courage, and lives the situation thus made.

The story lies in whether they did meanly or nobly. Compared to this drama, all that went before, including the illusions and misgivings of those who directed it, have only the importance of the orchestral overture. The play's the thing.

Part of the setting is here described only that those who read will not enter the battle blind, and in the modest hope that if there is to be an end to unjust criticism, it will be made not by indifference but by that compassion which is born of better understanding.

American forces in the Far East had long been well aware of the close affinity between the Chinese Communist armies and the Red cohorts of North Korea. During the American occupation of South Korea, North Korean regiments had shuttled into Manchuria and back to gain battle seasoning fighting the Chinese Nationalists. Under heavy pressure, Chinese units used North Korea as a sanctuary, crossing into one corner of it when pursued, pausing a while for rest and rehabilitation, and then slipping into Manchuria again across Korea's northwest border.

The significance of these reciprocal accommodations was understood at full value by the American establishment. News of the movements was supplied mainly by an indigenous intelligence network which had been procured catch-as-catch-can and was compensated in the same way. When the occupation ended amid signs that Amerian policy was tending toward a forswearing of interest in the Korean Republic that network disintegrated. Work began on another net under the auspices of the Far East Command. It was just past the cocoon stage when South Korea was invaded, and it never fluttered thereafter. In the overrunning, its individuals may have been caught and either killed or made prisoner; at least nothing was heard henceforth from this group of agents.

Beginning its war under that handicap, Eighth Army understood early and well exactly what the handicap meant. Before its first-arriving regiments had formed up for defense of the Naktong Line, General Headquarters took steps to school new native agents who could be dropped into enemy country. The start was made 9 July 1950, and the school had to be moved from place to place as the battle line shifted. That was of minor concern to the Koreans who had been accepted for this crude and abnormally hard enterprise. There were no parachutes in Korea to facilitate their jump training. In lieu thereof and until parachutes arrived, they were hardened to their jobs by practice in stepping from the rear of a speeding jeep, so that they would master the knack of tumble-and-roll.

In due course, those who survived this rigor were taught how to make a night descent by parachute, what to look for, and how to get the word back. These are complex and deadly tasks for the fully skilled and war-wise hand; in this case the human material were simple Asiatics who knew little of military operations and less about the treachery of a descending silk canopy. The one point in their favor was that they were willing to try.

All of the drops into that formidable country of ups and downs were made under cover of dark. Such was the shortage of air transport that frequently the Commanding General's plane was used to carry these men into nowhere. Only the loss rate fulfilled expectations. Less than 50 per cent of the men parachuted into enemy country during the summer of 1950 ever got back to American lines. Of these marked missing, the record is mute as to how many were killed and what number defected; the circumstances whisper that all are entitled to the benefit of the doubt.

The ones who made the round trip returned laden with information. But such were its vagaries and contradictions that when sifted by intelligence, it shed but little light. There had to be many more drops and the agents had to acquire wisdom through hard experience before the net could pay real dividends on its heavy human cost.

The story of that period contains the minor footnote that the most productive line-crosser serving Eighth Army was a Korean woman. She didn't jump, she walked. Her cushion was not a parachute but a year-old baby strapped to her back. She figured rightly that she would be above suspicion because of her cargo. She made many trips, she observed carefully, and reported clearly. It is not a pleasant picture—the power of the United States using a Korean weanling as a shield. But though it is not pleasant, in that hour it was the device that best served.

Still other agents were put ashore in small boats behind the enemy lines. The fault in the work of these castaways was that most of what they learned which might have been of value didn't get back to the army in the essential time. To supplement this deep casting, Eighth Army trained and installed from thirty to forty Korean agents in each division Intelligence section. Their contribution was to roam behind enemy lines during periods of contact and return—if possible—with news of what the Communists were doing. It is not good work even when one can get it.

In World War II, the great boon to intelligence procedure was the perfecting of photo interpretation, particularly in Pacific operations against the Japanese. The planes which hunted with cameras instead of bombs were without mercy. They killed insidiously by depriving military protection of its ultimate secret. Their still pictures came alive under the trained gaze of the truly qualified "PI" who could read out of shadows the probable size of a garrison and see in flecks of white the count and locations of its gun emplacements. So highly developed became this skill under the pressures of an unlimited national commitment that when the Gilbert Islands were to be invaded, an interpreter read an air photo of one target, counted the number of latrine pits, and estimated within twenty the strength of the enemy defenders.

Beginning its war in Korea, Eighth Army did not possess even the shell of such a system. There were no interpreters, no air crews adequately trained for the mission, and no production apparatus to process work had the specialists been available. This service had been one of the major casualties of the breakneck demobilization of 1945-46. The machinery was junked or warehoused. The experts doffed their uniforms and returned to their former tasks. They could not be replaced overnight. Brains aren't made in a hurry.

Getting along without air photo coverage imposes acute strain on a modern field force. But it is worse still to have to fight without maps. While the columns of 24th Division were falling back toward the Naktong, presses started rolling in Japan to print the maps to be dropped by planes to serve the already deployed force. One large strip of country over which troops fought west of the port of Masan had never been mapped; it was a nightmare for the American artillery.

These were grave, almost fatal, intelligence shortages. They put an excessive strain on all hands, simply to cope with the day-to-day operations problem. Even so, almost from the first shot, Eighth Army Intelligence was awake to the threat of intervention by the Communist Chinese. It was viewed not as a remote possibility but as the major contingency. In mid-

July, before the Pusan perimeter had formed, the first memorandum was sent down to troops urging them to isolate and report any appearance by Chinese soldiers in the ranks opposite.

The memorandum caused many alarms and not a few excursions. In late July one unit fighting southwest of Taegu reported the capture of a Chinese soldier. Army sent an officer to interrogate him. He proved to be simply a Korean idiot afflicted with mongolism. Again, in late August in the Castle area north of Taegu, 25th Division reported capturing a prisoner who told of a battle group in the Communist line which "held itself apart and spoke a strange language." Patrols were dispatched to prowl the area which he had indicated, but the tale remained unconfirmable. These were typical incidents among many such; all were investigated and none stood up.

From the air, watch was kept on the upper west coast road between Sinuiju and Sinanju as continuously as the weather permitted. Lieut. Gen. Walton H. Walker believed the Chinese would come by that route—the shortest line from Manchuria—if at all. After the Inchon landing and the mid-September breakout, Fifth Air Force became able to move its bases farther northward, and the watch was then intensified. But there were obscurations. The Air Force at that time had no means of detecting night movement unless the moon was bright. Furthermore, the Manchurian-formed 6th N.K. Division was operating along the coastal strip in this same period, thereby prompting false reports that the Chinese were on their way.

It was General Walker's view that either the Inchon landing, in a military way, or the crossing of the 38th Parallel, because of its political implications, would give the Chinese their hour of greatest opportunity, and that if they did not reach for one or the other of these openings, they would be unlikely to intervene. When both events had passed and the Chinese had not stirred, Walker and his staff felt a considerable relief.

But the respite was brief indeed. Eighth Army troops had hardly set foot upon Communist soil when Red China's Premier Chou En-lai made his declaration that his people would not "supinely tolerate seeing their neighbors being savagely invaded by imperialists." Thereupon a dread apprehension gripped the headquarters. Whereas the threat was greatly discounted in the United States, Walker and his staff gave full weight to the words and to the warning which came from the Indian Ambassador in Peiping that Communist China was preparing to enter the war.

Also, as October opened, Eighth Army published to its forces the Chinese Communist order of battle along the Yalu River front, an evaluation which subsequent events proved to be amazingly accurate.

But so delicate was this subject that Intelligence promptly came at cross-purposes with itself. At the merest mention of Chinese intervention in the official reports, our South Korean ally had a tremor phasing into paralysis. The psychological impact upon the field agents was tremendous; they acted like men hexed and their interest in their work dropped to zero. If the periodic report took a pessimistic tone, the effect on the Koreans was such that officers had to be sent forth to calm them with assurances that the words were probably exaggerated. KAMAG—the group of American advisers serving with the South Korean divisions—reported that troops had become highly nervous, with signs of demoralization increasing. The Defense Minister, Shin Sung Mo, urged that the advance toward the Yalu be halted. With some mental reservations, Intelligence therefore took a more conservative tone.

Its words were in any case written on sand, for all impressions of what portended were quickly recast on the basis of two greatly differing events, both widely reported in the press of the United States. From Japan, a five-star commander flew to Wake Island to confer with the President; in North Korea, nine simple-seeming Chinese prisoners were gathered in by troops of the ROK II Corps. The nine men had not been captured in battle. Several had been routed out of barns and other hiding places; some were walk-ins who had entered the ROK lines in voluntary surrender.

These events—the Wake visit by the General and the first appearance of a new enemy in his theater of war—happened just three days apart. They were not unconnected.

There is invariably a lag in intelligence flow between the frontal unit where the thing happens and the higher headquarters where it is evaluated. ROK II Corps at first reported possession of two Chinese prisoners, then later added to the number. Summary interviews conducted on the spot revealed mainly that the captives belonged to small provisional units of Chinese which had entered Korea as "volunteers" after being dragooned from their regular formations.

These morsels of information—hardly significant in themselves—were about all that had reached topside when two days later General MacArthur flew to Wake Island to tell President Truman that Chinese intervention was not a plausible or potent threat in the war.

From ROK II Corps, the nine prisoners were flown to Pyongyang. There, in Kim Il Sung's former headquarters, they were given a prolonged grilling by Eighth Army Intelligence. All were more than ordinarily responsive and quite willing to tell what they knew. They described in great detail the forced draft by which they became "volunteers." They identified themselves as coming from the 54th, 55th, and 56th Special Units, which had been cadred out of the 38th, 39th, and 40th Chinese Armies. The special units were each "the size of an infantry regiment, about 3,000 men." Then they named the places and dates on which the columns, totaling about 9,000 men, crossed the Yalu River. The prisoners wore no insignia of rank or unit. Their uniforms resembled the North Korean. They belonged to that Army now, they said, having been told by their leaders before departing from Manchuria that they no longer counted as Chinese. One of them piously added, "Only God knows what we are doing here."

In that hour it impressed no one as extraordinary that this small group of enemy soldiers who had played such a mongrel part on the field, having quitted the fight without firing a shot, should possess so much vital and detailed information. They had played their parts with broad-faced innocence, and quite likely they were nothing more than they seemed. If it is an intriguing thought that they were a deliberate plant, steeped in Oriental cunning, it still must be dismissed as idle speculation. The nine men were quickly lost to sight in the anonymity which cloaks the small prisoner in war. Today there is no item in proof that they were enemy agents assigned to carry a misleading story into the opposing camp instead of mere malingerers fleeing a fight. What is known is that, innocent or otherwise, the act became the perfect prelude to the Chinese deception.

At Pearl Harbor surprise had come against the United States like a bolt from the blue. The surprise in South Korea had been another full-armed effect, landing sudden and total. There was less chance that it could be done a third time in the same way, and besides there was something better.

Surprise could be won by eschewing all of its conventional methods. The new way entailed the slow creep forward . . . the appearance of confusion and weakness in commitment to screen a well-laid offensive plan . . . the pretense of picking around with a finger to cover the raising of a mailed fist . . . the schooling of troops on details of the order of battle so that they would be always communicative and in the beginning always wrong . . . the hiding of armies in motion by marching them only under cover of night and holding them under rooftops during day . . . the staging of little actions to divert attention from the chosen battlefield.

These things were warp and woof of the enemy pattern of deception. All were suited to the Oriental nature. But what most favored their cunning was the wide-front deployment of Eighth Army and the great spaces intervening between its tactical columns as they neared the Manchurian border.

By 24 October that prize looked almost won. The 7th ROK Regiment of 6th ROK Division descended into the Yalu gorge near Changju while at the same time the American 24th Infantry Division staged to the river's mouth near Namsi-dong. It seemed in that hour that Eighth Army and X Corps had but to close ranks along the frontier in leisurely fashion to bring the war to a close.

Then occurred the first shock warning. At Unsan on the night of 26 October one squadron of the 8th Cavalry Regiment entered into a fully prepared enemy ambush, got cut off, and lost a great part of its strength. Its parent, 1st Cavalry Division, was on a rescue mission at the time. Two days earlier one of 6th ROK Division's columns had been hit and broken in a fight east of Unsan. Already north of the Chongchon, the cavalry division was rushed along to stiffen the ROKs. These developments signaled more than a brief flare-up of organized resistance after weeks of desultory skirmishing. Both traps had been sprung by Chinese troops in superior strength.

The full significance of these events is revealed only by the map. Unsan is about fifty miles southeastward of the position which 7th ROK Regiment was holding on the Yalu. Beyond the mouth of the Chongchon River the Korean coast runs almost due west to Manchuria. Because of that accident in geography, the Chinese force which had staged the ambushes was in correct position to cut the highway serving 24th Division by making a short march directly south.

Of 344 enemy prisoners taken during the Unsan mêlée, however, only two were Chinese. Their stories started in much the same way as the revelations by the original nine deserters. They also were involuntary "volunteers." They, too, had no interest in the war. They had crossed the border with the 54th, 55th, and 56th Special Units. Then came the surprise! These units, they said, were not regiments; they were full-sized divisions.

Extrapolating, Intelligence concluded that somewhere between 30,000 and 60,000 Chinese had already crossed into Korea.

General Walker had not waited upon this estimate. The affair at Unsan had convinced him that the piecemeal advance toward the frontier was a bid for disaster. He ordered his forward elements to give up their ground and reform along

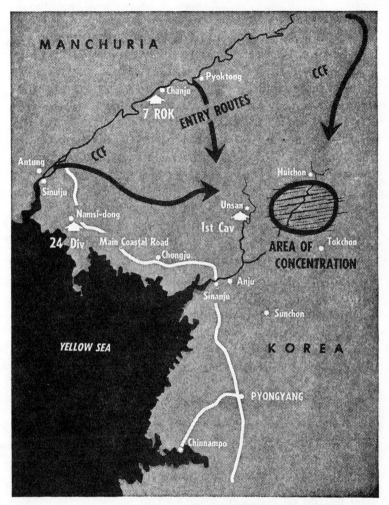

**DEVELOPMENT IN OCTOBER**

Eighth's Army northern thrust and the CCF advance to the build-up
area.

the line of the Chongchon to the south amid the main body of the army.

From its advanced ground near the Yalu River mouth, the 24th Division beat back to the new line without seeing any Chinese. The 7th ROK Regiment was less fortunate. One enemy column from the 42nd Army, after crossing the frontier at Antung, at first marched straight toward 24th Division, then took an east-turning road which put it across the 7th ROK rear. To save themselves, the ROKs took to the hills, abandoning all equipment. When at last the weaponless regiment reached friendly lines, it had lost 500 men but was not altogether empty-handed; a bottle of Yalu water had been brought back as a present for Synghman Rhee.

The halt called by General Walker was by nature a normal military precaution for which the besetting conditions within his own force strongly argued. The 2nd and 25th Divisions were not yet up to the Chongchon. The other divisions were north of it and feeling pressures which might prove uncontainable. Although the army had taken greater than average risks during the period of unlimited pursuit, the new situation obviously called for marking time and closing ranks to the limit possible until some better measure could be taken of the unknown.

All of the factors bearing upon this decision cannot be read out of the Intelligence periodic of 29 October, though the words show that eyes were open to the danger: "The imperative considerations are at present: Are these reinforcing elements the beginning of a commitment in piecemeal fashion so as to secure approaches to the border area by emphasis on defensive tactics? Or is this the beginning of open intervention on the part of Chinese forces to defeat UN forces in Korea? At present, the evidence is insufficient to say."

Not less in magnitude was the G4 (Supply) problem. During the period of pursuit, Eighth Army had been marching into enemy country with only one day's supply at hand, and it was hard pressed to keep it at that level. All air bases were still in South Korea, Kimpo being the main center. The port of Chinnampo was in the process of being cleared of enemy mines. Air Force had got its advanced detachments and some planes into Pyongyang, but because of highway traffic congestion couldn't get supply forward to maintain operations. Competing for road space, Eighth Army had perforce run low on all of the goods men require for living and for fighting. So the time had come to get things in hand and store a few cakes against tomorrow. Winter was coming and the troops were not yet winterized.

In Eighth Army G3 (Operations), what had happened at Unsan had scored a deep impression. The operators took it as proof that China was in deadly earnest: it was not to be a game of run-sheep-run. Their further conclusions were based simply on the developments diagramed on the overlay sheet. There was indicated the undertaking of a major build-up by the Chinese to the west of Huichon, within the highway triangle which has Unsan at its apex. G3 continued to give that area somber regard. Its main idea was right. But its pin-pointing was off about the width of a lead pencil (on an average map) from the ground where the enemy was concentrating. A small difference—but decisive.

Such, then, were the doubts and the problems which pressed upon this headquarters during the early days of November while the army was gathering itself along the Chongchon. It would be inaccurate to say that all saw the storm signals clearly and cried warning. But there was a sense of impending change and a realization that the army must replenish toward it. China's intentions remained the great riddle and the key was still missing. There were three interpretations of the object sought by this new enemy on Eighth Army's immediate front: (a) a limited assist to help the North Koreans hold a defensive base within their own country; (b) a show of force to bluff Eighth Army away from the Manchurian frontier, and (c) a screening movement to cover the advance of armies from behind the Yalu.

According to the knowledge then present in Eighth Army, each of these was a reasonable estimate. But all were equally wrong. The enemy armies were already there.

In the conduct of military operations, great illusions are born out of a poverty of information coupled with a wealth of confidence that the enemy in any case is unequal to the task of promoting a decisive change in events. This illusion was nearly complete. The enemy was standing in depth right over the county line. Begun on 14 October, the Chinese movement into Korea had thickened rapidly during the next two weeks. What the Unsan prisoners had described as "divisions" were but components of armies in transit. As Eighth Army began to form along the Chongchon, the 38th, 39th, and 40th Chinese Armies, in aggregate strength of about 100,000 men, were already inside Korea. By the time the battle began, they were backed up by three more, the 42nd, 50th, and 66th. The main columns had crossed the Yalu at Antung and Manpojin and, avoiding the coastal road on the way south, had moved to the concentration area among the ridges on the far side of the valley along which Eighth Army was gathering.

Both the movement and the concentration had gone undetected. The enemy columns moved only by night, preserved an absolute camouflage discipline during their daytime rests and remained hidden to view under village rooftops after reaching the chosen ground. Air observation saw nothing of this mass maneuver. Civilian refugees brought no word of it. The remaining chance for its discovery therefore lay in deep patrolling by fairly heavy combat columns, which was not done.

That it was not done does not require excuse. It is easy to cast blame if one has never seen the North Korean countryside or is unmindful of Eighth Army's strained situation. Within that hill country, a primitive army, lacking in heavy equipment, can be stowed away in less space than a hunt would use for the chasing of foxes. And Eighth Army did not have a sufficient troop strength to probe and prowl every corner of the outland where hostiles might be hiding. In the

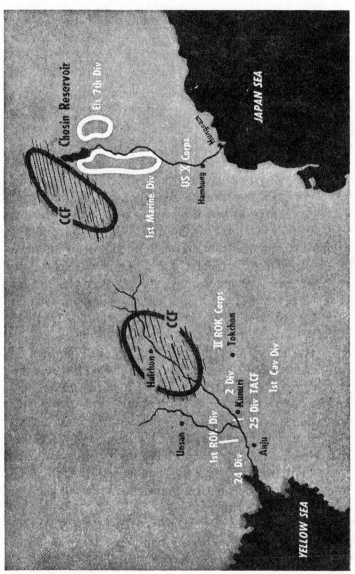

UN DISPOSITIONS AS BATTLE OPENED

The tactical strength of American X Corps was distributed mainly around the lower end of the Chosin Reservoir and the MSR leading to the coast.

preceding days, it had been several times clipped for just this kind of enterprise. Detachments had been cut off for striking too deeply while on their own. The army had reassembled along the Chongchon partly to stop such losses in detail, and the days were heavy with the tasks of accumulating supply, winterizing, and fitting green men into units.

But time was not permitted for thorough attention to these things. Almost as the period of reorganization was ordered, a directive came to Eighth Army from General Headquarters, Tokyo, that it would attack toward the Yalu as quickly as possible. General Walker was deeply disturbed. He replied that he was still moving troops up and that his army was beset by great logistical difficulties. It could not be ready, he said, before 15 November. When that day came, he was still not satisfied with the condition of his army, and not less dubious about the inferences of the order. Again he said he would have to delay. No new signs radically altering or amending the intelligence picture developed during the interval. On the far side of the peninsula, X Corps was only beginning its march north from Hamhung. The Chinese Army had not yet arrived in any strength on that flank.

There remained for Eighth Army the question of when to go. On 20 November, the Commander published to the army the directive for the attack which was launched the day following Thanksgiving. General MacArthur flew to Korea and gave his message to troops pointing them to the Yalu and to the prospect that the war would be over by Christmas. Communiqué No. 12, published on 24 November, included the sentence: "This morning the western sector of the pincer moves forward in general assault in an effort to complete the compression and close the vise."

By then X Corps, with 1st Marine Division and 7th Infantry Division in the van, already had penetrated deep into enemy country. There, as in the west, the Chinese counteroffensive would strike suddenly and with full power, following by three days the collision with Eighth Army. But these were two battles and quite separate, each from the other. All that happened on the eastern field for good or evil influenced the fortunes of Eighth Army scarcely at all. Another epic story, it someday must be told.

Here we look only at the unequal struggle along the Chong-chon between one army which, though attacking, had no expectation that it would be strongly resisted, and a second host which, hidden, watched and waited the hour opportune to its own offensive design.

One knew.

The other didn't.

So to begin.

# 2

# The Stonewall Company

Of all of the units in eighth army which became engaged by the Chinese in the great November battle along the Chongchon River, Baker Company of the 9th Infantry Regiment was the first to fight and the last to yield its forward ground.

It was a mixed company, being about 30 per cent colored, 60 per cent white, and 10 per cent ROK troops. This is the story of that one company's experience. As an example of courage, unity of action in the face of terrible odds, and the ability of native Americans to survive calamitous losses and give back hard blows to their enemies, there is nothing better in the book, though we look all the way back to Bunker Hill.

They were 129 able-bodied men when they started forward on the morning of 25 November in the great advance which was intended to reach the Yalu line and terminate the war. And though they had but recently dined on turkey and the Thanksgiving trimmings, they were in a black and resentful mood.

By their own account, it griped them all, from Capt. William C. Wallace down to the latest replacements. Their beef was that they had been given the dirty end of the stick.

During the preceding week, the regiment, along with the rest of the division, had been toiling northward opposed only by light screening forces of unidentified guerillas. It had been hit-and-run all the way. These casual enemy bands would stand for a few minutes on a hilltop, fire a few Parthian mortar and machine-gun rounds at the forward fringe of the American column, and then fade back into the dun-colored scenery.

Baker Company had been attached to Second Battalion in this period and had taken its turn in being rotated to the van. But it had just happened that every time Baker got forward, the enemy grew nasty, and there was consequent fire and loss, whereas the other companies had moved along relatively unscathed.

So it was not without cause that the men grumbled when they got the order just as sunrise touched the village of Sinhung-dong. Once again Baker was to be in the front row, orchestra. It would attack northward along the Chongchon and secure Hill 219, the most prominent ridge along the east bank. Captain Wallace was given four medium tanks and two Quad-50s * for supporting weapons.

Two of his platoons were mounted on these vehicles and they promptly hit the road. The other two platoons took it on foot under the Executive Officer, Lieut. Ellison C. Wynn, the Captain having accompanied the armor. The distance to Hill 219 was about three miles airline. But the cart track followed the river twists and looped over the lower folds of the ridges, which approximately doubled the strain and the distance. Even so, the marching men closed on the western end of the target hill almost as rapidly as the motorized column. For all its heaviness of spirit, Baker was remarkably light of foot on that particular morning. In fact, it was much too light.

This was what the preceding days of relatively light action and the promises that the war was wearing to an end had done to the company. All but twelve men had thrown away their steel helmets; the pile cap was better insurance against frostbite and the steel helmet wouldn't fit over it. Only two men —new arrivals—carried the bayonet. The grenade load averaged less than one per man. Some rifle and carbine * men carried as much as two extra bandoliers or six full clips. Others had as little as sixteen to thirty rounds on their persons. About

* See Glossary of Main Weapons.

one half of the company had dispensed with intrenching tools. The one light machine gun with each platoon had four ammunition boxes; there were 120 rounds taken forward for the feeding of the two 60-mm mortars.*

Completing the logistical picture, Baker Company had breakfasted on hot corned beef hash and coffee at sunup, and only a few men bothered to carry tinned rations on the march. Bedrolls and overcoats had been left behind. A party of thirty-five Korean bearers remained with the rear element, and the bedding, food, and extra ammunition were supposed to be brought up by A-frame after the hill was taken.

Neither the tanks nor the quads put Hill 219 under a preliminary fire. Baker assembled and got ready to jump. Its only link with the rear at the moment was the telephone wire of the artillery forward observer. The one SCR 300 * with the company wouldn't work. The company quota of SCR 536s * had been lost one week earlier in a trailer accident and hadn't been replaced. That was not a particular irritation, Baker having already concluded that the 536s weren't meant to operate in Korean terrain.

To Captain Wallace's eye, 219 did not appear formidable. The south facing of the ridge was virtually a cliff, and there was little chance that his line could be outflanked from that direction. The north slope was gentler, the only interruption to its graduated embankment being a series of rock outcroppings which ran nearly the length of the ridge. At the crest were two peaks, the lesser being directly above the head of the company, while the 219 height was at the far end. Both were slab- and boulder-strewn, and their approaches and the saddle between were covered with thicket. The eye could not detect a sign of life anywhere along the summit.

Wallace deployed his Third Platoon along the base of the north slope and faced it southward. First and Second formed in an arc around the base of 219's western end and started upward, with First Squad, Second Platoon, serving as point and leading the other people by about 10 yards.

* See Glossary of Main Weapons.

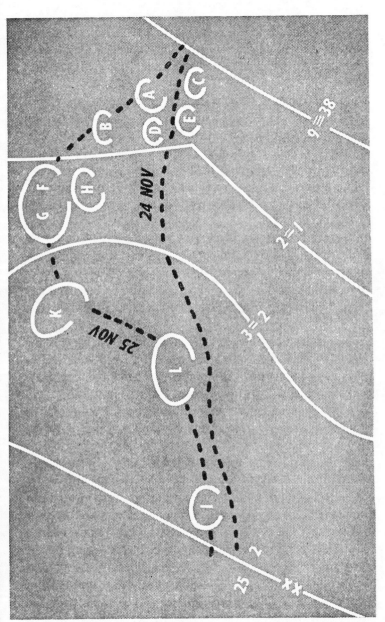

DISPOSITIONS, 9TH REGIMENT

Goose-eggs show company locations on 25 November 1950. Dotted lines trace the approximate front then and on the preceding day.

head, even before pulling him back to cover. But the cry had a more electric effect on Pvt. Robert Noel, a colored BAR man. Until then he had been firing intermittently into the thicket, careful not to expose himself overlong. Now he stood alone in the clear, working his BAR until he had emptied two magazines and his last bullet was gone. That was enough. Temporarily the thicket grew quiet.

Wallace reeled down the hill. He was still in the fight but he was bleeding heavily and his mind was fogging. He had called to Lieut. Theodore J. Weathered to take the company. At the mortar position below the first knob, he told Wynn, his Negro Executive, to take over from Weathered. The mortar battery had been doing its best to work over Hill 219 but the results spoke for themselves; another eighteen men of Baker had been brought down from the hill, some dead, some wounded.

From his aid station, Wallace walked north along the road, looking for the tanks. It was in his mind that if the armor couldn't bear by line of sight against the top of 219, it should cross the Chongchon and keep moving west until the hill came into clear view. But the track was cluttered with ambulances and ammo trucks and he had difficulty finding his way. There had been quite a bit of traffic along this feeble artery during the early afternoon. The Regimental Commander, Col. C. C. Sloane, had come forward, cocked one eye at the fight, then called Division and said: "I think this is different; it may be the real thing; we had better watch it." But his premonition was discounted. Lieut. Colonel Wolff, the Battalion Commander, had also been a witness from the roadway. He did not share Sloane's alarm. His other companies, to the rear of Baker, were still uninvolved. Able Company, echeloned to southeast of Baker with its right flank dangling in air, was covering more ground than it could hold if hit, and any gap would provide easy entry to the division rear. Because Sloane was playing a hunch and firmly insisted on it, Charley Company was brought forward to backstop both Able and Baker, facing east-northeast toward 38th Regiment's sector. The

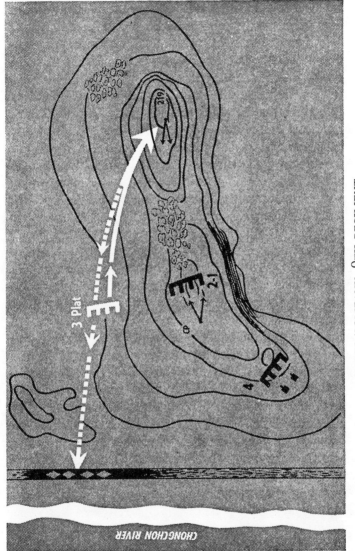

BAKER COMPANY, 9TH REGIMENT

The Daytime Attack, 25 November.

surrender. They were close enough for Noel to see the buttons on their uniforms.

All fire suddenly ceased. The platoon stood there, in an extended skirmish line, within 20 feet of the enemy, waiting for whatever might happen next. They watched warily for any untoward movement and noted that an earth bulge in the intervening space made it unlikely that any Chinese within the strong point could cut them down with rifle fire.

One of the platoon's ROK soldiers, known to his mates only by the name "Moonshine," speaking Chinese, said to the enemy soldiers: "If you want to quit, you must come down." One of them answered: "No, you must come up and get us." They argued for a few minutes. Meanwhile more Chinese had joined the line, hands in air.

Suddenly the hands jerked forward, and grenades showered down on the platoon as the Chinese dropped back into their pits. The line went flat. Moonshine had part of his hand blown away by a grenade explosion. Others were hit by fragments in the back, shoulders, buttocks, and arms. The platoon took it stoically and at good tossing distance continued the grenade exchange until the last bomb was gone. Then, for lack of any sensible alternative, they recoiled to the road, taking it on the run.

This was the action they described to Wallace when he met them by the tanks. He told them to reload and attack 219 again. SFC Jesus Cantu said to him: "Captain, you can't send us back up there again; it's plain suicide." Sorely shaken physically, and ready to trust the judgments of his men, Wallace at last agreed. He told Cantu to round up the rest of the platoon (half had remained on the low ground covering the approaches to the hill) and take them up to the lower knob where they were to fill in on the right. The hour was about 1600. Wallace figured that the main thing to be done during the remaining hours of daylight was to get the company tied in and ready for the night.

It was then that Hinckle found him, took one look at his bloody head, and ordered him out of the fight. In fact, the

Exec was so concerned for Wallace's life that he put him in his own jeep and sped back to the battalion aid station.

Up on the hill, Lieutenant Wynn and his men had made no progress. Kjonaas and his group had been vaguely aware that Third Platoon was attempting its wide end run, but knew nothing of its fortune. Wynn told Kjonaas to take his survivors and some of First Platoon and again buck the center in an effort to assist the move on the left.

It couldn't be done. The Chinese had returned to the thicket, bringing a machine gun. About twenty-five men got ready for the rush, Kjonaas leading them. As they made their charge around the left side of the knob, the dense brush erupted with grenade and bullet fire. Half of the group was cut down by a gun sited not more than 35 yards away. The other half stopped—naturally.

That ended the day's aggressiveness, though the Chinese continued their automatic fire from 219 and the thicket until dark. Both sides were wearing down.

The Korean porters got up to the company just as the hill became quiet. They brought ammunition, mainly. Also, a truck came up with hot food and bedrolls. Kjonaas was bleeding from a bullet in the arm and the grenade fragments in his foot. Wynn looked his wounds over, then ordered him to an aid station.

The main force formed in a narrow perimeter around the big knob. The Fourth Platoon—a handful of men enclosing the mortars—made their circle next a small knoll about 140 yards down the hill from the main body. Half of the men crawled part way into their sleeping sacks for warmth, and sat in their foxholes. The others, paired off with the resting men, remained at full alert.

It was an eerie night. The weather was about 15 degrees temperature but brisk and clear. A full moon lighted the scene except when there were occasional dimouts by the light clouds. Looking to rearward, the men could see tracers firing both ways across the Chongchon and across the road. From the same direction came the distant rumble of artillery. There

armor had quit its ground and gone back. Some of the Chinese were running forward; others walked. They fired rifles and burp guns as they moved, with the pipe spurring them on. Bullets were already chipping the rocks along the crestline. The defenders saw just one other thing before the fire build-up made them go flat: one Chinese was running laterally from group to group in the skirmish line, as if he were the leader. Pfc. Lawrence E. Smith, Jr., of Sandston, Virginia, noted that fact, and he also called to Wynn that he could hear the sounds of fighting from Fourth Platoon's position.

Then came a report from Third Platoon on the other side of the big knob. The enemy had set up machine guns in the field at the base of the south slope and the platoon was under a pinning fire. As Wynn saw it, that fixed the issue; Baker was surrounded and nothing remained but to fight it out on present ground.

These things happened almost as quickly as they can be related. Perhaps three or four minutes passed in rousing the men, deploying the main strength toward the danger line, and getting weapons going. By that time, the Chinese, using marching fire, had charged three fourths of the way up the slope, and their forward skirmishers were within 30 feet of the foxholes. It was then that they met Baker's fire in strong volume. Like other mortals, they went down, and slid off to any point where they could find cover behind a rock outcropping or an embankment.

The fire exchange continued at that distance. Other Chinese crawled up the slope and added to the pressure. They tried grenading but their weak-armed throws couldn't make the distance. However, their bullets took toll, and Wynn's small band of forty-odd men steadily grew less. Gradually the resistance line which had formed along the ridge crest was bent back once again on both flanks to make a last redoubt of the big knob. There the one machine gun was still going strong. Smith, Jr., and two other men were posted on the south side of the knob, covering a big draw which provided the best entry to the defensive ring. If the enemy charged from that direction, these three would have to meet it.

By the end of the first hour, the Chinese were in the foxholes which the platoons had held when the fire fight started, and Wynn's men were a little knot, fighting back from amid the rock slabs on the knob.

Among Lieutenant Weathered's men on the knoll by the mortars the situation was not less desperate. The skirmish circle still held them in a noose; the main body of the enemy had taken cover among the foxholes in the mortar position. That was about 20 feet away—convenient distance for the enemy grenadiers. So tight was the space that when a grenade landed on the knoll, the defenders could not roll away from it. They had no choice but to throw the grenade out, or kick hard if it landed near a foot.

Crawford and Cpl. James C. Curcio, Jr., played in this fight as dangerous a game as any ever undertaken by two teen-age Americans. Strong throwers, and agile of body, they cleared the surplus, heaving back such enemy grenades as the other men could not reach. The party estimated that sixty grenades dropped upon the knoll within two hours; of that number about forty were pitched out again while still hot.

But most of the others exploded, and some of them found flesh. Seegar had his nose shattered by a grenade shard. Sgt. Joseph Bellinger got riddled through the buttocks. Pfc. George Chapel was hit in the hand. Pfc. Whitehurst was taken out by a bullet.

The fight slackened at times, either because the Chinese grew arm-weary or the Americans, worrying about their diminishing stores, tempered their reply. Then a sharp whistle blast would sound from somewhere beyond the mortars, and each time it shrilled, a few Chinese jumped from the foxholes and rushed the knoll. The defenders got used to it. They timed themselves so that they grenaded in unison at the sound of the enemy whistle. The Chinese kept repeating their mistake.

From down on the knoll, Weathered yelled up to Wynn: "Fall back on us; it's better here." Wynn called to his survivors: "Get ready to run and I'll cover you."

But the big fellow had no weapon. Watching from the knoll, Crawford and Curcio saw the lieutenant stoop down and come up with an armful of rocks and canned C-rations. Then he ran to the north side of the knob and standing in clear silhouette on the skyline began heaving his missiles at Chinese heads not more than 25 feet away. The enemy was so startled by the fury of this personal attack that momentarily the fire slackened. One white enlisted man stood with him, swinging his empty rifle as a club, ready to brain anyone who tried to rush his lieutenant.

Smith, Jr., also saw these things as in the several minutes of grace in which this modern David was trying to save his command with rocks and rations, he attempted to lead the blinded man, Denny, down the slope.

But Denny couldn't get away fast enough. A Chinese lying behind a rock and armed with a tommy gun shot Denny through the heart while Smith, Jr., was tugging him by the arm. So Smith, Jr., picked up the tiny man, the bullet-riddled Brassfield, and threw him across his shoulder.

Brassfield asked: "Where are you taking me?"

Smith, Jr., said: "To first aid."

That was all from the little man. He didn't say another word or utter a moan while he was being packed down the slope.

Others made it without further hurt, except for Wynn. All of his subordinates save one had cleared the hill. Wynn turned to follow. The man guarding him threw his rifle at one Chinese who tried to close in. Then a grenade exploded in the air right next to Wynn's head and blew the side of his face away.

Pvt. Frost, who had stuck with him, was ready to give a helping hand. But Wynn shook him off, though his wound would have felled and ended an average man. The lieutenant staggered down the hill under his own power. That they escaped was just one more miracle among many.

Weathered had already taken over, knowing that Wynn had had it. Even before Wynn had thrown his last rock, he and Seegar had seen clearly that the consolidation put the company in worse case than before, unless the Chinese could be prevented from gaining the knob by fire from the low ground. Should they mount a machine gun there, every man would die.

The enigmatic enemy, though possessing Baker Company's mortars for two hours, had neither used them nor dismantled them. Seegar, Crawford, and Curcio had rushed to the tubes the moment the Chinese on this flank had departed. There were only ten rounds of high explosive and three of white phosphorus remaining at the position. So they decided to work only one mortar.

Wynn was still standing in profile on the knob when Weathered gave the order to fire. It was a little bit over, but still so close that Crawford at first feared his round had struck Wynn. They adjusted. Then as the lieutenant came down the slope and the mortar party saw the Chinese rush for the knob and deploy around its edges, the second round struck it dead on. There were shrill cries from above, and the knob was promptly vacated.

That was a warning to the enemy, but the mortar rounds had to be harbored. Weathered took council of his NCOs, and they agreed on their elementary tactics. Seven riflemen were put on the knoll with no mission except to keep eyes glued on the knob and fire when they saw a Chinese head pop up. The mortar would not be fired unless the enemy attempted to emplace a machine gun on the summit.

These were the terms on which the fight was continued for the next four hours. At about 0930 an air strike came over and hit 219 with napalm, rockets, and .50 machine-gun fire. That seemed to cool off the Chinese more than a bit. But they persisted in attempting to establish themselves on the knob, and the small party of sharpshooters had to stay at

awarding of medals requires the writing of many polished words on reams of paper. There was neither time nor material for that. Those who survived had to concenter their effort on rebuilding Baker into a battleworthy unit.

But probably that made little difference to Wallace and his men. During the company assemblies at which the story of 219 was reconstructed, the subject of awards happened to be mentioned.

Crawford spoke up, saying, "There's a little girl in Virginia with whom I happen to be in love. The honor of being returned to the United States so that I can marry her is the only award I want from a grateful government."

But then Crawford was only seventeen.

# 3

# The Affair at Chinaman's Hat

I<small>F</small> DIVISION HAD PAID LESS ATTENTION TO BAKER COM-pany's lone fight up forward than the facts of that engage-ment would appear to warrant, it was in part because there had been grave trouble at Chinaman's Hat, which was much closer to the command seat.

In this tempest-in-a-teapot affair, both the artillery and the infantry had shared, though not in their normal relationship to each other. It was more like a page out of the wars in Napoleon's time.

Toward an understanding of how and why it happened, it is first necessary to view briefly the artillery position and problem as a whole.

To assist it in the drive north, 2nd Division had been re-enforced by the 61st and 99th Field Artillery Battalions from 1st Cavalry Division. That was good so far as it went, but it did not solve the main problem of finding enough flat tracts of land along the main axis of advance to base satisfactorily such artillery as the division already possessed.

This was a chronic ailment in all Korean operations, and both the season and the peculiar characteristics of the Chong-chon countryside exacerbated it. The rice paddies were iced over, but not yet frozen solid; they forbade the guns. Other-wise the valley was almost barren of flat spaces given over to cultivation. The hills virtually overlapped one another. The

earth cover, no digging was necessary. The mounds and embankments were pitted with holes and short trenches left from some earlier military operation.

Outposting the general position, though not enfolding the 61st Battalion at its northern extremity, First Platoon of Able Company was in foxholes fronted on the river and looking westward, while Second Platoon held an extension of this same line looking northward toward the 61st's gun pits. Third Platoon was at ease within an interior position. Fourth Platoon had dug in its mortars about 300 yards back from the river and to the rear of the Company kitchens.

Interspliced with Second Platoon's line, six tanks of the 23rd Tank Company also faced northward toward the 61st's ground. So placed, they made the First Battalion's perimeter somewhat more secure, but were pointing right at the back of their own artillery.

At about 1820, Capt. Melvin R. Stai, Commander of Able Company, got a telephone call from Hutchins asking: "Do you hear rifle fire to the north?" Stai hadn't, but he asked some of the men in the foxholes; they said they had heard it, but it seemed far off and didn't sound dangerous.

Ten minutes later came another call: "Do you hear bugles blowing?" Stai listened and could hear them; they sounded at great distance across the river. But he left his command post near the kitchens to reconnoiter his front lines and give warning, and found to his astonishment that First Platoon, only 300 yards from where he had been sitting, had been fully engaged for five minutes; some of its men, so they said, were already running out of ammunition.

But Stai was not alone in his surprise. Unperceived from the east shore, seven enemy columns from the Chinese 94th Infantry Regiment had crossed the river straight into the front door of the position. The Chongchon, where it flowed past the camp, is about 85 yards wide and 3 to 4 feet deep. Each of the seven columns included between 100 and 200 men. They had waded the stream simultaneously as columns in line, with an interval of perhaps 75 yards between columns. Yet no part of this had been seen from the perimeter of the defenders; it is known only because Chinese who were captured in the fight later told how it happened.

Unfamiliarity with the eccentric methods of the new enemy, the late arrival at the site, the preoccupation with organization of the bivouac and the timing of the strike by the Chinese so that it coincided with the last minutes of dusk when vision is most impaired all entered into the total surprise of this encampment. So did the excessive optimisms of the hour, as evidenced by the Intelligence estimate of enemy capabilities on that day: (1) that the Chinese would delay from successive positions in withdrawing toward the Manchurian border; (2) or they might attack south in some force against positions on the Chongchon line. But taking all of these compromising factors into account, the lack of an adequate local security is still unexplained.

The wading columns of the left flank disappeared into the scrub poplars fronting the river next the 61st Battalion. They then exploded onto the camp. What occurred there in the next few minutes can only be conjectured.

In Able Company's line, M/S Roger W. Remillard was sitting near First Platoon's machine gun, manned by Sgts. Theodore A. Aspinwall and Robert Strahorn. The gun was in a large foxhole with a heavy earth bank covering it all around.

Remillard sat staring at the undergrowth lining the river bank about 75 yards away, and what he saw almost made his eyes pop out. There were men there, standing within the bushes, scores of them, naked from the waist down. They were moving frantically as if taking an exercise. Then Remillard could see what they were doing: they were putting on their pants!

Remillard yelled: "Look! They're gooks! Open fire!" He opened the volley with his own carbine. The machine gun joined him. So did a scattering of riflemen. The small arms stopped a few of the Chinese before they could start. The

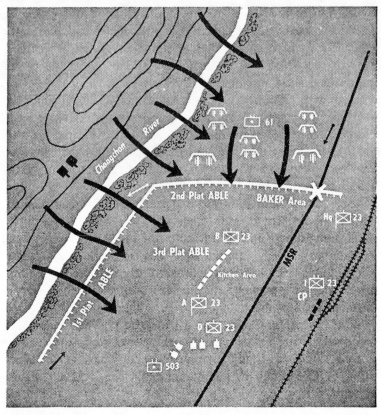

CHINAMAN'S HAT, THE CAMP AND THE ACTION, 25-26 NOVEMBER

The Chinese crossed the Chongchon in seven parallel columns to attack the entrenched camp.

of Baker's men, startled out of their wits, jumped from their foxholes and joined the flight. As Hutchins remarked: "We learned firsthand that panic is contagious."

But Gandy's men, and the increment from First Platoon, bore straight along, except as a file here or there was dropped by the machine-gun fire. They shouted at top voice as they moved along, some of them cheering, others screaming.

Most of the Chinese who had crashed the perimeter had already gone to ground, taking over holes in the already prepared position. But having gained cover, the majority remained inert and did not try to fight back with rifle and grenade. As many as five or six of them would be wedged in one foxhole. Gandy's men sprayed these works as they moved along, getting little fire back. They did not use area fire. It seemed like a waste of bullets; the ammunition was held until the firers saw live enemy.

That had to be done because about every third man in the line had suddenly discovered that his weapon wasn't working. The bitter cold and heavy frost had locked these pieces, chiefly the carbines.

As weapons went out, men swung with their fists and grabbed rocks. Cpl. Tracy Young threw his carbine at a Chinese, missed him, then grabbed for a pistol in the man's hand, only to find that it was tied to his belt. They grappled and went down. Cpl. James White shot the Chinese as he lay on the ground, with Young holding him.

Cpl. Raymond P. McDaniels, finding his carbine frozen, used it as a club, and killed two men in the same foxhole.

Pfc. Robert L. Echard, finding his BAR frozen, urinated on it, got it warm and working again, and probably killed more men than did McDaniels.

There were a dozen such encounters and episodes as this during the infighting. About twelve men in Gandy's force had bayonets fixed during the advance; it occurred to none of them to use the blade for any purpose save to tickle an enemy body to see if the Chinese were feigning death.

At last they got up to the foxholes where First Platoon had stood, and the three sergeants in the machine-gun hole were still holding forth. Gandy had carried out his order. At that moment an enemy machine gun firing from the artillery position hit him through the heart.

Stai was there to see it. He moved immediately to get some of the tanks grouped with Second Platoon to shift leftward and support First Platoon, lest new pressure come against its front. About that time, Sloane of the 9th Regiment called Freeman of the 23rd and asked: "How can I help?" Freeman

on through the greater part of the night. The enemy held to the position among the 61st's gun pits. From the west shore, re-enforcements continued to wade the river, while mortar batteries from amid the ravines of Objective 25 intermittently shelled the American camp. It was inaccurate fire and did little damage.

About two hours past midnight, Baker Company of the 72nd Medium Tank Battalion reached the scene with its tanks. They went into line with First and Second Platoons of Able Company, each tank becoming wedded to a small knot of infantrymen which fought right beside it. The regimental tank company gave its concentrated support in the same way to the line of Baker Company. For tankers as well as for infantry, this was a hand-to-hand contest, though the main missions of the armor were to interdict the river and keep the north flank intact by putting a general area fire on the 61st's old position. In frequent attempts to knock out the tanks and strip the defenders of their fire shield, Chinese infantrymen crept forward carrying charges improvised by combining a bazooka round with a stick of TNT and a friction cap. Utmost vigilance on the part of both elements in the line beat down these efforts. The tanks were kept inviolate, not one charge being set off against them. But as indicating the persistence of the enemy, when the morning light came, seventeen dead Chinese were found around one tank position. Most of the dead men had been carrying explosive charges. Their attack, however, had lacked unity from the time the armor went into action. They had participated as individuals and died that way rather than as members of a cohesive group.

From greater distance, the artillery at Kujang-dong had supported the defense with steady fires against Objective 25 and the approaches leading into the position from the north.

The enemy, however, had already begun to veer in a different direction before the armored re-enforcement insured the defense of the camp. Hill 329 is in reality an extended ridge with three pronounced caps, the highest being at the northern end. But from the perspective of the camp only the conelike peak at the southern end, bordering the camp, was visible. Hence the name, "Chinaman's Hat." What strength the Chinese had established on the ridge prior to engagement is not known for certain; no marked attention was given it because it was believed that only a handful of guerillas was skulking there and that hunting them was like seeking the needle in the haystack. Ninth Regiment had occupied the lower heights on the day before without trouble.

In setting up camp, First Battalion, 23rd, put a security outpost of five men on the same ground. They were driven off in the first stage of the fight. Thereafter "The Hat" acted as a magnet to those enemy fractions which, having broken into the American position and felt the fire, became discouraged both about facing it or recrossing the river under the guns of the tanks. It was not a preconcerted plan but one of those accidental recongregatings which occur from the pressures of a battle. They proceeded to assemble there and reorganize, building up with rifles and machine guns.

Able Company got official notice of this change in situation sometime after midnight when a machine gun, firing from "The Hat" at about 550 yards' range, found Second Platoon's position and eliminated two company cooks, Sgt. Oral Swindle, and Cpl. Kenneth Widdis. More men were hit in Baker Company's line. The fire quieted by about 0330. The American tanks long since had switched their fire to the peak. However, before morning the Chinese were using mortars from the heights and had formed along the ridge in sufficient numbers to entrench themselves around all three peaks. This grip was never shaken. Chinaman's Hat remained an abscess on the Division's rear until the hour arrived for full retreat. So while losing the objective in the fire fight, the enemy columns had neither withdrawn nor been denied a final prize.

Yet the price exacted was considerable. They left 410 dead on the flat ground and 111 Chinese were made prisoners; the full score is not known because during the night they evacuated most of their wounded. On the American side, the total casualties were somewhat less than 200 killed and wounded.

Their prisoners seemed to tell a straight story but did not possess much information. They were all from the CCF 94th Regiment. They said that the columns had been sent forward with the mission of destroying artillery which would be found in the river bottom; they had not expected to encounter infantry. About half of their men had no small arms but were carrying the special charges with which to blow up the guns. No secondary mission had been given them. When asked whether, having hit the artillery and destroyed it, the columns were supposed to recross the Chongchon or go on to some other object, the prisoners, including the officers, said they had not been told.

Even so, they had failed in the main task given them, though the door of opportunity for many hours had remained wide open. Having the guns in their possession, they became diverted by the opposition of the armor and made little effort to wreck the artillery. The artillerymen who had fled the pits were rounded up by working details from the force at Kujang-dong. Early in the morning, they were marched forward to the advanced camp, and for the sake of their own discipline, were ordered to advance out of 23rd's sector and re-establish their position. By then, nearly all of the able-bodied enemy had pulled away. The batteries were in the same positions where they had been deserted, little the worse for wear except where they had been nicked by fire from American weapons. Only two pieces had been damaged beyond repair.

What had happened at Chinaman's Hat alarmed 2nd Division, though the significance of the incident, in grand tactics, was not perhaps estimated at its proper value.

The fight was construed as a more or less isolated event, unrelated to any far-reaching enemy plan of maneuver generating a universal threat against the friendly front.

All appearances aided this deception and the estimate which derived from it. The enemy had seen the artillery set up in the river bottom. Its camp, viewed from the brow of Chinaman's Hat, looked invitingly vulnerable. Probably an enemy command post had sent a message by radio. Responding to that message, an infantry regiment had been dispatched on the moment to destroy the artillery . . . that was how the action was interpreted by the staff officers whose task it was to read the situation. It reduced the affair at Chinaman's Hat to the status of an accidental foray.

Considered alone, the several parts of the action dovetailed snugly toward the supporting of this limited, and therefore dangerous, conclusion.

Only as they were viewed in proportion, and assessed against the measure and timing of everything else that the enemy did on the same day elsewhere along the general front, could the attack across the Chongchon become recognized as an integral action in the grand design of an enemy army which, already coiled to spring, was now fully in motion.

There is no more startling example in the record than this of how intelligence fails at the central point when the breakdown of communications with forward units thwarts the prompt correlation of all pertinent information.

The battle facts considered, Colonel Foster's Intelligence estimate of enemy capabilities on the evening of 25 November, which saw the Chinese as continuing a screening action back to the Manchurian border, was already twenty-four hours cold.

When by 1800 on 26 November the blows dealt the division on the prior night had at last been approximately assessed, he revised his estimate and stated the enemy's probable intent in this order: (1) to attack south in force against positions on the Chongchon River front, or (2) to attack along the Tokchon-Kunuri axis to cut the division's main supply route and lines of communication.

But again, because Foster was not hearing what he needed to know, he was running one day late. The dam had already broken; the envelopment was in motion. But the data which might have made this convulsive change apparent did not get back. As Foster later said: "That was what killed us."

# 4

# The Fate of King and Love

In the breaking up of the 9th regiment's front on the night of 25 November, the misfortunes of King and Love Companies were virtually of one piece.

And that of itself was a strange thing since they were not physically connected.

In theory only, they were holding mutually supporting positions, which is to say that they were next neighbors in the middle of enemy country.

But they were separated by distance through which the Chinese could have marched an army once dark fell. They were not in communication one with the other. There had been no patrolling between them. Each had but a vague idea of where the other was located and no knowledge whatever of what it was experiencing.

Both were light of strength and, had they been consolidated, they would still have been ten men short of Table of Organization company size. The weakness was mainly in King Company, which had only sixty-five men and officers including its ROKs.

Nonetheless, when the sun went down, this small band was in mournful isolation at the apex of advance, farther out on the limb than any other element within Eighth Army.

It held a small ridge 2,500 yards to the north of Love Company's ridge, and there was a prominent hill mass in between them, though both mistakenly supposed that they were within fire-supporting distance of each other.

As for why things were not better coordinated, part of the fault was in King Company's sheer fatigue and small numbers. The men had made a long march during the day through the ravines and across the ridges. On arriving at Objective 35—a ridge with two peaks and two conspicuous extensions which compromised security in that direction—Capt. Benjamin J. Benton did not feel that his command was strong enough for active patrolling.

In fact, as Benton judged the ground, King Company did not have enough men present to round out a reasonably sound perimeter. So the men set to work digging in. No patrols were sent to look for Love Company and no call for help was sounded.

The ridge on its western end abutted a dry creek bed. It was sandy-bottomed and about 30 feet across, and it hooked around the ridge for perhaps 500 yards. For a marching force, it was as useful an avenue as an open road.

Concerned with this one feature, Benton disposed his company with only one platoon holding the westernmost of the two peaks. The higher eminence to the east was left unguarded. Third Platoon was put on the low ground at the southwest corner of the hill. Second Platoon faced south overlooking the narrow valley as it turned eastward.

It is a fair presumption that the company was thus disposed because the low ground made easier digging than for any other good reason in the tactical situation. As events were to prove, Benton's apprehensions were more acute than his deployments. Having conceded the higher ground, King Company still did not take a firm and balanced hold upon the lower hill. Its position was vulnerable from any angle.

Though at the forefront of Eighth Army, the company remained out of contact with every element to its rear. Distance and the terrain features silenced the SCR 300. Sgt. Alfred Bigger was sent from Battalion to run a telephone line to King Company. But as Bigger told the story of his failure, he was given "heavy wire" instead of the light 130 which is useful on such missions. So he couldn't carry it over the hills and thereby take the shortest line between two points. Instead, he followed the waterline, and his wire ran out before he had covered two thirds of the distance. There his personal striving ended, and with that failure King Company, left alone in a great void, ceased to operate as the outpost of an army.

Its men were insufficiently equipped for a lone-handed fight. A few of the riflemen carried two extra bandoliers and full belt. The greater number had less. Some of the carbine men had less than sixty rounds. No man carried more than two grenades; some carried one, others none. There were only five BARs and two light machine guns present on or around the hill. The company had breakfasted at 0630 and gone without food thereafter.

These were the rough details of the situation as the day drew to its close.

The moon was already up. Pfc. Louis Giudici noted how it shone like silver on the frosted stalks of the cornfield where he was lying with his machine gun, just a few paces to the northwest of the company's hill.

Giudici at that moment was the outguard of the company, as the company was of the army. Supported only by two ROK riflemen, he was posted at the most remote corner of the position, covering the creek bed as it approached the hill.

He had watched but no one had come that way. The evening was profoundly quiet. He looked at his watch; it read 1900. Right then he heard a scattering of rifle and carbine fire from south of the hill where Second Platoon was posted. As if in answer, a bugle call came from the north, then another from the west, and several from the south where he had heard the firing. And then he heard the tramp of men. He saw them coming down the creek bed, following the turn which would bring them to within 35 feet of his gun.

At first there were just small groups of men, moving about six in a bunch with a 10-yard interval between them. They moved at double time, and though there were five of these small groups, none seemed to be carrying small arms. He had sighted them first at about 250 feet. The first were just drawing abreast of him when he reached for the trigger with the intention of opening fire.

But things had changed, and he stayed his hand. A whole column of enemy infantry was now pouring into the creek bed, right on the heels of the reconnaissance groups. They seemed to be very large men, perhaps because the conspicuous white bandoliers which crossed their breasts and the overcoats which almost touched the ground increased their bulk. They carried rifles and tommy guns at the port as they, too, moved down the creek bed at a run. The column was four abreast. With every company or so rode a man on horseback, who shouted orders at the others as he moved along.

For seventeen minutes this solid column moved at a run past this nineteen-year-old gunner, its closest files within 35 yards of his weapon. The time interval shows that at least one Chinese regiment raced by. They did not see him, and he felt that if he fired, it would mean the destruction of the company.

But Cpl. Robert Howell had come into the cornfield armed with an M1. As the last of the Chinese swung around the bend, Howell emptied his rifle at the backs of the disappearing column. That done, he tore out of the position and ran back up the hill.

Realizing that the jig was up, Giudici opened fire with the machine gun. It coughed a few rounds and then quit. He cranked it, it coughed a few more rounds, and quit again. This was repeated four times. All that saved him was that the Chinese had hit the ground as soon as the automatic weapon opened fire. Then the gun finally quit and Giudici saw the prone enemy riflemen get up, deploy in a V formation, and start to walk straight toward him. That was enough. He left the gun straightway and ran back up the hill with the two ROKs hard on his heels.

Giudici and Howell were the only two Americans who saw at close range a solid Chinese regimental column during the Chongchon battle, but on getting to Third Platoon's position, the two men didn't bother to tell 2nd Lieut. David P. Krueger

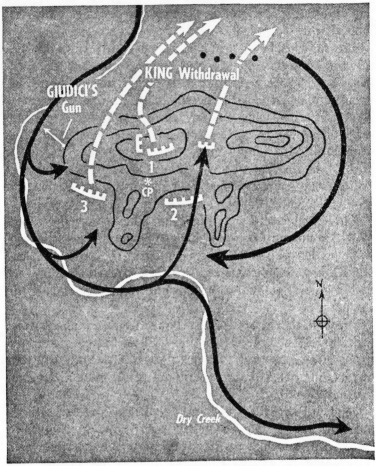

KING COMPANY, 9TH REGIMENT, 25 NOVEMBER

what they had experienced. Things by then were breaking so fast against King Company that the information seemed unimportant. They took their place in line and said nothing. Giudici still had his .45 pistol and he used it for tne remainder of the fight. Thrice he picked up carbines which had been discarded only to find that they would not fire.

A Chinese scouting party which had come into the small valley apparently from the other end of the ridge had drawn the first fire from Second Platoon. Its working relationship with the regimental column which simultaneously was moving to by-pass King's left flank on the double remains unknown. All of the circumstances argue that neither the scout group nor the column knew that King was there. When Second Platoon's first fire was returned, the men gave ground and fell back toward the hill. Thus they were never in position to see the Chinese mass pouring down the valley. When Giudici fired, most of the regiment had already cleared out of sight around the bend. The main body continued on southward at a run. Perhaps two companies peeled off and moved against King's hill from the south and west.

This shock fell on King in its moment of greatest confusion. The platoons were falling back to regroup on the high ground. Their ranks still believed falsely that they were dealing with another minor guerilla group such as they had engaged in recent days.

As the greater number of King's men were never seen again, much that happened during the next few minutes remains a subject for conjecture.

There was a steady blast of whistles and shepherd's pipes from all around the little valley. Bugles blew from the west, then from the north and from the south.

At Third Platoon's position, Pfc. Lawrence Brown had remained with his machine gun, a ROK soldier covering him with a rifle on one side, and an unknown American on the other. Cpl. Eugene Mann was in a foxhole a few yards to his right rear, holding a BAR. They saw no targets and they hadn't fired. Suddenly a hand grenade dropped into Brown's foxhole; the explosion killed him and blew the gun over. The ROK scrambled out, running for the hill; the other American didn't stir and Mann figured he was dead. Mann put about fifty BAR rounds across the draw in a scattering fire, and then ran for the hill. There he met 2nd Lieut. Al Raskin, who told him that the company would have to get out. Mann saw only about fifteen men around Raskin at the moment, and he saw no other sign that there were additional survivors on the hill.

But there was another group of about fifteen men under Captain Benton and Lieutenant Krueger to the westward of this central party. This was the remnant of Third Platoon which had managed to hold together during the forced withdrawal. They were at the base of the ridge. The enemy had not yet located them and they were doing nothing.

Pfc. Clarence V. Williams was in a position on the saddle between the two peaks. With him were Lieut. George Williams, Sgt. Leroy Davis, and two ROK soldiers. They saw a solid body of Chinese swerve from the creek bed and advance up the draw straight toward them, firing rifles and submachine guns as they walked. Williams' men had only rifles and carbines. They squatted behind rocks.

At about 35 yards' range, he yelled to his men to fire. A few of the Chinese went down at the volley, but the others kept right on coming until the lead skirmishers were within 10 yards. The Americans had continued fire. Even with only five rifles going, they at last forced the enemy platoon to check momentarily. But as the Chinese in the lead body sought ground cover, more fire built up behind them and another platoon came forward up the draw. At that point the two ROKs broke and ran north along the saddle. Williams and his men kept shooting until their pieces were almost empty. Seemingly the Chinese were also short of powder, for their forward line quit firing. There was a moment of relative quiet while the Americans wondered what to do next.

Then a large number of the enemy arose from behind the rocks and came straight on, without firing a shot. The trio in the saddle just stood there waiting.

One Chinese rushed in and grabbed Pfc. Williams by the right hand. Williams hit him with a left hook and knocked him back down the ridge.

Lieutenant Williams did equally well. The Chinese who grappled with him went down with his skull smashed by a carbine stock.

Davis kicked his man in the groin, and landed right where he wanted to. The Chinese doubled up with a scream.

Then Davis yelled: "Pull out! Pull out! There's nothing left here. They're trying to capture us."

He took the lead as the three men raced on across the saddle. Escaping capture by inches, they continued running until they got to low ground on the north side of the hill. The enemy rushed into the saddle and set up positions there. Getting only a few hundred yards beyond the ridge, the trio ran into another company of Chinese digging positions in the flat. With Lieutenant Williams leading the way, they crawled on their bellies through this line and at last gained open country.

The sounds of the fire fight within the saddle (there was no flash whatever from the Chinese small arms and neither side had used grenades at this point) stifled any possibility of continued resistance by the disorganized and scattered American fractions remaining on the western hill. According to M/S John R. Inyard, Benton decided that if he fought on, his survivors would all be enveloped and would die uselessly. The parties separately moved northward, since the Chinese had not yet closed from that direction. Continuing on to the next ridge, they then swung around in an almost complete circle, traveling toward the Chongchon via the eastward extension of the ridge on which they had fought their action. Along the way they encountered numerous small enemy groups and were engaged repeatedly. Further losses led to greater dissolution. Some of the men, including Inyard, at last decided to hide in rocky crevices until daylight to avoid further shooting. Others tried to leg it to the river as quickly as possible. Those who waited in the main survived. The word "missing" applies to most of those who took the other course.

Lieutenant Raskin and his group withdrew fighting, under close pressure, and did a good job of it. Corporal Mann and one other man (he did not survive and his name is unknown) formed their rearguard getting away from the hill. Both men were using BARs and the weapons, firing perfectly, provided enough discouragement to stop the enemy pursuit. After the getaway, Mann turned over his BAR to another soldier, then went out and acted as scout for the party.

Two somber judgments were drawn on the fate of King Company by soldiers who participated in the fighting of that night.

Said Inyard: "We got hurt because we didn't fire soon enough. In this company, we were so afraid of firing lest it give away our position that we withheld fire when nothing else would save the position."

Said Mann with equal realism: "In my opinion, on that night our error was that we had too few men, too few automatic weapons, and too much territory."

But the meaning of that fight had to be read much later by all others who were concerned. Of what had happened to King Company, and what the enemy was bringing forward, Eighth Army's other parts heard not a word. This was the price paid for the telephone line that didn't stretch the distance.

By sheerest chance we are able to follow the further progress of the main enemy body down the dry creek bed. One thousand yards south of Objective 35, there is, or was, a small Korean schoolhouse on the east bank of the valley. Hiding within it were two ROK soldiers who ten days earlier had escaped from the Chinese after a brief period as prisoners.

They saw the column jog by in the light of the full moon and judged it to be about 2,000 men. Before the dust had settled, they took off like hares across the ridges, running south to carry the word.

Already they knew where they wanted to go. On a ridge 1,500 yards to the southward, they had seen the glow of numerous fires, and they guessed it to mean that American forces were bivouacked there.

It was a good guess. From that distance, they had sighted Love Company's position in outline. The night was cold. The men had neither bedrolls nor overcoats. So Love Company was authorized by its commander to light squad fires. It was a mistake. But he was not the only soldier who had misread the mind of the enemy.

The two ROKs won the race to the perimeter. Love Company's hill was still quiet, and many of its men were warming at the fires. The two ROKs were taken at once to Lieut. Gene Takahashi, a Nisei, who commanded one of the platoons. They described what they had seen, estimated the enemy strength at 2,000, said every man seemed to be carrying a weapon of some sort, and added that they had counted twenty-five men on horseback riding alongside the column.

Takahashi accepted the men and their story at face value. But since the ROKs had said that the Chinese column was following the creek bed, and the stream took a sharp left turn to the north of Love Company's hill and ran eastward to the Chongchon, he concluded that the regiment had already gone by and was headed for the confluence of the two valleys.

One of the ROKs, speaking in his own tongue, said: "You are in terrible danger here. You must get out."

However, Takahashi did not further alert the company. And when he walked down the hill to the command post to tell what he had heard to Capt. Maxwell M. Vails, the two ROKs vanished and were not seen again. Vails heard him through, and accepting Takahashi's thesis that the enemy body was marching toward his right rear, he swung part of his Third Platoon around to cover a draw which entered the perimeter from that direction.

In one sense, the lieutenant was right about it. The enemy main body was continuing its march straight toward the river. But once again several companies had peeled off the column to dispose of the work right at hand.

Love's squad fires had not been extinguished. The men stood around warming themselves. Love's position would hardly have been better revealed had the ridge been floodlighted. Its strength was distributed quite evenly along the length of a narrow ridge shaped somewhat like a boomerang with its elbow pointing northward. Third Platoon was on the rightward elevation, facing north. Second Platoon held the high ground on the left flank, its foxhole line facing roughly west and northwest. First Platoon was on the knob in the elbow of the boomerang. That put its outpost within perhaps 200 yards of the dry creek bed.

Lieut. Lynn R. Raybould, forward observer for the 37th Field Artillery Battalion, had set up his OP at this point in the farthest extension of First Platoon's front. However, in this critical period of transitory indecision, when all that happened to his front was to have extreme significance, he had gone from his post for a few minutes to see Vails. He did not approve of the warming fires. But he soon saw that Vails had one of the largest ones next his own command post behind the hill and so he said nothing. He tarried there for a few minutes, but he did not hear the conversation between Takahashi and Vails which concerned the enemy movements. This was a bit unusual as the intelligence would have been of great moment to the artillery net.

His absence left SFC Lionel King as the senior in the forward ground. King had not been told that enemy forces were in the vicinity; moreover, he mistakenly supposed that King Company (already destroyed) was in position on a low-lying ridge which he could see to his immediate front about 100-150 yards distant. Two of Love Company's own ROK soldiers were in an "outpost" about 10 yards forward of the other foxholes. One of them told King that he could hear the sounds of men digging to the front; the other said he heard the diggers conversing in Chinese.

King listened, heard the digging, but was still only half convinced. There were seven men near him and he placed them in fire position so that they faced toward the diggers. But he sent no word to others in the company of what he had heard or what he was doing because he still felt that the diggers might be King Company men and he didn't wish to be embarrassed.

Finally, he yelled out: "Hey, you out there, are you from K Company? Are you GIs?" Immediately everything became deathly silent. That made up his mind, and he said to his own men: "Fire!" They shot off perhaps sixty rounds with their rifles and the BAR, and they heard one loud, piercing scream from the darkness; it rose above the clatter of a machine gun firing from the same direction.

These bullets hit the ridge among Third Platoon's foxholes. But SFC Lyman B. Heacock didn't know whether an enemy attack was on or he was getting jitter fire from some part of his own line. So he told his men to hold fire. A few minutes later from north of the hill he heard a vigorous whirring of rattles, making about the same sound as a Halloween rattle. He concluded that the Chinese had come, but he still saw no targets.

Hearing the fire from Sergeant King's group, 1st Lieut. Clinton Jackson went running to the forward position to learn what King was doing. King said: "There's enemy out there. They're firing a machine gun. I've already hit one of them." Jackson told him that he would get a machine gun forward to put a covering fire on the hill, and that King was then to withdraw his group to the general line of the company.

Part of the enemy body had already closed around the right of Love's position. Cpl. Carl J. Bly was on duty as an outpost for the company command post. Fire began sweeping the ground, coming from the right flank. He thought it came from Third Platoon's weapons. His squad leader went to the command post to protest. Cpl. Wilfred Matthews came back carrying the word that, according to Vails, there was a "Chinese regiment" somewhere between the company and the river. The men were told to get into their foxholes, ready their weapons, and hold their ground.

At about this moment, Takahashi, having tarried overlong in his conference with the Captain, came suddenly awake. He moved from platoon to platoon, shouting to the men to pass the word down the line that the warming fires should be put out immediately. Men had to move directly into the glare to do it; the Chinese, already maneuvering to a set pattern, ignored these targets.

There was no blowing of bugles or piping of shepherd's horns. This deviation in the Chinese deployment is explainable on one count: they had no need to feel out Love's position; they had already seen it.

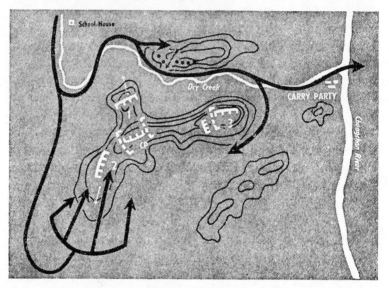

LOVE COMPANY, 9TH REGIMENT, 25 NOVEMBER

While these events were maturing on the hill, a supply party of ten Love Company men under Sgt. Charles Clark had been laboring toward the position from the west bank of the Chongchon. This was an all-Negro group. It had expected to arrive early in the evening, bringing food, bedrolls, and additional ammunition to the company. A hitch developed because Sgt. Joel Henry, Jr., in charge of the small convoy of one 2½-ton truck and one jeep which was moving the material north along the Chongchon found that he couldn't ford the river at any point parallel to Love's position. He strayed into 2nd Battalion's sector and got lost among the ridges. Clark and the nine men who were to carry the supply piggy-back from the river to the ridge waited in a house on the west bank until long past dark. Finally, guessing what had happened, Clark sent a man out to scout for the trucks.

The contact was made, and the convoy moved south haltingly, logged by the deep sand along the river bank. At the unloading point, Clark's men had time only to remove three bedrolls and one case of rations from the truck. At that point they heard the staccato sounds of a sharp fire fight coming from their own hill to the westward. Then Clark saw large groups of men running east along the creek draw directly north of him. He withdrew his men from the trucks to a small hill about 100 feet to the southward. A few of the men fired toward the running men. Clark yelled: "Are you GIs? Are you GIs?" But the running men neither answered, returned fire, nor turned aside. Clark then told his men to hold fire. He had noticed that the running men were wearing long overcoats and he assumed for that reason that they must be Americans, even though Love Company was overcoatless. So there were minutes of silence as most of the Chinese cleared by. But Clark's men were getting restive. They yelled that they wanted to fire and some of them said that they now saw other forms moving directly on them from the north.

At last, reluctantly, he told them: "Fire when you see somebody move." They did, and the fire was immediately returned from out of the foreground, in fairly heavy volume. Clark recognized the sound of a BAR operating within the other force. He yelled to his men to cease fire. Then came a call from out of the darkness, "We're GIs from K Company." They came on in—six of them—and they told Clark that King had been overrun and that most of its survivors were trying to get to the river. The two parties then formed as one.

Henry, who had stayed with his jeep, decided at that mo ment that he had seen enough. He drove straight for the river, with the truck following hard after him, and Clark, on the hill, cursing and screaming for them both to come back. By some fluke both vehicles escaped drowning and, after making it up the far bank, headed south along the road, bound for the artillery position. They got only 300 yards and ran into an enemy roadblock. The Chinese had strung mortar shells on a wire stretched across the road about shoulder high. When Henry stopped his jeep to look things over, a tommy gun opened fire on him from one side of the barrier and several rifles cracked from the other. Henry reached for his .50 machine gun, pulled the trigger, and found the weapon frozen tight. Looking northward, he saw a Chinese company marching down the railway embankment about 200 feet from his vehicle. That was when Henry, in his own words, "started deploying." Making his getaway, he was thrice wounded by grenade fragments. Wilson, the truck driver, was not again heard from.

Meantime the Chinese main attack against Love's ridge had been sprung in the quarter from which it was least expected. From the hill north of the company the enemy machine gun continued its grazing fire against the positions along the crest. The enemy main body had marched east, and a few small groups of skirmishers had split away from it to harass the right flank. This was the extent of the early pressure. Continuing for perhaps fifteen minutes, it did not seem ominous.

Habitually, the Chinese will attack via the gentlest slope of a ridge, though this was a point Love had not yet learned. On that particular ridge, the ground fell off most gradually to the southwest, the area farthest removed from the initial impingement.

Takahashi walked that way to see how the men were faring in the outwork of his own platoon's position. For a moment he stood at his forward foxhole listening. He saw and heard nothing.

Then from not 10 yards away, a man spoke, saying: "Hey there!" Takahashi called out: "Are you from K Company? If you don't answer, I'll open fire."

The night silence was split by a burp gun firing directly at him from a few yards away. He dropped flat and his men returned fire. The Chinese in the foreground apparently moved off immediately. Then from about 200 yards beyond the lower end of the left flank, rifle and automatic fire broke out all along a line which curled around that corner of the ridge for about one quarter mile. The men counted at least four submachine guns and one heavy in the line; there seemed to be several hundred rifles.

At that range all of the fire was going high and doing no damage. But the static fire exchange continued for somewhat less than ten minutes. Then the enemy force arose and moved toward the ridge, firing with all weapons as it advanced.

In the interval, there had been just a brief foray at Heacock's position, possibly purposed as a feint by the few Chinese skirmishers who had closed on the right flank. They had wiggled forward to within Third Platoon's lines. One campfire was still blazing there. Cpl. John Leeper had gone to put it out, but as he stepped into the circle of light, bullets buzzed all around him, and he had to pull back and leave the beacon burning. Heacock thought he saw a Chinese run past him. He yelled: "Who are you?" The man, running in a crouch, made straight for the command post and a rifleman near Matthews shot him down. Two or three others who had broken into the circle met the same fate.

But the marching line approaching from the southwest came straight on and was now within 50 yards of the base of the hill. The bullets no longer were going high. SFC James Woods, who had the forward squad in Second Platoon, had already lost three of his ROK soldiers. Unnerved, they had risen from their foxholes as if to quit their ground, and a Chinese with a burp gun had cut them down.

Coming out with all weapons, First Platoon completed its withdrawal to the main ridgeline as this U-shaped body of Chinese closed around Second Platoon. The enemy machine gun on the northern hill then shifted its fire to the ground where the two platoons joined. Takahashi sent a message to Vails: "I've got to have more men if I'm to hold," and back came the reply: "Take First Squad of First Platoon." But King's squad, cut to four men by this time (in the darkness the others remained unaccounted for) never got to the mission. When he passed the command post Vails told him:

"I'm getting direct fire from my right rear; they must be right upon us at the base of the hill." King didn't have to be told. Bullets were zinging all around him, and Vails was making good use of his foxhole. Lieutenant Jackson told King to move his men back and cover the draw behind the command post. He figured that if Second Platoon was beaten back, King could serve as a blocking force preventing its envelopment as it withdrew along the ridgeline.

Takahashi again moved down toward his forward positions. The advancing enemy skirmishers seemed to be within about 30 yards. He yelled to Sgt. Napoleon Cross, who was on a machine gun at the extreme point: "Cross, can you hold?" Cross yelled back: "No sir!" (By then he had lost three men and Woods had lost four.) Takahashi called: "Then fall back on me!" Doubling back to the crest, Takahashi yelled for others to rally around him. Two BAR men and about sixteen men with rifles and carbines jumped to it, quitting their foxholes and lying prone among the rocks to fire.

But the confusion was almost overpowering. As Cross and the other Americans had arisen to withdraw, the Chinese had rushed right in among them, and now they were coming up the hill together. Amid the smoke, dark, and excitement, it was impossible to distinguish friend from foe. The men on the crest took the chance and fired anyway. Woods got back and flopped down next to Takahashi. A Chinese came at the rifleman who was lying next him. He tried to fire, but when he pulled the trigger, there was just a click. So he swung with the stock and brained the Chinese. Another American, his carbine gone empty, heaved a boulder accurately and knocked a burp gunner back down the ridge.

This one quick, resourceful riposte enabled a few friends to come into the position and stopped the charge of the Chinese riflemen and submachine gunners at a distance of 20 feet. They got in among the rocks and for a few minutes only the Americans fought them on fairly even terms. But their own fire power began to diminish. Takahashi heard it from all around. "My carbine won't work." "I'm out of ammo." "The

BARs are almost empty." The men had been firing uniformly and steadily. Insofar as he could, Takahashi had mixed his shouts of encouragement with exhortations to his men to hold fire where possible. He knew that the company had come into the position critically short of clipped ammunition, the carbine men averaging only about two magazines apiece. Third Platoon, though less directly threatened, had been engaging the enemy with fire in three directions; its supply was running low.

But already the enemy was changing tactics. Two purple flares had gone up. The riflemen and submachine gunners had pulled back from the slope, giving over their places to a line of grenadiers. Grenades began to explode around the crestline. What with the distance, the weak throwing and the relatively light effect of the percussion potato mashers, the attack at first had only a nuisance value. A few men were hit by fragments, but their wounds were light, and there was no moral jolt to the defenders.

In this interlude, had Love Company been able to battle the enemy on his own terms, the fight still might have been won. But there wasn't one grenade in the American position. The grenade supply which might have served the purpose was on the truck with Sgt. Henry somewhere along the Chongchon. So to keep the grenadiers at distance, Takahashi's men had to continue to waste rifle ammunition on forces which they could not see.

There was a cry of "Banzai! Banzai! Banzai!" from down the slope. The Chinese grenadiers sprang up and rushed the hill, throwing as they advanced. They were met by well-directed fire, from the BARs particularly. Some of them dropped, and the others recoiled. For a few moments Takahashi thought that the fight was turning.

But the Chinese on the right shank of the U-shaped line had built up their fire against the command post area. Heacock was on the rear slope of Third Platoon's position, facing the south and trying to give the command post a covering fire. One BAR man and two riflemen were with him. They saw a man spring from the bushes on their right and run toward them yelling: "Cease fire! Cease fire!" in perfect English. Heacock sang out: "Who are you?" The man yelled back: "Sergeant Riley." It happened that Love Company had a Sergeant Riley. The name threw Heacock momentarily, and he lowered his rifle. One of his men yelled: "Hell, that's not Riley's voice!" and the Chinese scuttled back into the brush before anyone could fire. Then rifle fire in heavy volume began splattering the rocks and Heacock's group had to go flat.

Right after that, two things happened very close together. Several Chinese got close enough to the crestline to lob grenades into Takahashi's group at about 10-foot range. One landed right in Cpl. Glenn Huff's foxhole and blew off without hurting him. Two ROKs were wounded by a second explosion. Then from down in the draw next the command post a cry went up: "The Captain's hit!" It was heard by everybody on the hill. The words were true enough. Vails had gone down with two bullets through his arm and shoulder. But it was the outcry, more than the Captain's wounds, which finished the company.

Raybould, the artillery observer, noticed this phenomenon. He was just to the rear of Takahashi on the hill. Vails had been yelling moral encouragement to his men throughout the fight. So long as he was up, and Takahashi appeared to be acting with the backing of his authority, the men obeyed his orders. But when the word flashed that the Captain was down, control passed immediately from the lieutenant's hands.

There was a great blowing of whistles. The Chinese along the lower slope arose and walked straight toward the crest. Takahashi screamed to his men to fire; they paid him no heed. Already some were getting out and moving down the ridgeline. The Nisei fell back about 25 yards and tried to make another stand. Lieutenant Jackson yelled to him that, if he could hold on just a few minutes, he'd rally some men from Third Platoon and bring them forward. From down the slope Vails' voice could be heard crying faintly: "Stick together! Keep fighting! Hold your ground!" The men recalled afterward that they had heard his exhortations as they drifted back along the ridge; but it did not change the situation at the time.

Takahashi was doing his personal best. The ridge top was thick with dust and smoke from the smudged fires. He stood his ground shouting: "Regroup on me!" Perhaps a dozen men from his own platoon and the First responded, but they did not stick it very long. The Chinese came forward again, and as rifle fire began to strike around them, the Americans gave ground.

Love Company had fallen apart. Some of its fractions were already headed for the river, trying to get out in any way that they could.

There was one last attempt to rally the remaining force on Third Platoon's ground. That unit had not been closely engaged and its losses to enemy fire had been quite moderate. Takahashi still hoped that this rump of the position might be held for the remainder of the night. The enemy was slow in regrouping and coming on. In the interval, the survivors had time to set up a west-facing line and divide their ammunition. But as the fire exchange again got underway, Lieutenant Jackson was hit by an early bullet.

That left only Takahashi and twenty of Jackson's men. He told them to get out. It was an unnecessary order. They were already going, and there was no military order or dignity in the way they were doing it. The moral dissolution was almost complete. Singly, or in groups of two to four men, they took off, looking for sanctuary. The enemy was swarming over the countryside. Many of these small groups were ambushed after quitting the hill.

But on the record, it is self-evident that these were good fighting men deserving of a much better fate.

Given a harsh assignment, they were thrown upon their own resources to get forward the fighting supply which might have enabled them to carry it out. It is clear that these resources were not sufficient.

They were badly informed as to where their friends were located.

They lacked grenades in a fight tailormade for grenade action.

They were low on rifle ammunition.

They had no mortar shells though mortars might have saved them.

At any stage of the fight, artillery would have been helpful, and possibly decisive. But they were not in communication and the guns could do nothing for them.

Their immediate leaders had been negligent about security.

The bivouac fires were like a magnet to the enemy, but when the enemy appeared, the error was not redressed by sharp decision and immediate action.

As the enemy attack developed, the power of the company was not reoriented toward the point of danger. One second lieutenant was left to carry the main burden with a handful of men.

Riflemen, unhelped by any other weapons, cannot in any desperate situation do much more than these men did. But though they were more failed than failing, what happened to this company and to King Company still cost dear. The main Chinese column, after crossing the Chongchon, clamped down on the main highway between the forward infantry line and the artillery base at Kujang-dong. It was part of this force which overran the command post and aid station of 9th Regiment's First Battalion.

The blow was irreparable. From this one slash deep into the vitals of the 2nd Division, the Eighth Army front in North Korea never recovered. The breach continued to widen as the battle progressed. King Company's lonely machine gunner, Giudici, squatting in the frosted corn patch, had witnessed the loosing of the pebble which became an avalanche. And in everything that followed from the moment when he first saw the Chinese column trotting along the creek bed, the lesson shines forth clear that when battle troops lack effective communications, and when they do not understand down to the last man that fullness of information is the mainspring of operations, the fight is already half lost.

There is a final personal entry. Takahashi was captured before he could quit the vicinity of the ridge. Eight Chinese grabbed him. They told him in sign language that he would yell for other Love Company men to assemble on him or they would shoot him. Then they stood him in a ravine and from behind rocks covered him with their rifles.

He cooperated—at least halfway. For five minutes or so he stood there shouting: "Anone! (*Hey* in Japanese) Love Company, don't answer. Love Company, don't come." At last his captors wearied of the sport and led him back up to his own hill. As the party walked along, the Chinese picked up rifles and carbines which Love's men had thrown down. Each had about four or five extra weapons by the time they got to where Takahashi had made his first stand.

There the Chinese had set up a battalion command post. The commander talked for some time to the group leader, but didn't interrogate Takahashi. Another Chinese group appeared. In the middle of it was Clemmie Sims, first sergeant of Love Company.

The commander gave a sudden order. The prisoners were taken in charge by two Chinese bearing tommy guns and marched to the small hill where the enemy machine gun had opened fire early in the evening.

As they walked along the path, Takahashi sang a song, "The Fatigue Blues," which had been popular in Love Company. But for the obscene lyrics known to the company, he substituted other words, singing to Sims: "We will move along a certain distance, then I will give you a signal, then you will jump the man in front and I'll take care of the guy behind."

The rear guard didn't like the singing, and prodded Takahashi in the back with his tommy gun. Takahashi said: "I wonder how far these bastards will take us before they shoot us."

Sims mistook these words for the signal and sprang for his man before Takahashi was set. They went down in the dirt together. Too late, Takahashi jumped for the rear guard. The man was pulling back and in the act of firing even as Taka-hashi lunged. The bullets ripped Takahashi's left sleeve.

He did a running dive for the side of the hill and went roll-ing down the slope. That was how he made his breakaway. As he ran, he kept listening for the sounds of tommy-gun fire on the hill where he had left Sims. But he never heard it and that was the only thing that comforted him.

# 5

## In the Middle

During all of these terrible hours when Baker Company was having its ordeal east of the Chongchon, and King and Love were being ripped apart west of the river, Second Battalion, which held the middle ground of the 9th Regiment front, kept the greater part of its strength composed and intact.

The notable exception was Easy Company and the battalion's forward command post. Whereas the other companies were united around Objective 26, a great circular hill in the angle west of the river where the Chongchon met its tributary, Easy Company, assigned to Objective 15, was in fact assisting First Battalion to break a trail along the east bank.

Maj. Cesibes V. Barberis, one of the youngest and ablest infantry battalion commanders in Korea, after leaving his forward command post in the vicinity of Chinaman's Hat, elected to accompany Easy Company. He reckoned that the artillery positions which he had seen that morning were much too close to give decisive support to his objectives on either side of the river, but that, comparatively, Easy Company would run the greater jeopardy.

Forebodings such as this were not uncommon on that day. They were in part due to the abnormal difficulties which the Chongchon countryside presented to a modern, motorized field force. Though the ubiquitous hills and ridges were not of formidable height, the area was uniquely devoid of flat spaces, suitable for guns, command posts, aid stations, or supply points. Thus no element could be kept in a normal or practical working alignment with anything else. The distances were at once too great and too short.

Compartmented by the hills, operations were critically deprived of the techniques which promote combat unity. If the guns were not too close to companies in the assault, then the wire wouldn't stretch or the radios wouldn't work. Within the main valley, installations were often jammed close together, and even some of the infantry was short of elbowroom. But proximity did not of itself lessen their sense of isolation. The uneven ground foreshortened vision and redistributed the varied sounds of battle so that nothing could be measured in its true significance.

Much that happened to 9th Regiment—the successive shattering of some of its components and the survival of others—must remain all but inexplicable to those who have not labored in the same terrain.

On the morning of 25 November, Fox, George, and How Companies got up to their big hill beside the Chongchon without sweat. With the column went one platoon of tanks and two Quad-50s. The three infantry companies dug in on the south slope of the hill so that they faced toward the river and the dry creek bed. How Company was in the flat ground next a native village. The armor and the antiaircraft vehicles were put back of How Company, ready to fire along either the main valley or its tributary.

In the same hours that Baker Company was beginning its attack on Hill 219 (Objective 16) Easy climbed and took its ridge, Objective 15, slightly to Baker's rear. There it dug in, and for the remainder of the day played only a minor hand in the battle.

Barberis knew that First Battalion was meeting some resistance, but got none of the details. What mainly concerned him was that an interdicting fire by machine guns from Hill 219 and by machine guns and mortars from Objective 17 was playing constantly on the ford where Second Battalion had crossed the Chongchon and stopping his supply vehicles. By nature of the ground, the sources of this harassment were masked to fire from both parts of his battalion and their supporting weapons. During the day there were four air strikes against Objective 17 and the air claimed that it had eliminated seven mortars. And yet the mortar fire continued; Fox Company lost two killed to this distant fire, and three in Easy's ranks were wounded.

However, when the day closed, Barberis felt no real alarm about the character of enemy resistance. What worried him mainly was that a patrol of fifteen men from George Company had moved out 3,000 yards along the ridgetops to the westward just before dark, looking for some sign of King Company, and had found nothing.

Just at dusk, he set up his command post within the little valley south of Chinaman's Hat. There came a call from Lieut. Martin J. Kavanaugh of Fox Company that from their position they could see enemy movements along the railroad embankment on the east side of the river. One "mass of at least 200 enemy infantry" could be seen. The indicated target area was soon taken under fire from two directions. The division artillery at Kujang-dong fired north; the tanks with Second Battalion fired southeast. Though the results of this crossfire are unknown, the entry is typical of the confusions of the night.

Barberis walked out to make a personal reconnaissance. It was in this interval that the enemy forces fell upon the American camp south and west of Chinaman's Hat. His command post was overrun; his intelligence sergeant and driver were killed by mortar fire. The timing of this attack and the fact that troops in the bivouac area first saw the enemy columns when they were wading the river excludes any possibility that they could have approached via the main valley or its tributary during the daylight hours. Either they had been in hiding approximate to the river, or marching to the south of Love Company, they had attacked directly over Objective 25.

Second Battalion, encamped on Objective 26, felt little or no impact from the explosion which had occurred on its rear near Chinaman's Hat, except for loss of telephone contact with its commander. Nor in the hours which immediately followed was it alerted to the Chinese column which, moving down the dry creek bed to cross the Chongchon and attack the base of First Battalion, was passing almost under the shadow of Second Battalion's guns. The tanks and Quad-50s could have routed this enterprise had they but known. That they continued in their night laager all unsuspecting was not more unusual than that the Chinese, marching right across the front of this relatively strong force, missed its presence altogether, as was proved by subsequent developments.

These weird omissions were in the very nature of the struggle. The Chinese were fighting a battle of infiltration. Proceeding according to a well-set plan, they advanced on a generally southeastward-running axis along the natural corridors leading into, and out from, the central river valley.

Their forces were not "massed" or dressed linearly. As they came forward, they did not present a broad front in any quarter. They attacked with columns which proceeded along the drainage lines, seeking entry into the American rear.

The big fight was in the strict sense but a series of meeting engagements. When by reason of its location an American unit lay partly athwart the enemy right-of-way, or where the Chinese knew the exact location of a bivouac because part of their screening force had engaged the same troops during the day, there was a resultant collision. But some of the companies had closed on high ground in late afternoon. The enemy missed them in the same way that a man proceeding via a valley footpath will miss a beartrap on the far side of the hill. There is nothing in the record to suggest that as they advanced the Chinese were served by a superior intelligence system.

Night passed without Regiment or Division knowing that King and Love Companies, for all practical purposes, had ceased to exist. When Wolff and his staff from First Battalion, exhausted and shaken by their narrow escape, reached Colonel Sloane shortly after midnight and told him that their command post and attendant installations had been overrun, he thought this was the worst that had happened to his regiment.

It was perhaps three hours later that he got a telephone call from Lieut. Joseph Manto of Easy Company. The same enemy thrust from out of the north which had enveloped Baker Company on Hill 219 had closed down around Objective 15. A flash-and-sound crew belonging to the 1st Field Artillery Observation Battalion, which was under Easy's wing, had been hit hard. Manto also reported that Easy and elements of the 2nd Chemical Mortar Battalion were surrounded and under heavy attack. He closed by saying: "We're holding and that's what we'll continue to do."

He meant every word of it. Such became the pressure that Easy was beaten from the hill. But without waiting for daylight, it counterattacked and regained the ridge top. There were fifty-two dead and wounded Americans within the company lines when morning came, and thrice that number in enemy dead lay around the position.

Dog and Easy Companies on the extreme right had reported "negative" throughout the night. Item on the extreme left had been nonengaged. The main strength of Second Battalion on the big hill west of the river was relatively fresh and untouched. Otherwise, the 9th Regiment was a salvage operation. This was the score as breakfast time again came round.

As for how the higher levels had reacted to the collision, in which so much had already happened for the worse, though so very little of it echoed from front to rear, it wasn't until 2400 on 25 November that the Division Commander decided he was being brought to full battle and there was genuine cause for alarm. But that estimate was based less on what was known of 9th Regiment's situation than on the affair at Chinaman's Hat and the continuing reports that 38th Regiment was completely engaged. The Division Artillery Commander had reached an identical conclusion by about 1800, which perhaps bespeaks the greater sensitiveness of the artillery net, wherein what the man at the forward foxhole sees and thinks is more likely to be relayed straight to the top.

At 0630 men on outpost for George Company on the big hill saw a body of troops coming down the creek bed from the direction where Love Company had been the night before. Full light had not yet come; the column was about 700

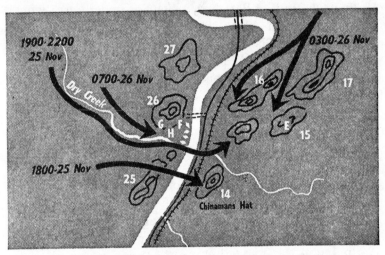

DISPOSITIONS SECOND BATTALION, 9TH REGIMENT

Showing CCF penetrations past the battalion and into the regimental rear. Main objectives are here numbered as in the American attack plan.

yards away when first sighted. Its closed ranks were walking boldly in the open. Hence the outpost concluded they were Americans and, except for one man, paid them no further heed.

Sgt. William Long kept watching. As the column got to within about 250 yards, he yelled to the others, "They're Chinks!" Within a few seconds, other men from George armed with rifles and BARs had built up a fire line facing up the creek bed. At 200 yards Long opened fire with his carbine, and on that signal, heavy volley fire riddled the column while still standing. Perhaps half of the Chinese were shot down before any could take cover. The survivors crawled behind rocks in the creek bed or flopped behind the embankments of the surrounding rice paddies, whence they sought to return the fire. The point of the column, which had come abreast of the little village when the fight opened, refuged to within the houses.

Capt. Frank E. Munoz of George sent a runner to Lieutenant Kavanaugh of Fox telling him what was happening and what to do about it.

Kavanaugh dispatched a tank which, moving via a trail with some of George's men pointing the way, took position on the hill flank of the village and shelled the houses from 30 yards' range. George's Third Platoon, meanwhile, had moved via the hillside to the far side of the village and come out on the enemy rear.

These arrangements made the sweep complete within thirty minutes. The tank killed ten Chinese in the village, and five survivors at that point surrendered to the infantry. In the fighting along the creek bed and across the paddies, George killed seventy-five of the enemy and took twenty additional prisoners.

They were clean-looking, well-set-up soldiers. Each man carried a pack complete with entrenching tool, blankets, and several bandoliers of ammunition. They were armed with American M1s, carbines, the old type Japanese rifle, and a new Russian-made submachine gun. All were supplied with two or more hand grenades. A party of porters with the column had been carrying a big pot and a large quantity of rice for the common mess.

But conspicuous by its absence was any sort of radio or signal equipment. There was one other item in solid proof that the enemy, too, was handicapped by communications difficulties. When it was struck, the column was serving as escort for thirty North Korean civilian litter bearers. They were sallying openly into the caldron of the prior night's fighting to help bury their dead and bring out their wounded, seemingly convinced that the issue had been decided and their friends had come into possession of the central valley. Here for the first time the Chinese enemy overreached because of the snap victory won from King and Love Companies. It was this same mixture of stupidity coupled with low cunning which was to make them a highly vulnerable antagonist once their tricks were fathomed. Along the Chongchon, our men were getting their first lessons.

With the dawn, a few survivors from King and Love straggled back to units still in radio touch with the rear, and higher headquarters for the first time learned positively about the gap in the 9th Regiment's front.

After that, Colonel Sloane decided on the shuffle which moved his remaining strength from the east shore, including Easy Company, to the west shore of the Chongchon, re-enforcing Second Battalion. Regimental boundaries were shifted, and the 23rd Infantry, which had belatedly assembled in the Chinaman's Hat area because of the slowness of the motor shuttle, was put in on the right with its right flank refused toward the southeast.

These movements, however, and the expected solidifying of the 9th-23rd front (the exact situation of the 38th Regiment continued obscure) were more easily ordered than done. The Chinese still held the peak of Chinaman's Hat; their machine guns interdicted the main road. Easy Company had forty wounded men within its lines on Objective 15, and a way had to be found to run them through the enemy fire block and on to hospital, before the able-bodied could ford the river.

Lieutenant Manto carefully destroyed the 4.2 mortars which had been left behind by the chemical battalion, and the radar equipment of the observation unit, before quitting the hill. He then split his company. One platoon waded the Chongchon and, joining up with Second Battalion, began to prepare a night position for the company. The other was given the task of evacuating vehicles and the wounded through the fire block.

It was done in this manner: Riflemen and BAR men took cover along the road embankment just underneath Chinaman's Hat. From their line, they could see the enemy positions on the crest. It was realized that the lead vehicle would receive the opening volume of heavy fire.

For a space of about 100 yards, that risk would have to be run. This was right under "The Hat." For the rest of the distance, the embankment put the road in defilade.

Cpl. James L. Brown and three members of his squad were in the lead jeep. They volunteered to dismount and, while trying to protect themselves behind the vehicle's metal, push it through at a slow pace. The decoy would draw full fire from the hill. The deployed rifle line would spot the positions and start to fire. Then when (and if) the jeep completed its run through the gauntlet, the firers would open up with everything. At that point the rest of the convoy would race full speed ahead through the fire gap.

The plan worked to perfection. The jeep was shot to pieces during the crawl forward, but by a miracle, the four men escaped unhurt. When the convoy made its run, not a shot was fired from the hill.

In mid-afternoon, just after Easy Company had again formed on the Battalion, Barberis got orders to move his troops back to Hill 153 (Objective 25). The retrograde had an elementary purpose—line-straightening. It put Barberis directly across the Chongchon from the perimeter of First Battalion, 23rd Infantry. That unit had need of a friendly shoulder; its lines were bumping Chinaman's Hat. The question might be asked why this festering sore had been tolerated within the American rear. No clear, wholly satisfying answer is possible. But its almost sheer rock walls appeared too formidable for infantry attack, and its recessed machine-gun bunkers defied artillery.

The new front along the Chongchon formed that evening about two miles downstream from where the positions had been the night before. Barberis closed on Hill 153 about one hour before sundown. A patrol went out to search for the

right flank of First Battalion, 9th Regiment, which had crossed
Barberis' rear during the afternoon and moved up on his left.
The four M4 tanks under Lieut. Charles Haywood, Jr., and
the two Quad-50 vehicles were put on the river side of the
hill with the infantry screening them to the front.

Thus on both sides of the Chongchon the enemy had as
his springboard the same hills which the division had held
the preceding night.

At about 2100, the 23rd Regiment's front on the east shore
was hit and broken by a strong enemy thrust coming from
the north. The Regimental Command Post and Headquarters
Company were overrun first off. Both First and Second Battalions, knocked off balance, withdrew down the river about
600 yards before they again steadied.

When Colonel Sloane got the word, he envisaged the Chinese, from their new ground, wading the river and attacking
his Second Battalion in rear. About one hour after Colonel
Freeman's front buckled, Sloane called Barberis and told him
to load as many men as he could on his tanks, trucks, and
antiaircraft vehicles and cross the Chongchon into 23rd Regiment's ground. Such troops as could not go out on wheels
were to search westward and join the First Battalion.

What further jeopardy might have resulted from this gam-
bit was never to be learned. The battalion hardly started.
George was on the high ground and the men were just vacat-
ing their foxholes. Fox was trailing down the hill bound for
the river. How Company, lodged in a small ravine in the
center of the ridge, was holding its mortars in readiness to
cover Fox, if necessary.

At that moment the battalion came under full attack from
the precisely opposite direction. The patrol had gone that
way looking for First Battalion. It had not come back. The
enemy closed in through this intervening space, and as his
fire crackled suddenly from around three sides of the hill, it
revealed that his skirmishers, unseen, had crept to within 40
yards of the foxhole line.

From the start, the pressure built up directly against Captain Munoz's position on the high ground. George Company was well set for all-around defense—so it looked. Second Platoon held the cap of the main hill facing north. Third Platoon was on line with it to its right, but on a slightly higher elevation. To the rear was a shallow saddle and beyond it a lesser rise, perhaps 100 yards distant. On this elevation, a platoon from Easy Company faced generally west so as to cover the company's left rear, while First Platoon guarded toward the river. However, two light machine guns from First Platoon were so positioned that they could put a flanking fire across the Easy platoon's front.

From the beginning to end, this Chinese action appears to have been perfectly coordinated and timed, according to a predetermined plan.

It opened with a heavy volley of rifle fire which had the Easy platoon as its direct target. The platoon held its ground and returned fire. First Platoon's two machine guns got into action; they were in good position; a line of Chinese riflemen was walking straight up the hill toward Easy's foxholes, firing as they marched. But the ground was uneven and the night dark. That gave them a measure of protection. Some were shot down but the others kept advancing.

One hundred yards behind the enemy rifle line, three of the little 57-mm mortars were also moving up the hill. Their fire was loosed against the machine guns. The first few rounds were erratic. The mortarmen displaced, moved closer, and began to hit home. The two machine guns were knocked out. With that, the enemy line came right on up and over the knoll. Both platoons were overrun; less than half of their strength was able to get away in the darkness.

While the force on the rearward knoll was being pinned and then destroyed in this manner, Second and Third Platoons had taken no part. Out along their open flanks, they could hear voices yelling: "Don't shoot! GIs! Don't shoot! GIs!" M/S William G. Long thought that the cries were on the level, and that the other platoons were breaking and coming into his lines. But he was doubly perplexed because he thought he could hear men speaking Chinese out somewhere beyond his front. He called to his men: "Don't fire yet!" The fact was that though they had heard fire all around, they had seen no targets.

Then Long heard a bugle blown from rearward—four sharp notes, twice repeated. That was the enemy call from the other hill, signaling that the point was won and that heavy weapons should come up.

Right afterward, whistles shrilled from many points, and bullets thickened around Long. Cpl. Henry Miller yelled: "Here they come! I can see them!"

By then Long could see them also. Perhaps a score of dark forms stood out clear against the starlight within a hand toss of his foxhole. They were stooped over, looking like hunchbacks, and they moved in perfect silence. Long and several others fired. The figures hit the ground and returned fire. Several grenades exploded near the position.

Munoz had previously instructed Long that if any such thing happened, he was to sideslip his men and form with Second Platoon on the other half of this bifurcated peak. He didn't want the platoons split and the other rise, though slightly lower, had more fighting room.

Long gave the order. The men made a dash for it. So far none had been hurt. As the two platoons united, there came a continuing whistle blast from directly in front of Second Platoon's ground. Then a heavy machine gun opened fire from the knoll where First Platoon had been. The aim was dead on, and the fire caught the line in enfilade, ripping it from end to end. As yet, there was no fire from the rise which Third Platoon had vacated—and for a good reason.

Munoz wasn't there to see that part of it. He had slipped away to his command post in the ravine behind the hill to telephone Fox Company for help. Kavanaugh—an ever-willing hand—replied that Fox was beset on all sides, fighting for dear life, and could do no more.

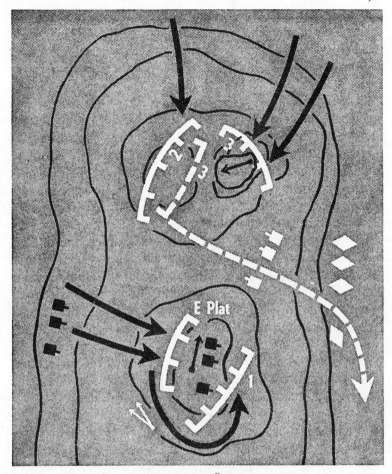

SECOND BATTALION, 9TH REGIMENT

The CCF attack on the George Company perimeter, night of 26 November, ending in the defeat and withdrawal of the Battalion.

The mortar platoon in the ravine was feeding the tubes as fast as they could fire, in an attempt to break the Chinese force moving upslope. They continued until the last round. By then there was no time left to evacuate the mortars. They thermited the tubes and then made for the tanks.

On the hill the Americans still fighting—some in foxholes

and some flattened against the rocks—could no longer raise their heads to see what was coming against them. They fired mechanically with their small arms and heaved such grenades as they had, but the grazing machine-gun fire from their flank made it impossible to take aim.

Munoz, looking up at the fight from his post in the ravine, could see the play in silhouette, as if looking at a puppet show. Chinese topped the rise, only to be cut down by their own gun firing from the other direction. Some fell into the foxholes. There were screams as men grappled for life and death. The scene was lighted occasionally by the exploding of a grenade. Still, Munoz could hear his men shouting words of encouragement to one another.

It could not last long. From the knoll which Third Platoon had vacated, another machine gun opened point-blank fire against the hill. Other Chinese got into the hollow and tried to grenade the defenders, but their throwing arms weren't equal to the 15 yards of distance. The machine-gun crossfire exploding across the knoll top, however, settled the issue.

Munoz called Capt. Marsh Stark, the senior officer present with the battalion, and told him the company was finished, the position gone. Stark told him he could withdraw.

But no order was given or needed. The survivors on the hill had spent their last grenade. The BARs and most of the carbines were empty. Long yelled to his men to jump for the slope and try to roll down into the saddle. In some manner, a few of them made it.

This had been a short fight: from the firing of the first shot —perhaps twenty minutes; the final stand of the two platoons —perhaps seven to eight minutes.

But Long, who had gone onto the hill with thirty-four able-bodied men, had only seven at the end. Second Platoon's losses were in ratio. Total loss for the company was seventy-three men.

There were four who had not cleared Third Platoon's hill in the move to the final position. One was Pfc. Gaskins, the machine gunner. Long told Gaskins to follow and bring the gun, but he neither answered nor followed. He sat there working his gun while Third Platoon joined its brother. Long heard him firing down the slope for several minutes afterward. Then the Chinese bore him down, turned his gun around and fired against the final position.

Three who witnessed Gaskins' stand were Pvt. Albert Smalley and two of Long's ROK riflemen. They were in a foxhole when the order came to move. Before they could obey, eight Chinese had pinioned them. They were moved at rifle point farther up the slope in the thrust which killed Gaskins. Then they were held by the machine gun while the Chinese used it to accomplish the final defeat of the company.

The enemy, after closing on the big hill, did not pursue, but turned to organization of the position. Fractions of George and of Fox worked back toward the tanks and the Quads, carrying or helping such wounded as they could find. Of Easy Company there was little left to find. How had suffered only moderately.

To make possible this scant assembly, the Quads already were raking the hilltops with their .50 guns. The wounded—perhaps thirty to forty men altogether—were loaded on top the tanks. Munoz told the other men to follow along.

The little column started out via the base of the hill on which the Easy platoon was first struck. Chinese mortars were already firing from its crest toward the low ground. The lead tank fired on the mortars and scored a fluke hit immediately. But by the flash of the gun, Munoz and his men saw a line of Chinese infantry on the slope just above them, perhaps 35 yards away. A bazooka round banged out of the darkness, hit the tank in the engine compartment and started a fire. The riders jumped off and, along with the tank crew, ran for a half-track which was up ahead.

Munoz and six of his men, using the armor for a shield, stayed there to give the column a covering fire. They did it with two rifles, two BARs, and three carbines. Bullets from the slope splattered against the metal like rain, but the Chinese made no attempt to close down on the small party. There were two tanks still to clear the position. But the fire within the tank was blazing so high that Munoz feared it might explode. It was time to get out. However, they couldn't run for it. Sgt. Lester Heath had taken a rifle bullet through the foot and had to walk along leaning on Munoz. The latter said to the other five: "There's safety in numbers; better stay with me." They walked away from the hill at the pace of a cripple.

One Quad-50 was knocked out by a mortar round as it started toward the river. By then both Quads had burned up their ammunition supply. From the base at Kujang-dong, 37th Field Artillery Battalion had fired 477 rounds in defense of the hill, but the infantry action had been too closely joined for artillery to do much good.

Part of the infantry rode the tanks across the Chongchon and landed dry on the other side. The others waded the stream in 10-degrees-above-zero weather.

The able-bodied and the "dry" men went into position in the perimeter of the 23rd Regiment. Barberis evacuated his wounded and his "wetbacks" to a point near Kujang-dong where, beginning at about 0700, they were given the dry-clothing, hot-food treatment. Losses from frozen feet and exposure cut further into the battalion's slender strength. On 25 November, it had counted 28 officers and 750 men. By 28 November, it could muster 9 officers and approximately 250 men.

After making the east shore in the first withdrawal, Lieutenants Haywood and Kavanaugh volunteered to recross to the enemy side of the river with the tanks and prowl the far shore in search of stragglers and wounded. They continued this mission throughout the hours of darkness, and were the last men to cross the Chongchon after dawn, getting back to their own lines at 0900. But in the course of their work, two more of the M4 tanks had been shot from under them.

When the fight on the hill had quieted, Smalley, the prisoner, was told to get into his sleeping bag. He slept till first light and awakened to find a Chinese officer shaking him by the shoulder. Speaking perfect English, the officer began to question Smalley and the two ROK prisoners. Smalley said nothing. One of the ROKs looked at him questioningly, and when Smalley shook his head, the ROK also remained tight-lipped. The officer made a gesture toward several of his riflemen. The two ROKs were marched 20 yards away and shot, while Smalley looked on.

Then pointing south across the Chongchon, the officer said to Smalley: "Your outfit's over there; take off!" Smalley walked down the hill expecting to get a bullet in his back. But he got across the Chongchon without further adventure except that he had to jump for cover several times to avoid enemy patrols.

Smalley, as even his name suggests, was a tiny soldier, weight about 115, age nineteen, with no fire in his eye and little dynamite in his system.

About the mystery of why he was turned loose in such a manner there was much conjecture. The intelligence people finally decided it was for propaganda purposes, to create a more friendly feeling among Americans.

If that was the trick, it backfired. On getting back to George Company, Smalley said to Munoz: "I saw what they did to those ROKs. One of them was my buddy. Now let me have a machine gun. I at last feel like killing some of those sons of bitches."

The morning wore on quietly. As was their custom, the Chinese drew back a brief space into the hills to cook their morning rice, bury their dead, and regroup in preparation for the night. The 23rd Regiment moved forward into its old position with little difficulty. The command post was as the regiment had left it, the files still intact.

However, all of this was very small change. To the right of the 38th Regiment, the front of the ROK II Corps had been riven wide, its formations scattered, its men driven south in panic flight. The 38th, already under full attack from the north, was now having to reform its right wing to parry the major blow expected from the east. Terrorized South Korean soldiers were drifting back through its lines. It was difficult to tell an attacking enemy from a fleeing friend.

Yet as to the true nature of the total disaster on Eighth Army's right flank, 2nd Infantry Division, though it was next under the gun, got only an occasional hint.

Divarty had a liaison officer with ROK II Corps, Maj. John H. Sanguinetti. At 1100, by some fluke he got through to the headquarters by telephone. He said that he was with the KAMAG people (American officers in the Korean Army Military Advisory Group) at an airstrip just west of Tokchon, and that there was nothing to do but wait since the Chinese had cut all routes to the south of ROK II Corps. They had prepared their vehicles for demolition, knowing that escape was impossible.

Sanguinetti was brought out by one of Division Artillery's L-5s. The pilot made four more flights during the afternoon and each time brought out a KAMAG officer. But there was still a large group waiting at the airstrip when he made the final run. By then the Chinese had surrounded the field and the runway was under small arms fire. The reports had it that the KAMAG officers who didn't make it were killed that night.

From scraps of information such as this one, 2nd Division had to piece together "the friendly situation." It was becoming clearer that there weren't friends enough, and that from both flanks the division was being compressed into the strait jacket formed by its limited line of communications to the rear.

An understanding of developments, however, requires closer examination of what had happened to the 38th Infantry.

# 6

# The Long Patrol

Within the 38th (rock of the marne) regiment on the first day of battle, the blows dealt by the enemy fell heaviest upon Able, Fox, George, and Love Companies.

This was pure happenstance determined by the geography of the battlefield, abetted here and there by human error. As happened in the valley of the Chongchon against the 9th Regiment, the Chinese columns came forward in the darkness via the footpaths and stream beds, feeling for the American positions.

In their groping they missed some units altogether. Others were struck a glancing blow, either by a strong patrol or by a main body recoiling from some previous encounter. Still others were met head-on with full shock.

It just happened that these four companies became the chief targets in the opening round. They have no other common denominator. Their actions were not joined; they were remote from each other when the fight began. Each company engagement had a separate character. Each was distinct as to time element and the effect upon the regimental situation.

Their parts must be studied piecemeal because this was a piecemeal battle. Back of the regiment was a division, and back of the division an army, but the issue rested on how long a lone infantry company could stand unaided in defense of a solitary hill.

The 38th had got to its phase line in the late evening of 23 November, with Third Battalion on the right, First on the left, and Second in reserve. Northward from First Battalion's front, a narrow valley wound through the ridges, the trench of the Peangyong-chong, tributary of the Chongchon. It was next this stream that the worst hurts of the regiment were to be suffered in the hours immediately ahead.

For the moment, there was only one premonitory sign. Baker Company, proceeding to its hill beside the valley, encountered an enemy patrol of eight men crossing a bridge. In the ensuing fire, two in the patrol were killed. The others ran north up the valley, and Baker Company, watching their flight, saw them join a force of about company size, which promptly disappeared beyond the skyline.

They looked the dead men over, and then someone called Battalion, saying: "We can't be sure but we think they're Chinese."

On the next day, Regiment held in place, with Second Battalion relieving First along the forward line, in preparation for the attack order. But that promise of a respite was quickly dashed for Able Company. In late afternoon an Air Force pilot flying over Hill 1229 reported seeing six heavy mortars in action along its crest, and numerous small enemy groups moving along the ridgeline.

Whereas the regiment for the past week had been engaging phantom patrols and elusive small guerilla groups, this was strength of a kind which suggested the possibility of a solid defense line. It was decided that Able Company would move out as a patrol to test the reality.

Hill 1229, the most formidable ridge in the Chongchon countryside, lay approximately 6,300 yards north of the regimental front. That was map distance. But Korea is all up and down hill, and a dozen or so folds must be negotiated in the crossing of any one ridge. In short, Hill 1229 was at least sixteen walking miles distant through enemy country. Had Able Company been stripped down to sweat shirts, running pants, and tennis shoes, it still would have been an exhausting assignment.

Capt. Jack W. Rodarm got his order at 0130 on 25 November and spent the next hour at the Battalion Command

Post receiving his instructions. The company was routed out of bed and breakfasted by 0330, to be ready to move by 0400. Three trucks were supposed to lift it two and one half miles up the valley to the line of departure, which paralleled the footbridge where Baker Company had engaged the patrol. Only one truck arrived, the others having broken down en route. So the one truck shuttled them and they arrived at the appointed ground one half hour behind time.

We can see this small command in clear profile as its men crossed the footbridge and started up the narrow valley, moving Indian fashion. It was a strong company, as such things were counted in Korea at that time, with 125 armed men in its own ranks. Its attachments were numerous—three men from the battalion wire section helped by seven Korean bearers; an artillery lieutenant, with an artillery corporal to work his SCR 619 and a Korean to carry a spare 619 along; Capt. Leonard Lowery, the Battalion Executive Officer, shepherding a party of about twenty Koreans carrying 342 C-rations on their backs.

The fighters were packing two grenades apiece. Those with M1s had full cartridge belts plus two bandoliers; the carbine men had a minimum of ninety rounds apiece, and some had eight magazines. Full canteen, first aid pack, field uniform with only the pile cap and M43 jacket for added warmth—such was the total of the weights they carried forward.

Of heavier arms, the command contained fourteen BARs, two light machine guns, one 60-mm mortar and one 57 recoilless rifle.* This was normal armament, and less than an average march load, considering the help from the bearers.

A point of three men moved out 250 yards ahead of the company as they started forward into the dark. But flankers were dispensed with, since Second Battalion was supposed to be holding the immediate ridges on either side of the valley. So feeling no trepidation about the early situation, the company marched as boldly as it could, holding to the west bank of the Peangyong-chong. It provides some measure of the

* See Glossary of Main Weapons.

roughness of Korean ground that after four hours they were less than one and one half miles beyond their starting point.

By then it was broad daylight. Cpl. Renaldo Acosta, the lead scout, was suddenly startled by a burst of machine-gun fire directly across his path. It sounded as if it came from the right, but he could see nothing. The point went flat, but it held fire, seeing no targets.

Rodarm, hearing the same fire, decided it sounded like an American LMG.* But within one minute of the first burst, rifle and automatic rifle fire in heavy volume was breaking all around the company. Rodarm estimated that 500 to 600 rounds were fired while the men of Able, strewn along 350 yards of trail space, were gaining cover.

Three or four men were hit. Still he couldn't see anything or tell by the sound from which direction the fire was coming. The ridges were shrouded in mist, and it also lay thick in the valley. To Rodarm's ear, all of the fire sounded as if it had come from American weapons.

He called Battalion and asked: "Are there any American troops this far forward?" Capt. John L. Blackwell, the operations officer, told him: "I think Fox Company is on that ridge. They're supposed to have had some kind of an action this morning. I'll call Second Battalion and tell them they're firing on our patrol."

On breaking off the conversation, Rodarm again looked at the height opposite. He saw about ten men moving along the slope; they were in American uniform. He thought that confirmed it—that he had been engaged by friendly fire. What he didn't know was that these were men from his own support platoon who, tiring of the wait, had decided on their own initiative to prowl the ridgeline.

But the fire managed to outlast Rodarm's wrong notion of its origin. He at last concluded that whether it came from friend or foe, he'd have to stop it or return to home base. Second Platoon, in the lead of the company, was put forward about 250 yards through a draw where it could gain

* See Glossary of Main Weapons.

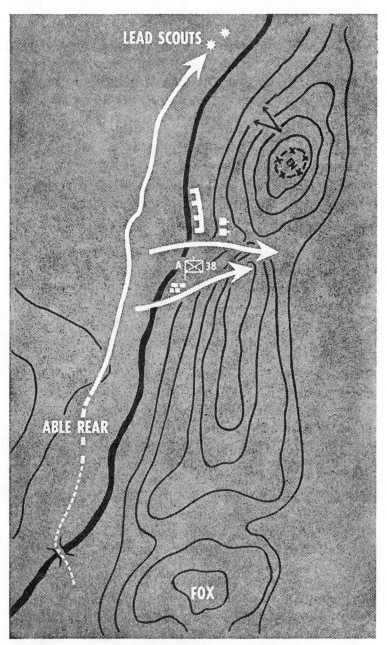

ABLE COMPANY, 38TH REGIMENT
The Morning Action.

fair cover and stop anything moving against the company from the north. First and Third Platoon were ordered to fall back about 150 yards, gain the summit of a connecting ridge (Hill 383) which Rodarm judged to be aflank of the enemy's fire position, trade fire with the enemy from that point until Fourth Platoon could establish its heavy weapons on the high ground, and then close upon the position.

That was what they did—approximately—there being no alternative. Lieutenant Claridge, the forward observer, had already called for artillery help, only to be told that the ridge was too close to Fox Company to permit fire.

The mortar was set up behind a knoll at the base of the hill to support the advance by the two platoons upslope. Directed by Rodarm, the two machine guns, supported by six riflemen, fired from the river bank. The 57 recoilless engaged from the same point.

The ridge was steep and rocky. First Platoon, on left of the line and therefore nearest the enemy ground, started working around the curve of the ridge in the hope of coming out on rear of the enemy machine gun. So doing, it moved right into the path of fire and became pinned, having mistaken the location of the gun. Third Platoon made the whole climb through dead space, without one shot interrupting its progress. Even so, it was forty minutes getting to the crest, such was the exertion of the journey.

By then, the surviving Chinese had fled the ground. From the position by the river bank Lieut. George Gardner had seen them decamp, urged on by a round from the 57 gun, which had exploded amid a group of riflemen. Sergeant Joseph, observing for the mortar, saw one round land square on the machine gun, wrecking it and killing the crew. These two chance shots from the low ground ended resistance.

Quite possibly, however, one other bit of pressure speeded the withdrawal. On reaching the skyline, Able's men saw a line of Americans moving toward them along the ridgeline from the south. They were from Fox Company. They shouted from the distance: "We've come to take over." The entrenched Chinese must have seen their approach much earlier and realized that the position had become untenable.

It may be coincidence merely. But Rodarm had looked at his watch and noted that this fight took place between 0945 and 1100—the same hour when Baker Company, 9th Infantry, was first encountering determined Chinese resistance on a hill, covering another river valley, and parallel to Hill 383. An identical condition was confronting the van of 25th Infantry Division still farther to the westward at the same hour.

By tapping an Easy Company wire, Rodarm got in touch with Battalion. Blackwell told him that he was to bring the company down from the ridge immediately and continue on to Hill 1229.

This was easier said than done. The Chinese fire initially had carried all the way back to Captain Lowery's Korean carrying party, which was stopped not far from the little footbridge. The porters promptly dropped their bundles and ran for cover. Lieut. Col. William Kelleher, the Battalion Commander, coming forward to look at the situation, helped Lowery to round them up. But another thirty minutes were lost that way.

Regiment was sweating out the slow progress. At their suggestion Kelleher joined the column, and he and Lowery moved up front with the point so that they could set the pace. The route was changed slightly, the column veering to the northwest so that it could pass through an Easy Company platoon outpost about 2,500 yards forward of the regiment.

The way was unusually steep and rocky, and Kelleher and Lowery were perhaps pressing a little too hard. By late afternoon the head of the column reached Hill 453, not yet halfway to its objective. Rodarm, looking back over the line which dragged haltingly up the slope, felt that his company was about spent. Men were strung out as far as he could see into the haze of twilight. About thirty had fallen behind the main body. They were mainly the ammo bearers and the men with radios or heavy weapons. To move farther would mean a loss of all tactical unity.

He talked over with Blackwell whether it was wise to press on. The Executive was undecided. He said the point would go another little distance while he thought it over. Lieut. John O. Crockett, who led the forward platoon, was listening to the conversation. He started to move uptrail. Just then a grenade came out of the bushes not 10 yards away and exploded between him and Rodarm. Crockett yelled: "Get the son-of-a-bitch!" but the grenadier slipped over the ridge and disappeared into a thicket.

The grenade settled the argument. Blackwell agreed that since the enemy knew their location, the only thing to do was collect Able Company as quickly as possible, set up a defense around the crown of Hill 453, and camp for the night.

Third Platoon was put on the left of the position, First Platoon on the right, weapons platoon on the left in rear of Third where the ground afforded fair cover, and Second Platoon in support to the rear, covering the approach from that direction. All of the native bearers were enclosed within Second Platoon's ground. Some of the men dug in; others did not, because they either lacked shovels or were too fatigued. Kelleher had returned to his command post after making the climb, but Rodarm was in touch with him via the SCR 619. The early part of the night was quiet.

At ten minutes before midnight, M/S Thomas E. Weikel, who was walking just outside First Platoon's foxhole line, collided bodily with another man in the darkness. As the man recoiled, Weikel challenged him and raised his carbine; his target rolled away into a pine thicket before he could pull the trigger. At about the same moment, Cpl. Renaldo Acosta, who was to the left of the forward machine gun outposting Third Platoon's line, saw a Chinese standing 10 yards from him. The man vanished before Acosta could move.

These were the only preliminary signs. There were no bugle calls, and no warning that an enemy body had moved up. But immediately from the ridge to northward, which was connected with Able's position, came a hail of bullets.

Rodarm and his men could see no flash or get any other indication of the enemy position. But they could hear distinctly two machine guns and possibly three submachine
guns firing in tune with "many" rifles. They judged that the
enemy line was about 200 yards or more away.

Though seeing no targets, Third and First Platoons returned fire, using mainly the LMGs and BARs. For perhaps
ten minutes, this was the extent of the engagement, with
both sides persisting in the exploratory fire.

Then a curious thing happened. Tracers from Third Platoon's machine gun started a grass fire about 125 yards in
front of the position, and the wind fanned it into a bright
blaze. Out of the darkness waves of Chinese rushed forward
into the glare, not to charge the hill, but to try to stomp
out the fire. As the targets came alight, the machine gun
mowed them down in sheaves. Other Chinese rushed forward
to take their places; they, too, were cut down as they hopped
about among the flames. The wind was getting stronger all
the time, the blaze brighter, and the enemy numbers more
numerous. Yet this mad act persisted for more than one hour
with Third's machine gun and the riflemen alongside doing
their work as methodically as if they were working on ducks
in a gallery. Said Weikel of this part of the fight: "It was
like dealing with mass lunacy. They acted as if a grass fire
bothered them more than death. Yet they didn't know how
to fight the blaze; they kicked at it with their heels. They
kept coming and we kept shooting. We killed scores and
scores of them, and they ceased offering themselves as targets
only when the fire stopped because there was no longer grass
to burn." It was a highly significant incident—the first straight
tip to Eighth Army that getting illumination in and around
the Chinese was the surest way to demoralize them in night
engagement.

But the diversion on the left could do little to stave the
pressure against the right. While the fire fighters were meeting their doom, the other enemy flank swung down from the
ridge onto the low ground eastward of the ridge, and then

climbed toward First Platoon's position through the scrub pine and thicket. The first warning of this outflanking maneuver was the sound of bugles blown from downslope. In between blasts from the bugle, the men within the perimeter could hear the peep-peep-peep of the shepherd's horn. Then these sounds faded and above all of the other noises of the battle came the voices of men chanting shrilly and in unison. The chant crescendoed steadily as they drew nearer. But the effect was too methodical to be unnerving. Said Pfc. Delino Horne: "It was an act, and we felt they were doing it less to scare us than to boost their own courage."

First Platoon, still seeing no man target, fired steadily at the thicket whence came the tumult. BARs, rifles, and the machine gun all joined the fire. Other weird noises pierced the night—the whirring of rattles, the simulated crowing of a cock (done on the shepherd's pipe)—but the enemy skirmish line never emerged visibly into the open. The intense fire against the thicket apparently disorganized the charge. However, as the enemy formation dissolved, it fragmented into small groups of grenadiers and riflemen who crawled to the forward line of brush and then wiggled along the gulleys in the uneven ground. First Platoon still had seen no Chinese when grenades (potato-masher type) began to fall along its forward line. They were coming from not more than 12 or so yards beyond the foxholes, but the rock and scrub pine cover adequately concealed the positions of the throwers. Weikel's weapons squad was the focal point of this upthrust. Within a few minutes, every man in it had been put out of action by bullet and grenade fire. The defenders had no fortune with their own grenades; they tried, but they could see nothing and hence the stuff seemed to be wasted; the position held by the strength of the bullet-firing weapons.

During these minutes, the enemy fire from the main base was building up ominously, and the impact was being felt elsewhere around the perimeter. Three additional machine guns were now firing from the Chinese hill, the effect of which was to increase the distress along the forward slope

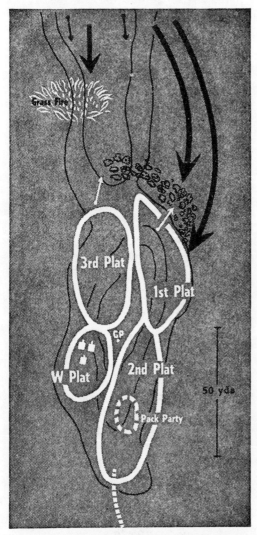

ABLE COMPANY, 38TH REGIMENT
The Night Action.

where Third and First were holding. The action had continued for perhaps fifty minutes when a battery of Chinese mortars also joined. About three tubes fired, and they did their work with precision. Within a few minutes upwards of seventy rounds had found the hill.

The first salvos struck Second Platoon's area. It panicked the Korean carriers and they fled the hill, except for those few who were saddled with radios and could not run or, being next a soldier when the fire began, were held in place at rifle point. Lieutenant Claridge, the artillery forward observer, was hard hit by one round. Further damage was done in Weapons Platoon's position, where several shells landed. But the worst blow came when a mortar round landed on Third Platoon's machine gun, destroying it and wounding several in the crew.

Rodarm, totaling the score, saw that he was approaching a degree of immobility which would soon make retreat impossible. He had five dead men and twenty-six wounded on his hands. At least five of the latter were litter cases. His Korean bearers had fled. He had no litters. They had started with the company in the morning but had been used to evacuate the wounded during the first engagement. In trying to rejoin the company, they had been intercepted by Chinese; two bearers had been killed and the others driven back. All of his badly wounded men would have to be carried back along the rugged trail slung in blankets or shelter halves. It would take six riflemen to move one casualty, for the distance was long and a blanket sling is very awkward.

At 0130, he told Lowery that he believed Able had to withdraw. Lowery called Kelleher on radio and the movement was approved. The two forward platoons were directed to fall back through Second Platoon's lines, bringing their wounded. They had been given as much rude first aid as was possible, but there was no plasma in the position and no skilled medical attendant. Weapons Platoon had expended all of its mortar ammunition in the course of engagement and was therefore relatively "light." To the extent possible, the mortar men were assigned the task of making the long haul with the blanket cases.

Second Platoon's machine gun and BARs were swung northward to form a strong point. With the walking wounded taking the lead, followed by First Platoon, the head of the company then withdrew through the tail. It was all done hastily, and perhaps that was just as well, considering what followed. All weapons were brought out, except one machine gun and one BAR destroyed by enemy action. But the men left their sleeping bags, rations, and other equipment on the ground.

There followed a few minutes of disorder as the column moved through Second Platoon's ground. A few cases of rations and ammunition lay open next the trail. One or two men fell out to reach for food or an extra clip; the example set was swiftly followed; others quit marching to grab for things they didn't really need. Officers and NCOs forced them back into line and motion, shouting curses and asking them if they wished to die on the spot.

It could have been terribly costly, had the enemy been alert and aggressive. But for the moment his tactical integrity also had succumbed to mortal impulse. The Chinese skirmishers, closing immediately upon First and Third Platoon's lines, had been stopped by the desire for loot. They had found the sleeping bags, rations, and other souvenirs, and their shrill voices could be heard to rearward, screaming in excitement as they collected the prizes. For the time being, they quit fighting and Second Platoon was able to form as the tail on the column on the way out without having to fight as a rearguard.

By 0220, Able Company was reassembled on Hill 526 where, on the way up, it had passed through Easy Company's outpost. The hill position, as Rodarm saw it, was even less tenable than the old perimeter, as one of the northward-facing flanks was bald and smooth-surfaced, and thus wide open to automatic fire. Further, ammunition for the BARs and machine guns was about gone, though forty additional bandoliers of M1 cartridges had been forthcoming from the Easy platoon; this was the only resupply.

Under guidance from Claridge, the 38th Field Artillery had supplied fires assisting the defense of Hill 453, though the shelling had not noticeably slowed the Chinese. Now with Claridge gone, his assistant, Cpl. Jack McKnight, took over as forward observer and called for fire against the hill which Able had previously defended. It was a bull's-eye; there were two direct hits, one by high explosive and the other by white phosphorus, and they fired the ration dump. From their new hill, the men could see the explosions and watch the Chinese moving in silhouette against the blaze.

Rodarm had called a halt on Hill 526 because he reckoned that the company was practically spent. At about 0300, Able was hit again. The Chinese had picked out the weak flank and set up four machine guns to bring it under fire. One BAR man was hit immediately. Another bullet found one of the blanket casualties and killed him. Lowery told Rodarm that it was time to withdraw full-length. They decided to retrace the course of the day before, Lowery trying to keep the other platoons together while Rodarm remained behind to direct evacuation of the wounded and help Second Platoon fight its rearguard action.

The Easy platoon had left its machine gun behind; that was a lucky bonus, for Second Platoon's own gun suddenly jammed because of a ruptured cartridge. Helping the one gun were approximately twenty M1s and carbines. SFC Floyd V. Chitwood and Sgt. Delwaine Coddington handled the fire party while Rodarm cleared the last elements from the position. There was no waiting for the enemy to get set and charge. All weapons were turned loose against the ground whence the machine-gun fire had come. This fusillade was continued for about ten minutes. Then Second Platoon arose and backed away, still firing. The Chinese pursued for about 600 yards. Periodically, Second Platoon halted, took ground positions, and gave them concentrated fire. The enemy pressure slackened as the distance lengthened.

Rodarm had correctly judged the condition of his force. In the fall-back from Hill 526, Able Company became disjointed. Lowery and the walking wounded, covered by the lead platoons, moved along fairly well at first as a group. Second Platoon couldn't catch up. Rodarm and the litter cases, covered by some elements of Third Platoon, moved at a still more halting pace apart from the fighting elements. There were other small fractions which found their way out alone. Before the head of the column descended into the river valley, Lowery's party broke apart under the stress of caring for the walking wounded.

During the night there had been heavy trouble in the valley, with Fox Company's hill as its vortex: Fox had stood like a rock, but the Chinese still swarmed on all sides of it. Of this fight, Able's men knew nothing; a few minutes before first light, their forward element, which included the more mobile members of the walking wounded, drew abreast of the ridge where the company had first engaged on the prior morning, just as the Chinese, recoiling from the fight with Fox, were making their reassembly in the valley.

Lieut. C. A. Wilkinson was with Lowery when suddenly they heard the sound of men marching parallel to them and only a few yards away. They froze instantly, and the men behind them followed suit, no one making a sound. Then through the morning murk they saw the enemy column—a battalion of men, judging by its bulk, headed south toward the footbridge. As quiet as hunting dogs, they stood there in the field while the Chinese marched on. When they were out of earshot, Lowery's group trailed them as far as the bridge, then swung right and up a narrow canyon, looking for Easy Company.

The second element of Lowery's group was a few minutes too late to see this happen. It included Lieuts. George Gardner and John O. Crockett, Sgt. Joseph Tistyan and about twelve men. The group crossed the footbridge and continued south. By then, the Chinese column had reversed direction and was marching north. Gardner was out front with his first scout, Pfc. Horne. Daylight was just coming. Dimly, they saw a few forms walking straight toward them, and beyond the individuals, what looked like a solid body of troops.

Gardner said to Horne: "Who's that?"

Horne said: "I think it's Chinks."

Gardner answered: "I think it's ROKs, but we'll hold up and make sure."

Someone behind Gardner yelled out: "Is that Baker Company?"

By then, the point of the Chinese battalion—two riflemen and a burp gunner—had come to within 15 feet of Horne and stopped. The burp gunner gave a gasp of surprised recognition but didn't raise his weapon. Then all three bolted back toward the battalion. Crockett fired with his M1 and one Chinese went down.

During these seconds both the Chinese main body and the American party had remained spellbound. Gardner's men, leaning on a rock wall, reacted as if they were witnessing a tableau. Then the battalion came forward at a run, and the American group, with one impulse, ran for the creek and the high ground on the far side. Their legs saved them. They covered perhaps 100 yards and were moving up among the rocks before anyone in the battalion thought to open fire. A third element of the company, coming down the valley by a different path, was already on the high ground. There were about ten rifles in the party; they stood their ground and fired toward the mass in the valley. Such was the moral flux in the uncertainties of the early morning that this pitiful effort turned back a charge by several hundred men.

Rodarm and his party limped along hampered by three litter cases. The light was fairly full when they descended into the valley, though mist hung unevenly over the scene. The Chinese battalion had made camp next the footbridge and had set up an aid station. Rodarm saw them in time. His party swung over to the ridge and managed to pass unobserved. But Rodarm wanted to get a closer look at the Chinese camp. Taking Corporal Acosta with him, he crawled forward behind a rock wall which ran diagonally toward the aid station. They soon had it under full observation. Rodarm noted that the enemy soldiers were all big men, conspicuously smart and strong-looking and with a very erect carriage.

Then Acosta drew his attention to a man sitting on the ground near the aid station. He looked like an American. Finally the man arose, and from the way he dragged his leg, they could tell he was wounded. A shot was fired by a Chinese standing near him and the man pitched on his face.

Acosta whispered: "Let's us attack those sons-of-bitches."

Acosta had an M1 and Rodarm a carbine. The latter answered: "I don't think it's a good idea." They crawled back along the wall and rejoined the group.

Because the aid station attendants and the Chinese troops in the valley were moving about unmolested, Rodarm reckoned that Fox and Easy must have been beaten back from the flanking ridges. At that, he was wrong, but it prompted his decision to keep moving downstream looking for friends.

Perhaps one half mile farther along, the group came to a ford. The water was deep and the rocks were icy. Rodarm and most of the group struggled through. Last in the column were Cpl. Ritter, Pfc. Tinkle, Pfc. Raymond, and Pvt. White carrying Cpl. Willard Smith in a blanket sling. As they started into the water, they staggered under their burden. Feeling that they couldn't make it and that Smith might drown, they pulled back to the bank.

Ritter yelled to Lieut. John D. Grieve across the stream: "We'll stay here and cover him and some way we'll get him out. Tell the Captain." By then the fatigue of the party was such that the others had to leave the five men to work out their own problem. Within an hour or so, Rodarm's group entered friendly lines.

By that time, Ritter and his party had fought another engagement. From the high ground, a party of six Chinese spotted them huddled on the river bank next to Smith, trying to keep him warm. Scenting an easy capture, they came running down the slope. The Americans held fire till they were within 100 yards. The volley killed one Chinese and wounded a second, and the others fled. But one of the Chinese had fired, also, and his bullet hit Private White in the leg.

For several hours, Ritter kept his party quiet and resting. Noon passed, and there was no longer any sign of the enemy. There were a few squat Korean houses on the hill behind them. Deciding that food was the main thing, Ritter left Smith well wrapped in blankets, and the others took off for the settlement, Raymond and Ritter taking turns at carrying White piggy-back.

A Korean housewife—just a North Korean peasant—took mercy on them and cooked a hot meal. They carried an extra portion back for Smith. The food revived their strength. The three able-bodied men tried it again, and carried both Smith and White through the torrent, making two trips.

By slow stages they moved along to friendly lines. The sun was again setting when they reached Able command post, and the long patrol ended.

# 7

# An Eddy in the Riptide

Shortly before noon of 25 november, george company of 38th Regiment got a hot meal and then moved out of Sinhung-dong on what appeared to be routine mission.

They were to establish a holding position on Hill 291, which was perhaps two miles airline to the southeast of the village. Trucks were used as far as the battalion assembly area. From that point to the objective was approximately 2,200 yards, map distance. Adding the extra distance up and down the lesser hills and around the abutments of the higher ridges, they hiked that day not less than 5,500 yards.

It does not seem a great distance as military marches under nonfire conditions are reckoned. Further, the company was not excessively loaded. The men with M1s carried full belt and one bandolier; a few carried an extra bandolier. The carbine men averaged out 110 rounds apiece. Add to this the full canteen, aid pack, light pack, sleeping bag, and about one grenade per man, and it is the average load. They carried no rations because there were none at hand to give them.

This was a better-than-average strength unit, counting all told 164 hands. There was thus abundant resource to spell men on the heavier loads, such as the flame thrower, the radios, and the mortars, which was done at regular intervals.

Even so, George Company did not close on Hill 291 until 1530; the advance had taken almost five hours. Two of its ROK soldiers, who were carrying machine-gun ammunition, passed out going up the first hill, though the air was coldly bracing; such was the roughness of the country that the column had to take five breaks while making this same grade. Thereafter, Lieut. Robert H. Rivet found that he had to rest his men at quarter-hour intervals.

By the time the company reached the vicinity of Hill 291 the column was strung out over three fourths of a mile of trail space. It took the stragglers—chiefly the men who were carrying the heaviest loads—about thirty-five minutes to close. The column had followed a poorly marked native track which wound from valley to valley, looping over five ridges in the march route.

At day's end, it was a question which had won the struggle —the men or the terrain. Though their condition of near exhaustion was attested by all participants, the degree of it is best marked by the actions and decisions which followed.

Charley Company had been in this same position without making enemy contact. Getting word that George Company was being sent to relieve them, Charley Company had failed to dig in.

Totally worn, and taking over just before dusk a position without diggings, George Company did not radically improve this situation. In First Platoon, the leader, M/S Felix Acosta, told his men to dig. But the shovelers found that there was loose slate just below the surface, and after they had got down a foot or so, their muscle and will power gave out. They built up revetments of dirt and loose rock around their personal positions, and Acosta found that was all he could get them to do. It was the same in Second and Third Platoons. The men tried to dig but their fatigue defeated them. There were plenty of boulders and slate slabs around. They perfunctorily threw this stuff together to form rude walls around each two-man "foxhole."

Even in the larger sense, Charley Company's dispositions were unsuitable and dangerous; afterward, George Company's leaders concurred that this was the case. The platoons separately occupied three hills which were not within sight of each other and could not provide mutual fire support. The company command post was approximately 1,200 yards to the rear of the closest platoon. Yet Lieutenant Rivet simply fitted himself into his predecessor's spot, and George relieved Charley platoon by platoon, sitting there on the same lines, with no one questioning whether this was the right thing to do. Later, the leaders put it this way: "We knew that it was a mistake, but we were so tired that we accepted the easiest solution."

Second Lieutenant Hollingsworth, leader of the Second Platoon, went back to talk with Rivet as soon as his men had got into position. Rivet told him to send out patrols on the following morning, but not to bother with any that night; as a footnote to this instruction, it needs be noted that the platoons did not know the exact location of each other when they bivouacked, and were without contact with friends on either left or right.

Sergeant Acosta, on leaving Rivet, was given an SCR 300 for use on his hill. After trying it from various locations, he was still unable to raise the command post. He then sent his radio man with a runner back to Rivet, with a request either to string wire or send another radio. There was no wire or other radio. The runner came back saying so. Trying to do the right thing by somebody, Acosta sent the runner to Second Platoon with the radio, hoping they could use it. It didn't work there, either.

Third Platoon had an SCR 536 by which it got through to the command post. At half-hour intervals, the commanders at the two points conversed. This element was, in fact, the only group that Rivet commanded after dark fell; otherwise, there was no contact between the several elements of the command.

Though most of the men felt dead beat, nerves kept them from sleeping during the early night. Far to the westward, they thought, they could hear the sounds of battle. Hollingsworth set up a rotating detail to visit the positions, prod the men, and make certain they didn't doze off.

At 0130, Third Platoon's leader, Lieut. Elster King, was called on radio by Rivet, who told him to take the platoon minus the machine-gun squad and the mortar (in effect, this meant two rifle squads) and take up new ground between his then position and the company command post. Rivet did not tell King the reason for this order. But King promptly took off, leaving Cpl. John J. Plunkett in charge of the men at the mortar position. This was the last Plunkett ever heard of the men who went with King. The SCR 536 had been left with him, and immediately that the two squads got beyond voice range, the company became powerless to aid them or to follow their fate.

Rivet had called rearward at about the same time, raising his Battalion Commander, Lieut. Col. James H. Skeldon, as rugged a fighter as is to be found in the Army.

He said to Skeldon: "I can see approximately 2,000 Chinese coming up on the rear of my CP"—an exaggeration for which he can be pardoned in the circumstances. It is instructive to note, nonetheless, how the air report made earlier in the day of a marching column of "2,000 Chinese" adjacent to Eighth Army's front must have fired the imaginations of some of the younger line commanders.

Rivet said that this force was coming against him "from the east."

Skeldon asked: "What are you going to do about it, Bob?"

Replied Rivet: "I will take them under fire as soon as they get close enough."

This was the last Skeldon ever heard of Rivet or of his platoon at the command post. By daylight, they had been wiped out and for days their fate remained unknown. A few minutes before the conversation with Skeldon, Rivet had dispatched Cpl. Kenneth F. Johnson to serve as a guide to a carrying party which from rearward was bringing hot chow and ammunition to the company. In the course of his mission, Johnson had several close brushes with death, but afterwards, he could shed no light on what had happened to Rivet.

The persistent search for at least one survivor of the fight at the command post who could fill in the piece missing from the company story led at last to Pvt. An Jong Sup, a highly intelligent and aggressive twenty-one-year-old ROK soldier, who had been one of the main actors in the drama from the opening curtain until the death of the platoon.

In fact, with his own hand, he had unwittingly sprung the trap. This is the tale that was told by An Jong Sup, while Skeldon and the company survivors listened, awed by the revelation, but convinced from their knowledge of the man, and his manner during the recital, that he was telling the absolute truth.

Until past midnight, Rivet had felt no cause for special alarm. The hill on which the command post group had formed its perimeter was not a commanding position with suitable fields of fire. Heavy gunfire could be heard far over on the left in the direction of the Chongchon, but right around Rivet the night was quiet and a clear moon provided a fair view of the surrounding countryside.

About 150 yards to left of the perimeter lay the trail along which the company had marched during the afternoon. At just a few minutes past 2400, Rivet's attention was drawn to strangely muffled noises coming from that quarter. He could hear no men, but only the sounds of scraping, as of metal being plied against rock.

Rivet called An Jong Sup and said: "Go over there and *see* what is happening." The order was translated by another ROK soldier, and Sup, getting it in Korean, took it to mean exactly what it said, neither more nor less.

He moved cautiously down toward the trail, making use of natural cover. At last from within the shadow of a large boulder, 20 yards off the path, he could see all that was occurring.

Beyond the path, and extending in both directions along the draw for as far as he could see, were Chinese soldiers digging foxholes. There must have been several hundred of them. Sup watched fascinated. Then advancing toward him down the draw, he saw a Chinese column marching single file. They moved on through the men who were digging in and filed past his boulder, heading south. Sup counted them;

there were an even 150 men in the company. There followed
an interval of about thirty minutes, broken only by the sounds
of the digging. Then came another Chinese company, this one
113 strong, and moving on the same line as the other, deeper
into the American rear.

By his own estimate, Sup spent just under an hour making
these observations. Not once did it occur to him that he
should return and tell Rivet; he had been told to "see," not
to report. Neither does it seem to have struck Rivet to send
after Sup, or at least attempt another reconnaissance.

But as the last of the second Chinese company trailed by,
Sup decided on sudden impulse that the target was too inviting to be resisted. He jumped up and put about thirty
rounds of carbine fire into the stragglers. Perhaps four or five
of them dropped (among the Americans Sup had a reputa-
tion as a first-class firer). Then from the far side of the trail
where the shovelers still worked, a machine gun opened fire
on him.

Sup then sprinted back to tell Rivet what he had done.
Rivet was horror-struck. He realized that Sup's eagerness had
given the position away and that the marching companies
would now double back on him. It was then that he called
the forward platoons asking for King's two squads, and also
called Skeldon to report that he was under attack from "2,000
Chinese." But he failed to pass along the very real information which he had gotten from Sup.

Somewhat belatedly, a second thought struck him. On present ground, he was a sitting duck, with his position already
known to the enemy. He would move his men forward to
slightly higher ground; there was a chance that the Chinese,
in doubling back, would somehow miss his lines. So he led
off to a new hill about 150 yards north of the first position,
stopping there because of the dense brush cover.

King and what remained of his two squads arrived to join
the command post group just before the move to the new
location. They had come through the Chinese and had got
into a fire fight. Of those who had started, there remained

with King only five Americans and three ROKs; the others were either hit or made prisoner on the trail.

Rivet spread his men in behind rocks and among the trees. He told them they were to remain perfectly quiet, and even should they see Chinese coming straight toward them, they were not to fire until given an order. For about thirty minutes nothing happened, except that the men with Rivet could hear enemy fire—mainly from automatic weapons—breaking against the crest where they had been. Rivet had disposed his twenty-five supporters in a crescent-shaped line facing southward. Digging was impossible. The men crouched low and waited.

Came the piercing shrill of a whistle—two short blasts and a long one. Then from out the space short of the old position, three Chinese walked forward, moving boldly upright. They were spaced about 30 yards apart and they stopped perhaps 40 to 50 yards short of the rise where Rivet's line watched. The moon shone brightly; Sup noted that the men were unarmed but were carrying something that looked like a short stick. On halting, they raised the "sticks" to their lips and Rivet's men heard the clear trilling of flutes, playing sweet music. For at least five minutes, this terrible moonlight serenade continued. Rivet's men watched spellbound. Sup, lying between Rivet and another ROK soldier, heard the latter whisper: "I'd like to be home."

The flat just to the rear of the flutists was thickly boulder-strewn. Chinese arose from among the boulders, rotated forward around the flutists, then back to the rocks, and around and around again. There were three separate chains of men so moving, all perfectly silent except for the eerie music. It was like a scene from a nightmare—a lunatic's delight.

And it had its effect. The moment came when frayed nerves could stand it no longer. Someone along Rivet's line fired, and all of the others promptly joined in—a heavy volley, particularly from the carbines, and most of it going to waste.

At the first shot, the targets disappeared as if swallowed by earth. Promptly there followed a short bugle call, just four short notes like this—ta ta ta ta. It was the signal for reassembly somewhere back beyond the boulders, out of clear range. Immediately, nothing more was seen of the Chinese skirmishers. But at less than 100-yard range, three machine guns, several submachine guns and perhaps a hundred or more enemy riflemen poured fire upon Rivet's hill.

It was accurately put and began to take toll from the first minute. Rivet had found a slightly sheltered spot for double duty as command post and first-aid station. Four wounded men and one dead man were brought back to him from his line before he had scarcely started his fight. That appears to have unsteadied him for the moment. He went forward to the other twenty and told them that he would lead them in a charge against the enemy.

Of this order, Sup said: "We couldn't understand what object the lieutenant had in mind. It seemed hopeless in view of the fire then coming against us. Maybe he thought we could drive them back far enough to get better cover for the wounded."

The force didn't get out of its tracks. A few men strode forward a few paces from the hill, firing uncertainly as they took off. Two or three of them were clipped by Chinese bullets; the others recoiled to the cover of the hill. The enemy made no attempt to follow up the advantage coming of this momentary confusion. Unseen, he continued to rain bullets against Rivet's ground in steady volume, while the reply by the defenders grew weaker as more men were hit or personal weapons ran out of ammunition. For more than four hours it continued this way, a fight in slow motion, inexorable in its monotone. Rivet said nothing more to his survivors; those who still had ammunition kept fighting because there was nothing else to do. Wounded were struck time and again, and so the death count rose disproportionately.

Just before dawn, the Chinese opened fire on the hill with two mortars. The shells hit dead center. An early round exploded next Rivet, killing him. Another round knocked King down, driving a shard into his right arm near the wrist; Sup bandaged King's wound with his undershirt. Lieutenant Armstrong, who had joined the company only the day before, took stock of the situation.

There remained alive on the hill the two officers, five American enlisted men, and three ROKs. Of these survivors, five remained unwounded. The two officers had one full clip apiece for their Colts. Sup had one clip remaining for his carbine. All other firearms were empty; what stuff was salvaged from the belts and bandoliers of the dead had already been fired.

King found a thirty-round carbine clip in his jacket pocket and handed it to Sup. He said to the others: "We got to get out."

They sideslipped rightward off the hill and into a small valley, going the way the other platoons had headed the day before. As they came to a shallow creek at the bottom, they saw six Chinese standing on the skyline of the hill beyond it, about 100 yards away. The enemy soldiers were waving them to come in, as if expecting a surrender. Sup took them under fire. Though the range was prohibitive, both lieutenants joined with their .45 pistols, firing their last bullets. Sup thought he got two, possibly three, of the enemy; the others, after a brief exchange, ran away. One American enlisted man was killed by a chance bullet.

For one half mile or less the party followed along the creek. All was quiet and Sup began to be hopeful that they had outdistanced trouble. A whistle blew. Sup looked up and saw Chinese rising from behind the rocks on both sides of the valley. They were midway in a perfectly set ambush. At that moment came a roar from the sky and all the Chinese dropped to earth again. The pilot of an L-5 had told Regiment of seeing "300 Chinese moving northwest" along a small valley behind George Company's sector. The resulting air strike had arrived just at the right moment to discharge its napalm and rockets impartially against the enemy ambush and the surrounded Americans. King's party went flat as the hot stuff hit the ridges and sloshed down onto the low ground.

Whatever it did to the Chinese, it was sudden death to this small band. As the planes passed on, Sup jumped to his feet and raced up the ridge side, running through Chinese before they had recovered from the shock. He felt that one or two members of the party were following him out; also, he retained an impression of seeing in a quick glance backward that King and perhaps one other man were on their feet and trying to escape the valley via the ridge on the other side. He heard shots and cries behind him, though he did not again glance back. None of the others was ever heard from again.

At the top of the ridge, Sup found himself alone, and he walked on north along the highline, while behind him the fire still crackled in the valley. For perhaps ten minutes his progress was uninterrupted. Then as he passed onto a connecting ridge, two Chinese stood in his path, smiling and beckoning him to join them. Their arms were at their sides; they obviously mistook him for a friend. Sup walked right up to them and with his carbine muzzle against their jackets shot them both dead. These were his last two bullets.

He is to be excused that at that moment he panicked a little, ran blindly down the hillside and forth across the frozen rice paddies until at last he fell in total exhaustion. He was still out cold when somewhat later friendly hands found him and brought him in.

During all of these hours when Rivet and his die-hard band were being disintegrated, the main body of the company had felt nothing. Though it held forward ground, these ridges were just so much dead space in the main battle. Occasionally the men could hear strange bugles blowing far in the distance. At intervals a few .50-caliber machine-gun bullets, badly tumbling, fell in among the ridges, hurting no one. These were the only evil omens of an otherwise uneventful night. The platoons heard nothing of the fight 1,500 yards to rearward of them which had enveloped their comrades. They did not dream that Rivet was in a death grapple.

At the forward position, a baby-faced 2nd lieutenant, Dale Gordon Hollingsworth, was in command. This youngster did not look the part of a fighter. His thick-lensed glasses suggested timidity. He was green, age twenty, and smallish, and he talked very quietly.

About one hour after first light, Hollingsworth decided to make a personal reconnaissance back to the command post to see why he was hearing nothing from Rivet. With him went Cpl. Archie Edwards. They got perhaps 400 yards along the way when Hollingsworth, making a turn in the stream bed, saw about two companies of Chinese a few rods beyond. They were not in formation, but were moving in groups around a shack which seemed to be serving as a headquarters. He figured it must be their breakfast hour.

He sent Edwards back on a run to bring up an LMG. Edwards was told to return as quietly as possible, bringing only one extra ammunition bearer. It was in Hollingsworth's mind that if he could get the gun set without being heard, he could "clean up the whole business" single-handed.

But before Edwards got back with the gun, Hollingsworth heard still other Chinese moving up through the trees along the ridge to westward of the command which he had spotted in the valley. At that point he decided that instead of opening fire, he had better get back to his own troops just as quickly as possible. If the marching Chinese continued along the same line, he might be able to rig a deadfall.

The ridge held by Second Platoon lay square across the enemy path. But one of its squads was outposting the nose of the ridge which pointed northward toward First Platoon; so reckoning that its firepower would otherwise be wasted, Hollingsworth pulled it back to within the platoon perimeter. One thing he forgot in the excitement of the moment—to send a runner to First Platoon apprising them that a strong enemy body was advancing on the company. He had already sent one patrol that morning to look in on First Platoon and the patrol had not returned Now, busied with his own dispositions, he simply overlooked a normal precaution.

Hollingsworth's whole perimeter had been set up to defend primarily toward the north. In less than five minutes, he had to swing the thing completely around so that his main killing ground would be to the south. The machine gun was sited so that it could fire southeastward toward the enemy headquarters he had seen in the valley. One BAR was placed to fire along this same line. A second BAR was stationed to cover the approach to the ridge from directly south and southwest. The third BAR, already in position, would defend the westward slope. The fourth BAR was with the outpost squad; this force was deployed to protect the general rear of the position.

Swatches of fog blanked out some of the low ground and made the whole scene seem unreal. Nothing could be seen of the approaching enemy. Moreover, that was why Second Platoon's patrol had become lost, and why a reciprocal patrol sent out from First Platoon was also overdue. Both were wandering in a maze, looking for a friendly hill.

In the few moments still remaining, Hollingsworth's men, not having foxholes, piled up loose rock and slate in front of their personal positions. They were still hard at work on these revetments when to the southeastward, some hundreds of yards away, they heard a bugle blow. The instant the last note sounded, fire came against the hill in heavy volume, striking all along the line and out beyond the flanks. Hollingsworth's first impression was that an enemy envelopment was already underway.

The Second Squad, holding the eastern anchor of the south-facing line, was right under the hammer. This part of the hill was thickly wooded. Coming through the shrouded trees, the Chinese were within 30 yards of the rifle line before the defenders knew they were there. The first warning was a hail of bullets from out of the fog, coming mainly from Thompson submachine guns, supported by rifles. Such was the steepness of the slope beneath them that the defenders could not bring their rifles to bear on the enemy skirmishers without standing —clear silhouettes against the skyline.

Hollingsworth yelled to the machine gunner to fire.

The gun got off two good bursts and then quit.

Hollingsworth shouted: "Work the bolt! Work the bolt!"

The gunner did, and the bolt responded, but when he pulled the trigger, nothing happened.

The gunner yelled out: "My gun won't work!"

Almost as an echo came a cry from the BAR man standing next him: "My gun's jammed!"

Immediately came a call from the one other BAR man facing southward: "My gun's gone, too!"

These cries rang out high above all of the other sounds of battle. Every man on the hill heard them. They coincided with Hollingsworth's discovery that his own carbine wouldn't work automatically; the piece would eject but it wouldn't feed, and so he had to work the bolt each time.

As coolly as he had withheld his own hand from the machine gun earlier in the morning (twenty eye-witnesses spoke of his calmness at this moment), he decided that his force was morally lost on the ground it then held, and that his main chance lay in swift withdrawal and regrouping.

The reasons for this decision are indisputably clear. This was his subsequent explanation: "I knew that the crying out about weapons failures had unnerved my people. It hurt worse than the technical failure. The force knew in a moment that our automatic power had run out. I needed an interval in which to restore their confidence." His men all agreed that this was a proper statement of the case.

In fact, the weaker spirits among them were already responding to the moral pressure. A few of the ROK soldiers, who were interspersed among the squads, had jumped from their foxholes and started on a line toward First Platoon's ridge. Some of the Americans arose as if to follow them.

Hollingsworth did not give an order. He simply started backing away from his own position along the crest, firing as he went. Steadied by his example, his remaining riflemen did the same thing. The upgrade was steep and rocky; the Chinese, scrambling over ledges and through the underbrush, were slowed by the exertion of the climb. The men in the retreating line could get only a brief glimpse of a body at which to fire.

By now the Americans were shouting directions at one another, yelling encouragement and creating such a din that they could not tell whether the enemy was making any sound or using instrument signals.

Nine men became missing during the withdrawal. A number had been seen to fall; it is presumed that those who were not killed became wounded prisoners. One casualty was brought out—Pfc. Bostic who had been on the flame thrower, and had been hard hit in the arm and shoulder. He had been a cipher during the fight; after lugging the flame thrower forward, he found he had no cartridge for it. Two other men had to desist from fire to carry Bostic out.

The others backed away, still fighting, to a small knoll mid-distance between the ridge and First Platoon's hill. SFC Moises Jaronia Loquiao had already sped to the knoll to blockade every rifleman arriving in the backwash.

By now the fog had partly lifted. From First Platoon's hill, M/S Felix Acosta, in an outpost position, could follow every step of the withdrawal. He heard Hollingsworth yelling to his men to assemble on Loquiao.

But of the enemy he could see nothing. The far ridge was still swathed in mist. The Chinese, on topping the crest, had stopped there to regroup. Acosta didn't fire because he didn't know whether all of the Americans had got out, and he wasn't yet sure that the attack was real.

There was about a twenty-minute breathing space upon the knoll. In that time, Hollingsworth's men worked over the fouled weapons, trying to free them. But only one BAR responded; the other two and the machine gun were jammed beyond hope. However, the platoon's one 60-mm mortar had been brought out, minus its base plate. It was set up immediately and opened fire. About six rounds were put on the ridge just vacated. Such was the fog that the results couldn't be observed.

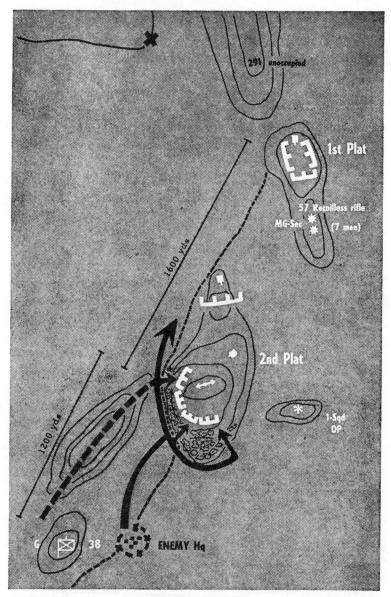

**291** *unoccupied*

**1st Plat**

57 Recoilless rifle

MG-Sec ✳ ✳ (7 men)

1600 yds

**2nd Plat**

✳ 1-Sqd
OP

1200 yds

G ⊠ 38   ENEMY Hq

GEORGE COMPANY, 38TH REGIMENT

The attack on the main position after the destruction of Rivet's platoon. Hollingsworth's secondary position is shown in the center.

After the last round, Hollingsworth personally scouted out to his right flank. He saw three or four Chinese moving down the ridge slope between his old position and the new location. He thereupon decided to abandon the knoll and unite with First Platoon. This movement was made by sending one squad rearward, along with the mortar, the wounded man, Bostic, and a medic. When they reached First Platoon hill, the other squads were then fed backward one at a time. The enemy made no attempt to rush them.

At higher levels, by 1000 on this morning of 26 November, the final pessimistic conclusion had already been reached on George Company. Colonel Skeldon, starting up toward George's rear command post, ran into four men from the company en route. Two were drivers with a rearward supply detachment; the other two had been on their way up to join Rivet the night before just as the Chinese closed in. From a distance, they watched the envelopment. They described to Skeldon the impressive numbers of the enemy. Skeldon immediately called Col. George B. Peploe at Regiment and told him that he believed George Company had been wiped out. Since that meant that a wide gap existed between the 38th and 9th Regiments, he asked for another company to fill the breach. Peploe gave him Charley Company and it was sent immediately to fill in along the main line of resistance.

There was need for these prompt precautions, since the Chinese were swarming over the rear. With the coming of morning, they had moderated their headlong assault, but the majority had not pulled back. Going about their tasks of burial, feeding, and reorganization, they set up their camps contemptuously on the nearest ground. This placed them, in many instances, between the American "front line" and its support element, with resultant compromising of supply lines and jeopardy to any small parties which traveled them.

The experience of Corporal Johnson, who had been sent the night before to guide the carrying party to George Company, was typical of what many others went through. With

Johnson went a ROK soldier, Che Jong Kuk. They got to the Korean farmhouse where they were supposed to meet the bearers. The rendezvous never came off, but later in the night two wire men from Easy Company came along. The four men decided to stay in the house until daybreak, with each pair mounting guard alternately for a two-hour trick. Just at dawn, Johnson dozed off a little. Kuk awakened him and said that he heard the sound of digging.

Johnson looked out the window. Not more than 75 yards away on both sides of the house he saw Chinese digging in and setting up mortars and machine guns. There were about 200 of them. Johnson got down on his knees and did a little hard praying.

About 0900 they looked out again and saw litter parties bringing in wounded from the northward. There were about forty such cases, and they screamed and groaned so loudly that the men could hear nothing else of what went on. Then they heard a door slam loudly; the Chinese were moving into the main room of the farmhouse and using it for a field hospital.

Johnson stood by the door of the inner room covering it with his carbine. The two wire men had Colt .45s. Kuk had an M1. They whispered to one another that if a Chinese opened the door, they would "blast" him and the hospital and break for the outside. The North Korean farmer who owned the house was out with the Chinese during this time; he knew the Americans were in the house, but he said nothing. A few days before this time the CCF had forcibly impressed his son to do hard labor; this he had told Kuk the night before. And by some odd chance, no Chinese in the outer room moved to try the inner door.

At about noontime the Chinese attendants left the hospital to go outside for a meal. There was a guard outside the door and he also left his post to eat.

The four men decided to strip down to their underwear and field boots and make a run for it. Going across the field for about 200 yards they would be in full view of the enemy.

Kuk left his M1 behind. Johnson removed the bolt from his carbine and left the rest of it. The two men from Easy Company kept their pistols. They exited by the back door, slipped around to the side of the building, and then took off across the field like sprinters. Halfway across the field they heard bugles blow, but they got to the base of the first ridge and lost themselves in the underbrush before the first shot was fired in their direction. Still, it was mighty cold.

During the same hours in which these four men sweated in the box and at last from sheer desperation broke out of it, the survivors of George Company were in an identical situation.

After Hollingsworth's men closed on Acosta's First Platoon on the forward hill, there were Chinese all around them. They held the high ground and they seemed to be swarming in the valleys. Still, they did not attack. They reacted as if daylight befuddled them, leaving them without ambition to gather in the prize which was right within their grasp.

Hollingsworth and Acosta talked things over. The position itself looked unsatisfactory to the lieutenant. Further, the men had been without food since noon of the day before, and there was not a drop of water to be found anywhere around the hill.

At about 1300 two patrols were sent out. Sgt. Frank Gibson led the group which scouted to the westward. He came back and reported that the enemy had set up a roadblock in the next valley 700 yards away. Further, he pointed out that the ridge over which he had traveled easily dominated the hill where the company sat.

Sgt. Dan Dykes took the other patrol northward. He reported that there were numerous enemy groups moving around through the underbrush not more than 400 yards beyond the perimeter. From within their own lines, the men among the foxholes had already observed part of this moment.

Again Hollingsworth and Acosta conferred. They agreed that the only thing to do was to put the company on the road back, even if that meant fighting all the way.

It didn't. Their luck changed when they hit the trail. During the passage through the valley, not a single shot was fired on them.

A strong company had gone forward—four American officers, 115 American enlisted men, and 44 ROK soldiers. Out of it came one officer and 55 enlisted men. Part of these losses are not accounted for in this narrative; they were the men lost on carrying parties and other line-of-supply work whose fate remains unknown.

Hollingsworth marched his column all the way back to the Regimental Command Post. There he ran into Skeldon, and Skeldon said: "I was never happier to see anyone in my life."

# 8

# In Battle Royal

CONCERNING FOX COMPANY'S FIGHT, A LACONIC SUM-
mary made at the battalion command post contains these
words: "F Company took the initial shock of the main Chinese attack, but being on strong ground, turned the enemy
thrust aside and to its right."

It would be hard to phrase a more moderate and less accurate capsule description of Fox Company's position, the
situation which the enemy fixed upon it, and how the men
of Fox met it.

In final sum, they had only two great advantages over Able
Company in the face of the common enemy. When their
hour came, the men of Fox were relatively in a condition of
physical freshness, and there were great quantities of ammunition at hand for all weapons.

Fox had the same number of fighters present as did Able.
Like Able, it possessed a better than average quota of keen,
aggressive NCOs and junior officers.

But otherwise, Fox was badly set for a fight. If overexten-
sion was the general condition in Eighth Army on 25 November, then Fox, within itself, was the most thoroughly rep-
resentative unit in the fight.

Just east of the footbridge which figured in Able's story,
there is a complex of small ridges and low hills which together form a boxed-in area next the river bank.

Some of the ridges run parallel to the stream, others at
right angles to it. The diameter of this complex as a whole
is roughly 1,200 yards. That means that to keep it inviolate,

and deny all high ground in the square to an invader, an infantry company would have to defend over far more than 2,000 yards of front. That was what Fox was trying to do.

Able's early morning brush with the Chinese on the hillside just a few yards up the stream had made no particular impression on Fox. That was understandable. It looked like another jab-and-run sortie by an enemy which for days had been using no other tactics.

Fox had sent two patrols north to probe the ground and see what the shooting was about. The leader of one, Lieut. J. E. Fox, got a Chinese bullet through his leg from the same band that had shot down eight of Able's men. He limped back to home base and reported that it was another brush with a small rearguard patrol.

The company then went about getting itself better set to defend its ground against any real pressure. What it bit off was truly ambitious.

Its strength was spread over parts of four different ridges and hills, not definitely joined or so aligned that each element of the company could be directly helped by the fire from some other.

The preponderant strength was disposed along two connecting ridges which were roughly at right angles to each other. The main elevation in this general mass was Hill 383 at the elbow where the ridges linked. But the hill itself was not manned. Its crown separated Third Platoon, which was on the ridge running diagonally northwestward toward the small valley, and First Platoon which, with the headquarters group and mortars, covered the lower half of the ridge capped by 383.

First Platoon, in turn, was split within itself. Capt. Nicholas Gombos still wanted a reserve, even if he was covering an excess of countryside. Two squads of First were put on a small hill backing up his general line. The other two squads were put in fire positions on the left shank of the main hill, facing westward and overlooking a long draw running to the ridge from the valley. As events proved, this was a key disposition. So placed, the First Platoon rifles could help cover an open flank of Second Platoon which had dug in on the extreme left flank, along yet another ridge running parallel to the river.

Slightly to the rear of Second Platoon and off to its right was a heavy machine-gun section from How Company. Its field of fire was thus in extension of First Platoon's two squads, and covered the mouth of the same draw. The word "perimeter" therefore hardly fits Fox Company's dispositions. The line was an attenuated horseshoe, with a bad break at the bend and an open side left unprotected, save for the mortar output.

The ridges were all extremely rocky, with outcroppings and strewn boulders. They were thickly covered with stunted pine, scrub oak, and thorn thickets. The only relief in an otherwise desolate countryside was the half-dozen Korean farmhouses perched along the walls of the draw leading to the main position. Each platoon was separated from its next neighbor by approximately 1,000 yards. Neither of the two flank platoons could see into First Platoon's position.

Because the countryside was totally unroaded, Fox had left its organic transportation 3,000 yards to the rear and from that point had lugged all of its ammunition and supply to the position by its own sweat. At each platoon position, the LMG had 3,000 rounds, and there was a 9,000-round reserve in the company area. There were ten working BARs present with approximately 2,000 rounds for each piece. The men with M1s had two bandoliers and a full belt. Each man with a carbine carried a full box plus his magazines. The one marked shortage was in hand grenades; the company averaged less than two per man. The light mortars had about 500 rounds per tube.

The company was only half set for housekeeping. The men had carried light packs and sleeping bags into the positions. But they brought no rations. Enough B-rations were brought into the command post in midafternoon to supply hot food to the men around First Platoon's hill. On the outlying ridges the men went hungry throughout the day.

The evening was quiet. There were no alarms, and no reports indicating that an action was imminent.

At 2100, the fight began, though the start read like a false alarm. There were two sharp bursts from one of the HMGs * at the mouth of the draw looking to the footbridge. M/S Eugene Smith, leading the Second Platoon, phoned over to ask what had happened. He was told that the gunner had seen four or five "enemy" crossing the bridge. When he cracked down on them they had scampered away into the hills.

One half hour later the gun resumed fire and sustained it. The second machine gun and several riflemen in the How attachment also went into action. Still, Smith could see nothing from his position on the ridge, and his own men held fire.

Then he heard mortar rounds crumping right down on the HMG position. Machine-gun bullets began to spatter the rocks around Smith's own men. There was no flash to be seen; the platoon could get no idea whence the fire was coming.

Already, though Smith did not know it, the HMGs were out of the fight. One gun had been killed by a direct mortar hit. Naked to the fire, the How survivors picked up their other gun and fell back along the draw toward First Platoon.

That stripped Smith's two forward rifle squads of any extra protection to their front. They were paired off in foxholes covering the gently sloping nose of the ridge which faced toward the HMG position. The deployment covered about 45 yards. The first warning to the men along this line that the enemy had closed tight came with the exploding of ten or more potato-masher grenades among the foxholes. This shower was mixed with a scattering rifle fire. Unobserved by Second Platoon, the Chinese had crossed the river on a line with the draw and, taking advantage of the heavy brush cover along the

* See Glossary of Main Weapons.

lower slope, had crawled undetected to within 15 yards of the Americans.

Smith gave his situation a quick size up. Along its length fronting on the river, the ridge was virtually a cliff; the Chinese could not come that way. On the other hand, his two forward squads were not only in position to be cut off, but they were effectively masking the fire of his own LMG which was farther up the ridge. If he fell back on the gun, it would have a good field of fire against the Chinese who had closed upon his riflemen. Though no one had yet been hurt, he yelled to the two squads to withdraw to the crest. Events proved the correctness of his decision. For so long as was needed the LMG, supported by one BAR and the riflemen, kept the ridge top inviolate, though the Chinese continued to press forward.

But the barndoor was now wide ajar. Smith's weapons were now concentrated against the few Chinese moving up his own ridge slope, and with the departure of the HMG crew, the draw was left altogether uncovered. The greater number of the enemy went straight for this alley and, so doing, threatened to split the company.

Mortar fire—particularly from the 81s—would have been the best counter against this direct menace. The steep-sided draw narrowed sharply as it neared the river; the Chinese had to advance via a footpath clinging to its left bank. In effect, they moved along an inclined slot leading directly into the mortar position.

This possibility had been anticipated by the defenders. But they had not envisaged the swift unhinging of the position where Smith's forward squads were linked somewhat tenuously with the HMGs. In the beginning, Lieut. John Knight of Fourth Platoon had placed a mortar OP among Smith's squads on the ridge nose to direct the 81 fire. But the OP had perforce withdrawn when Smith's forward element fell back on the LMG. When the HMG position broke, Gombos called Knight and asked if he could put 81 fire on the mouth of the draw. By then the Chinese had cut the wire between Knight and the ridge on the left and he was without means of ad-

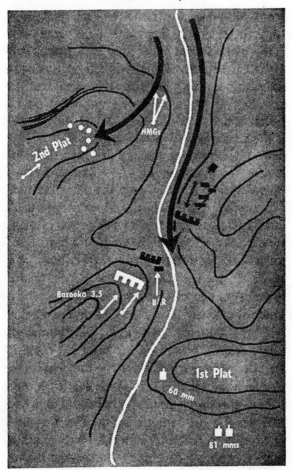

FOX COMPANY, 38TH REGIMENT
The attack up the draw as the fight opened.

justment. He called on phone to SFC John Reddick, who was in command of Third Platoon, which held the ridge on the extreme right of the company. This ridge hooked toward the river and from its height Reddick could see the footbridge. Knight asked Reddick if he could view well enough to phone corrections for the 81 fire. Reddick was already having his troubles. Lieut. Adolphus W. Roffe, who had reported to the company only that day, was trying to persuade Reddick to get his men into their sleeping bags so that they could rest, which Reddick didn't think was a very sound idea. Anyhow, he began to adjust fire for Knight, relaying directions through WOJG Robert C. Clark at the company command post. Soon the stuff was falling in the right area along the river bank just short of the bridge. Reddick saw a last round come right down on the structure and partly demolish it.

Just then, his wire went out. In fact, it was right at that moment that Reddick and his men had to begin fighting for their lives simultaneously with the First Platoon's being brought to brook by the Chinese thrust upward along the draw. These two platoon actions were as separate as two different wars. Each had to face its own problem.

The partial collapse and further contraction of the company left flank placed on the LMG covering First Platoon's left flank the main burden of stopping the enemy attack via the defile. There was a native hut to the right and slightly forward of the LMG. Lieut. Lemuel English, commanding First Platoon, had already posted one of his BAR men, Pfc. Cleo Wachel, at the right rear corner of the hut. He had been dug in almost shoulder high and there were sandbags revetting his foxhole. From this protection, Wachel could deliver a grazing fire right down the gut without unduly exposing himself. He was thus in prime position to help the LMG guard the draw, and in fact, as the fight developed, he became the main stanchion of the defense.

English deployed three riflemen to the rear of Wachel: they were told to fire in time with Wachel and to cut down any Chinese making a sneak run to his position. As the Chinese came along the footpath, Wachel was first to open fire upon them. He had to be pretty delicate about it. The How men who had been with the HMGs were not all accounted for, and whether Second Platoon had managed to hold to its ridge or was in process of sifting back toward the command post, remained unknown. So in the darkness, Wachel figured he must run extra risks to make sure he was not firing on his own comrades.

He waited until the Chinese got within 25 yards of the BAR. Despite the moonlight, he still could not see the faces plainly. So he challenged them. They answered with fire from two tommy guns, and he felt some of the bullets strike the sandbags. Wachel fired a quick burst in reply. Still the Chinese did not go flat. Only a few moved at a time, and they came on in short rushes, taking cover behind the rocks or at the far side of the house, but remaining standing.

As soon as the first skirmishers had moved up, the Chinese set up a machine gun on a piece of flat ground next the Korean hut directly in front of the BAR. Both Wachel and the riflemen behind him took the gun under fire, but they couldn't get a clear idea of its location though it was less than 100 yards away. The enemy gun kept firing.

More of the Chinese worked up to the house and took positions next it, with only the building separating them from Wachel. Grenades began to come in on the riflemen supporting Wachel, but the throwing was inaccurate and the explosions didn't worry them.

Then Wachel had a sudden inspiration—he set the house ablaze by firing into the roof. The thatch burned brightly and the scene became well illuminated. Together the light and the heat drove back the Chinese who had moved in next the house.

But it didn't flush the enemy machine gun, and its fire continued uninterrupted. For perhaps the next ten minutes, the fight was hardly more than a duel between the American light gun and the Chinese heavy gun at 100 yards' range. Then from behind their gun the Chinese opened fire with a 60-mm mortar against First Platoon's left flank and the command post position. As rapidly as the one tube could be served, they unloaded twenty accurate rounds on this critical area. Lieutenants Stevens, Coleman, and Benson and five enlisted men were hit by mortar fragments before anyone had moved to neutralize the fire.

Lieutenant Knight moved one of the company's 60s out to the left of the battery, set it on high ground, and opened fire on the enemy mortar. For several minutes there was a direct duel between the two pieces with both crews serving their weapons about equally. Then the Chinese dropped one round right among the American crew. Three men were wounded and, though the tube was not damaged, it went out of action temporarily.

Sitting a little way up the slope from Wachel and the machine gun was Sgt. Paul West with a 3.5 rocket launcher on his lap. He had been watching the action, but so far had taken no part in it. So he raised the launcher and let go one rocket. His first round hit the Chinese mortar dead on—at 225 yards' range. It was the luckiest kind of a fluke shot, and its impact cooled off the enemy force attacking up the draw. When the mortar and crew were knocked out, the Chinese machine gun went silent. The pressure against the company was then deflected to a new quarter.

When the wire went out connecting Third Platoon's position with the command post, Sergeant Reddick figured that it probably meant that the Chinese had filtered to within the general perimeter. The sounds of skirmish from the left flank were so diffused that he could get no impression of the scale of the fight. But he took his cue from the cut wire and alerted everyone along the ridge.

There was a twenty-minute hiatus in which the men simply waited in their foxholes. The platoon was set up in a perimeter of its own along the south slope of the ridge, so that its weapons faced toward the company. Four of its men were nested at the foot of the slope, serving virtually as an outpost 35 yards from the main body. The first sign to the platoon that the Chinese were on them came when perhaps a dozen grenades looped out of the underbrush and fell between the outpost and the men upslope. Lieutenant Roffe, the boy who had joined the company only that morning, went down to help cover them. The fire of a burp gun ripped him through the face and chest, and he fell. The medic, Pfc. Joseph Mc-

Carthy, crawled down to drag him back. He was back in a few minutes, saying to Reddick: "He was either dead or dying; I couldn't help him." The lieutenant had had perhaps five minutes of battle. Within the hour, McCarthy was also hit.

As the outpost dropped back, Reddick formed a fire line of about sixteen men. There was now a steady rattle of submachine gun fire from the left, biting in parallel to the defending line. But the defenders gave it no heed and concentrated their fire against the Chinese whom they could now see working up through the rocks to their immediate front. It was a good field of fire—maybe too good. The men in the blocking position soon began to run low on ammunition and had to send runners to the platoon's center along the upper ridge to keep the fight going. In these lulls, the Chinese worked upward around the flanks of the blockers, and when Reddick began to get grenades from both directions across his rear, he realized that the choice was one of further withdrawal or being cut off.

The party of sixteen was now ten. Private Marshall and Corporal Westmoreland were dead on the ground, both taken off by bullets. Four others were wounded so that they could not walk. They were carried upslope piggy-back by some of Reddick's survivors, while the others provided a covering fire. The rifles of Marshall and Westmoreland were also taken along.

But dissolution was already besetting the ridgetop. Three men from the HMG group of How Company, uprooted from the position by the river, had drifted cross-lots to Reddick's lines. All were wounded. One man with a bullet in his shoulder and another with a bullet in his leg had carried a third man shot through the stomach. Reddick gave the two mobile men the spare rifles and told them they would have to fight. It was a superfluous gesture; he soon found he had no ammunition to give them.

There were six of his men on the reverse slope of the ridge, covering his rear. He counted noses and found that three of his survivors from the blocking position had skipped the ridge during the retrograde. That left him with seven effective rifles and one machine gun to hold the height; he figured that he'd have to leave the rearguard where it was, and that he didn't dare pare off a man to serve as contact between the two positions. One and one half boxes of ammunition remained for the machine gun; he told the men with M1s not to fire until they saw targets and to hold their last three clips in reserve. When that point was reached, there would be no choice but to get off the hill as the survivors would probably encounter Chinese on the way out.

For perhaps another hour or more they continued their fire. The enemy did not attempt to rush them, though his skirmishers continued to poke forward among the rocks. Then downslope, where the six-man rearguard was posted, Reddick heard the sounds of grenading, and at the same time he heard the rattle of burp-gun fire behind him. It sounded as if the Chinese were moving up both sides of the ridge between him and the outpost.

He said to Cpl. Robert K. Imrie, the machine gunner: "Fan both sides of the ridge with all the ammunition you have left, and we'll start our getaway while you're doing it." Imrie sat there firing as the others took off, running as best they could while still helping the wounded. The Chinese closed in as they left. As Imrie arose from his gun, having fired the last bullet, a grenade sailed in on the gun, blew it right off the hill and over the cliffside; he heard it hit on the rocks below. But the explosion didn't get Imrie; he lived to die from a bullet the following morning.

By the time the "main body" came to low ground, Imrie caught up with them. Reddick yelled to the six men on the lower slope to join him as his party veered off to the westward, and they didn't need a second invitation. Still moving at a run, the column crossed the middle ground diagonally, heading toward the old position of the HMGs. The Chinese on the hill ceased to fire as Reddick's men got into this flat, boulder-strewn area. But there were other enemy soldiers all around them—"scores and scores of them, some almost within arm's length." The survivors described how their "uniforms shone like silver in the moonlight" and how they noted the surprised expressions on the Chinese faces. But not a shot was fired. Reddick's party had to withhold fire from fear of hitting their own men. It is presumed only that the enemy was similarly startled and embarrassed.

At last the column got to the point where the Chinese mortar had fired against First Platoon. They heard a stirring within one of the houses. Reddick and Imrie went forward to look things over. Two Chinese jumped from behind the door. Imrie shot one of them dead, and they saw the second man dive headlong into the waters of the creek and disappear. Right behind the Chinese came three ROK soldiers; they had been with the HMGs, and had become prisoners in the early stage of the fight. When Imrie felled the running Chinese, the ROKs also went headfirst into the creek.

Reddick yelled to his men to spray all the buildings with their remaining ammunition, and they went at it. From within First Platoon's lines, Lieutenant English recognized Reddick's voice and called to him to bring his men in. The survivors reported to the command post immediately and were given fresh ammunition by Mr. Clark.

But it was a dubious gift. The company had run out of clipped cartridges for the M1, and what Reddick got was a case of loose shells which had to be loaded on the spot. It was an agonizing, nerve-wearing chore. The M1 clips were scattered on the ground all around the foxholes and the men had to feel for clips before they could get going. Such was the strain of doing that under fire that after they found the clips their fingers would scarcely respond. At the same time First Platoon was given machine-gun belts cut up, fifty rounds to the strip. They lost twenty minutes or so in what could normally have been done in a twinkling, and it strained them even more than the danger.

So far as Gombos knew during this period, both of his flanks were now gone. He had lost all contact with Second

Platoon on his left and believed it had been destroyed. Reddick told him about the collapse on the right. The Chinese, beaten back from the draw, had shifted rightward and were now attacking the main hill from the direct front.

First Platoon's reserve and Reddick's men were committed at the same time and in the same direction. Gombos told them to space out the perimeter rightward and try to extend to Hill 383. The force was all too thin for such an assignment.

Gombos called Battalion and talked to Lieut. Col. James H. Skeldon.

He said: "I've lost the hill on the right and I've got to have more men."

Skeldon asked: "Do you suppose a platoon would do it?"

Gombos said: "Yes, I think that will be enough."

One platoon of Easy under Lieut. Carl Stevens was loaded onto two 2½-ton trucks. At the regimental aid station, 1,500 yards behind First Platoon's hill, they were met by a guide from Fox Company, and from there they hiked forward. Gombos told Stevens to fill in on First Platoon's right flank and build up the line. But Stevens sent one of his squads with a machine gun to the opposite flank so that it could fire against the crest of Hill 383.

The pressure from that point was mounting by the minute. Already second squad of First Platoon had been kicked back from its attempt to fasten on the base of the peak. One ROK soldier had been killed by a grenade in his foxhole. The others had pulled away, less because they were hurting than because their diggings were wide open to the grenade shower from the hilltop, whereas a small knoll just short of the hill afforded them some protection. The Chinese immediately dropped into the foxholes which they had vacated. M/S William C. Gamlin, platoon sergeant of First, stood on the knoll to fire his carbine at this new target. Before he could pull, a Chinese bullet hit him through the heart. But the bullet exchange between these two small groups continued with the Americans gradually getting the better of it. Ten dead Chinese, including one aid man, were counted around this foxhole cluster when daylight

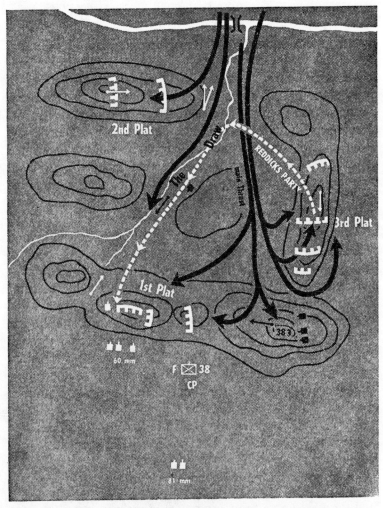

FOX COMPANY, THIRTY-EIGHTH REGIMENT

Showing the CCF Maneuver and the contraction of the defense.

came. There was no answer, however, to the Chinese grenading; Fox's cupboard was completely bare. Yet at this point the men needed grenades more than flat trajectory weapons.

The one squad which Stevens had sent to the left of First Platoon's line, along with the machine gun, lacked a gunner. As by this time every Fox soldier was on the rifle line, Gombos sent along his communications sergeant, John Parrish, to handle the gun. The tripod had been lost in the darkness. Parrish substituted his steel helmet as a base and opened fire. Aiming on the crest of Hill 383, he fired only when he saw live enemy moving and then he sprayed liberally. This seemed to cool the Chinese off, but only for a bit. By this time, all ammunition was running low and Gombos sent word to his junior leaders that the men should fire only when they saw a live target.

What the enemy was attempting throughout this period seems to be rather clearly indicated. Those elements which in the opening round had struck against Third Platoon's position and then advanced up the draw must have been the vanguard of a major enemy body. This column had subsequently crossed the river from the north, moving on both sides of the bridge. Its strength was then divided, part of it advancing through the middle ground against Reddick's platoon and the other part striking for the crown of Hill 383, which though unoccupied, was the dominant terrain feature. In trying to advance up the hill from the inside, the Chinese became partially exposed to fire from First Platoon's line on the lower hill. The fight was approaching its culmination in this struggle for the peak.

Once again Gombos phoned Skeldon for more men. He pointed out that the collapse of his own right flank left a hole through which the Chinese could march across the regimental rear; he said that if he could get enough manpower to take and hold Hill 383, he would at least be able to look into Love Company's sector.

Skeldon promised him another platoon. About thirty minutes later, fourteen men under Lieut. Ronald C. Bowshier arrived at the command post. This group comprised what remained of the reserve strength of the entire battalion.

Bowshier and his men started out the same way that the group under Gamlin had gone. They got just a little way past the knoll where Gamlin had died. There they were stopped by rifle and machine-gun fire which was beating on the ridge like rain. It was coming from the top of Hill 383, where the enemy now quite obviously was strongly emplaced. This same fire enfiladed the length of First Platoon's line and bounced off the high ground westward of the draw.

Knight, keeping busy with the 81-mm mortars, had fired most of his stuff toward the mouth of the draw and on both sides of the ridge to the south of it, in the hope that in so doing he would block the enemy's main entryway and at the same time enable Second Platoon's survivors to hold out.

He was still persistently working over that ground when suddenly from the top of Hill 383 three 60-mm mortars opened fire on his battery. The salvo was his first knowledge that the Chinese had got heavy weapons onto the peak. Knight started to adjust backward from the draw, through the middle ground, and onto the hill. In the middle of the act, one enemy salvo came right down on him. Five of his men were hit and both of the 81-mm mortars were destroyed. That ended Fox's defense by mortars for the night. The enemy 60s continued to bang away from the ridgetop until daybreak. They hit the regimental collecting station and the company command post. Most of their fire, however, was directed against the supply route connecting Fox with the battalion, to prevent the upcoming of supply and support parties.

There was one other unusual variation in the Chinese order of attack—having collapsed or neutralized the wings by rushing, the enemy thereafter made no attempt to crush the center in the same way. There were no banzai charges, no group rushes, and no marked infiltration by snipers. The whole effort was directed toward driving the Americans from the ground by developing superiority of fire. Machine- and burp-gun fire and the rifle were the main weapons employed toward that end.

This hail of steel continued unremittingly until about 0300. On First Platoon hill, the men simply stayed in their foxholes and took it, approximately half of them becoming casualties in the process. Gombos had told English and Bowshier that there would be no retreat in any circumstance and that if the enemy charged in strength, they would fight it out on that ground.

Perhaps two hours before dawn, two bright red flares exploded above the river valley somewhat to the north. Immediately thereafter the volume of enemy fire fell off noticeably. Within a few minutes following, Sergeant Smith, on Second Platoon's hill next the river, heard a great pickup of activity around the bridge; it sounded as if the greater number of the Chinese were giving over the attempt to break Fox Company and, after pulling back from the ridges, were reassembling in the valley.

But an intermittent fire—probably that of a rearguard set to contain Fox Company while the main column withdrew—continued to harass First Platoon Hill. The banging of the mortars and occasional machine-gun fire showed that the enemy was holding fast to Hill 383.

When daylight came, Gombos ordered Bowshier to extend to the peak. The group started hopefully, but had taken only a few strides when machine-gun fire from the crest hit two men and pinned the others. Bowshier yelled back for some of Reddick's men to help out. Imrie, the young machine gunner, volunteered.

When he reached Bowshier, he was told to get down and seek cover. He said to Bowshier: "What's the matter? Are you going to let just a few guys hold you up?" Then he started marching up the hill. He got halfway up. Then a bullet hit him. Death overtook him while he was going it all alone.

Fox's preoccupation that morning with Hill 383—the abscess on its right flank—explains why it missed the marching and countermarching of the Chinese columns in the valley on its left, as witnessed by Able Company during its return from the long patrol. Shortly before 1000 an air strike was put on the height. Then a scratch platoon drawn from Easy, Baker, and Love Companies attacked from the far side of the hill and killed or drove off the remaining Chinese.

Twenty-eight dead Chinese were found in the draw in front of Wachel's position. Fifty-eight more were counted in and around the ground defended by First and Second Platoons. There was never any chance to assess the toll taken by Reddick's fire.

Two Chinese prisoners said that these were troops from the CCF 113th Division, which had crossed the Yalu River on 10 November and, marching only by night, had reached the Chongchon trench three days before the battle.

# 9

# Edsel Turner and Outfit

To RECAPITULATE WHAT 38TH REGIMENT KNEW OF ITS situation up till midnight of 25 November: Able Company was fully engaged far to the fore of the regimental line, Fox Company was just coming under the gun, and everywhere else the units were standing steady. George Company had not yet been hit, though Regiment was hearing nothing from it. Love Company, which held the ridges directly to the right of Fox Company, was still quiet.

On form, Love Company should have been a main pillar of the defense. It had strength—200 men, including seventy-five ROK soldiers. It was moderately weaponed, the M1 carriers having a full belt and bandolier apiece, the carbine men averaging between forty-five and ninety rounds. Half the men had two grenades apiece, others one, and still others none.

Each platoon had three BARs, one LMG, and one 3.5 bazooka.* The BARs had twenty-five magazines apiece, the LMGs 1,000 rounds per gun within the position. There were six rocket-launcher rounds with each weapon. The company also had three 60-mm mortars, with a total of 147 rounds, and one 57-mm recoilless rifle with nine rounds.

The men were dug in soundly and their foxholes were three to four feet deep. They had had a hot meal late in the evening. Each man had his sleeping bag. The company had not moved that day and had done no extraordinary labor.

Though the company perimeter sprawled over a considerable area, the platoons were tied in to each other, their flanks

* See Glossary of Main Weapons.

within easy seeing distance and their weapons set to give the other fellow help. In the little valley which defined the company right flank, there was a roadblock formed of one M26 tank supported by one of Love's rifle squads and one bazooka team. The infantrymen were dug in on the two sides of the tank, the bazooka team on the right and the riflemen next the company. There was also a second M26 roadblock on the company's left rear where it met the Fox Company area, the detail at that point being led by Lieut. Florian Lis.

The dispositions of the company are as shown on the sketch map. Slightly to the rear of the tank roadblock guarding the right of the company were a few native huts—the Korean village of Somin-dong. The battalion command post had been set up within the huts. The company commander, Lieut. Elmer J. Kallmeyer, was told that he would be responsible for the security of the battalion installation in the event of an attack. This charge and its adverse effect upon an otherwise brave soldier are deserving of particular note. The added responsibility seems to have prepossessed him to an extraordinary degree, so much so that while the fight was on, he tried personally to carry out his extra mission, and his company, left without any real central direction, was ripped apart piece by piece with no one helping anyone else very much.

Likewise, the time lag in communications is an instructive element. Fox Company first came under fire about 2100. But it was not until 2230 that Third Battalion got word that anything untoward was developing on its left. Kallmeyer, who was between his company line and the battalion command post, was not given the same advice until 2330. The message he received was: "Enemy attacking F Company." From these few words he gained the impression that the threat was not particularly serious.

But he called Lieutenant Lis on the roadblock detail next to Fox and alerted him. He also called Lieut. John Barbey, leader of the First Platoon. Barbey replied: "I can already hear Chinese voices and signals in the hollow just below me." Then Kallmeyer tried to alert the two squads of Third Platoon which held the hill on his right flank, and he mistakenly thought he had got through to them. Their SCR 300 wasn't working, and the two squads remained unaware.

By this time, the company ground was figuratively crawling with CCF soldiers, while Love Company, bedded down, remained in a doze except for the few soldiers actually on guard detail. Yet three hours had elapsed since Fox Company, over on the left, had received its first warning.

Pfc. Robert Stevenson, doing guard duty at the company command post in rear of First Platoon's line, saw a light—as if from a pocket flashlight—wink suddenly three or four times from halfway down the hill to his fore. Immediately, he heard a prolonged whistle blast, as if in answer, from the top of the next ridge beyond the foxhole line. Then came the clatter of machine guns and rifles and the exploding of grenades. There had been an earlier warning, heard by Sgt. Gaines C. Roberts and a few other men in First Platoon's line. Perhaps ten minutes before a mournful bugle call had come out of the darkness. It had been repeated three times from three different quarters, the calls coming about one minute apart. At about the same interval, they had heard the short blast of a whistle —just an instant of sound. But they had not reacted by spreading the alarm through the company.

Already, though the men did not know it, their defensive circle had been violated. First Platoon had one squad about 400 yards beyond its line serving as an outpost for the company. One group of about thirty Chinese moved into this outpost. Someone speaking good English said: "We're GIs," and the group was allowed to pass. Continuing south toward Somin-dong, they were stopped by the tankers at the roadblock covering the right flank. Again they said: "We're GIs, we're GIs," and once again were waved on their way. This put them in the draw intermediate between First and Third Platoon positions, and they continued on their way to the latter target without one shot being fired.

This penetration by stealth had about reached its climax when the first assault wave of Chinese reached and rolled over

First Platoon's outpost squad. That was where the fire fight started. It was the noise of the attack on the outpost which Private Stevenson heard and mistook for the beginning of the Chinese action.

They got the ground immediately. Sergeant Bender and his squad had been holding the nose of an extension of the ridge which jutted to the northward. Before the defenders were aware that the Chinese had come, thirty or forty men came in on the foxholes, grenading as they moved. Only four men got away; they came running back to Roberts to tell him what had happened. Part of First Platoon's line was then shifted rapidly to the right to take over a knob of high ground between the flank and the lost outpost position. But for the next twenty minutes or so, there was only silence from the spot where the squad had been rubbed out. The Chinese were using the interval to set up a 60-mm mortar battery where Bender had been.

While that was being done, the enemy column which had sifted through the roadblock after shouting "GI!" proceeded to jump Third Platoon's two squads on the hill to rearward.

Pfc. Bobby J. Gillem, who was in the squad on the left, was still in his sleeping bag, trying for slumber. His leader, Sgt. Joseph Rodriguez, had heard the firing up forward, but had concluded it came from "trigger-happy Americans." The first warning to this squad was a yell from SFC Charles E. Cot'e, who led the squad on the right: "Rodriguez! Watch out! They're all over your position!"

It came not a split second too early. The CCF column had climbed the hill via a small gulch running between the two squads and was already turning right against Rodriguez when Cot'e spied its lead files. Gillem scrambled from his sack and grabbed his rifle. So did other men. In the excitement, Rodriguez couldn't find his piece. Gillem saw Chinese only 20 feet away. They were advancing silently at a walk, rifles at port arms, almost as if they were seeking higher ground and hadn't yet seen the Americans. Rodriguez yelled to Gillem: "Fire! Fire!" then got down on all fours, searching frantically for his own weapon. Gillem pulled the trigger of his M1; there was a soft click, but no explosion. He tried it again twice with no better success; the shells ejected but they did not fire. (Probable explanation: the chamber needed cleaning.) Gillem backed away; the Chinese kept walking straight toward him. The fourth and fifth rounds fired and two Chinese went down. The sixth again drew blank. He put his seventh and eighth bullets into a third Chinese. By then he was out of ammunition, having left his belt with the sleeping bag. Rodriguez joined him, disconsolate, not having found his own rifle; weaponless, the two men pulled a little distance up the hill out of the line of fire.

There was a nice, stiff grade between the crest on which this squad stood and the path in the gulley along which the Chinese had made their climb. When Gillem polished off the first three men, those behind them recoiled toward the gulley and got in among the rocks. Because of the sharpness of the embankment, the Chinese couldn't get their grenades up to the foxholes; they tried, but the grenades rolled back on them. Pfc. Hampton, the squad's BAR man, poured a steady fire into the draw. Pfc. Edsel Turner, who had stuck to his own foxhole while Gillem and Rodriguez were backing away, may have been a bit slow in coming out of his sleep. But once awakened, he made up for lost time. He could look right down into the gulley. In the clear light of the moon, he could see the Chinese trying to work along the path, moving in bunches, four or five at a time. So he stood there picking them off; it was good shooting. He saw at least eight Chinese fall to his personal fire as they tried to advance up the gulley. But their mates had already found a soft spot lying opposite. Cot'e had with him an assistant squad leader, Sgt. Charles G. Thibeault, and eight ROK soldiers. His hill was only 20 yards off the gulley, its banks were not steep, and the crown was devoid of rock cover. By crawling just a few yards upward, the Chinese were able to lob grenades in among the foxholes. Four of the ROKs were hit by grenade fragments within a few minutes. Cot'e thereupon ordered the position abandoned, and the survivors ran down the forward face of the hill toward the main body of the company. Having taken over Cot'e's hill, the Chinese mounted a machine gun there and turned its fire against the crest where Turner (hometown: Kalamazoo, Mich.) was holding forth.

But the gun was now exposed, even as Cot'e's men had been. Hampton trained his BAR on it and used the last of his ammunition in knocking it out. Just as he fired his final round, a Chinese bullet creased him in the head. Bleeding badly, he walked to the front of the hill, heading toward the aid station at the Battalion Command Post. Another bullet got him through the shoulder before he could make it.

Rodriguez and Gillem had gone that way. But in scrambling down through the rocks, Gillem had sprained both ankles, and Rodriguez had badly injured his back. They were bandaged at the first-aid station, where Gillem got an M1 from one of Cot'e's ROKs who had been shot through the head, and Rodriguez was put to bed because of his injuries. Gillem, starting to return to the hill, was stopped by Lieut. Harry E. Dodge, leader of Third Platoon, who told him to go to the roadblock and help cover the M26. Dodge said to Gillem: "By now, those two squad positions are destroyed and the rest of the men have been lost."

He was quite wrong about it. Turner was still holding the fort from his foxhole. With him was Cpl. Edward F. Stucke, wounded and weaponless, and therefore unable to give help. With Stucke watching him, Turner continued to fire away at the Chinese trying to come at them from the gulley. His tactics were simple; periodically, he would play quiet and let the Chinese get in close. Then he would cut loose with grenades, and as the Chinese hesitated, he'd resume fire with his M1. Three times he stopped their advance in this manner, using nine grenades and five clips of rifle ammunition.

Turner had no awareness that other Americans were still on the hill. But four other members of the squad had stuck to their ground on the opposite side of the knob. Cpl. Glenn I. Dill, Jr., who had a BAR, Cpl. Raymond W. Baumbach,

Pfc. Colin Hulse, and a ROK private were conducting a little war of their own. Stopped in the gulley by Turner's fire, the Chinese were attempting to turn his flank by attacking up the front of the hill. There were three thrusts altogether. The first was just a probing patrol action. The men with Dill could hear the rustle as the Chinese tried to work up through the weeds and underbrush. At last they came into clear view, about 10 men, deployed in line, at not more than 20-foot range. Dill heaved a grenade and it exploded right among the Chinese. Hulse and Baumbach were ready with their M1s; as the explosion lighted the scene, they fired rapidly in the same direction. The Chinese faded back, dragging away their dead or wounded.

In the next two attacks, they advanced firing and yelling "Banzai!" to the accompaniment of bugle calls. What with the night and the music, it was difficult to judge their numbers. But to the defenders it seemed that they were hearing the fire of not more than fifteen to twenty weapons—rifles and tommy guns, mainly. Dill's BAR fire was the main agent in cooling off both of these attacks.

Then the hill quieted for perhaps an hour. The quiet was at last broken when a mortar battery—three tubes—began dousing the crest from about 225-yard range, out beyond Dill's line. The first rounds fell near Turner. The next batch landed right next to Dill and he got fragments in the hand, shoulder, and head. Dill gave Hulse his belt to carry, and with Dill still lugging the empty BAR, the four men struck off down the slope, trying to find a few friends.

That left only Turner and Stucke, the wounded man who was watching him. The hill was now being held by one rifle. Perhaps it would be more accurate to say that it remained temporarily secure because of the extraordinary spirit in one man.

During the interval when Third Platoon disintegrated from pressures which were beyond containment, First Platoon had met its ordeal, and failed for lack of coordination. Ten minutes after Bender's survivors got back to tell about the collapse of the outpost, and perhaps twenty-five minutes after the event itself, the Chinese assault wave hit against the right flank of the platoon line. In this interim, the enemy had put his mortar battery into operation from the outpost position. But the attempt to shell the platoon line resulted only in "overs" as the target was not more than 115 to 120 yards from the tubes. The Chinese quickly realized this and switched their mortar fire from the foxhole line to the general area containing the Battalion Command Post, vehicle park, and first-aid station.

Their infantry was in squad column when it started the climb to First Platoon's line, but it rapidly fanned out and thereafter advanced as little knots of skirmishers, rushing from rock to rock and hiding in the shadows cast by the moonlight on the uneven ground. The hill was barren of tree growth or underbrush.

The natural approach to First Platoon's line was an evenly eroded draw which cleft the center of the position. The platoon felt sure the Chinese would take that road; the LMG was set to cover it. But the enemy scrupulously avoided this natural shooting gallery. His squads and half squads, stalking the hill, pressed hard only at one point—the open flank of the right-hand squad.

They were fairly numerous—perhaps fifty to sixty Chinese soldiers engaging in this limited envelopment. In the moonlight, they should have been conspicuous targets. Their quilted uniforms had white collars and they wore crossed white bandoliers over their clothing. But even so, the defenders could see just an occasional flash of movement as the attackers dashed from shadow to shadow.

Getting to within about thirty feet of the first foxholes, the Chinese then began to heave their potato mashers from behind the rocks. From behind the grenade line came a desultory submachine gun fire. None of this was particularly damaging. According to Sgt. Roberts and Sgt. Martin F. McCreary, the men on the American right did not make a strong effort to reply with their bullet-firing weapons, and no power was dispensed from other parts of the line to rally this type of fire. They stayed down and tried to counter the grenades with their own grenades. This possibly would have succeeded if their supply had not been limited, and if, in the middle of the futile grenade exchange, the Chinese had not got into operation a machine gun which fired into the open flank from about 75 to 100 yards' range, where it was based on a fold in the same ridge. It grazed right along the top of the foxhole line. Again, the effect was less lethal than constricting. Only two men were hit. But the others "could not get their heads up," and crouching lower in their foxholes, they slackened their grenade fire. That encouraged the Chinese grenadiers to come in closer. A few men were hit by grenade fragments, the grenades falling in such numbers that it was not possible to clear them.

What followed thereafter provides a graphic illustration of how men and squads can topple one another just like a column of dominoes unless they react to the crisis with greater unity under the persuasion of strong leadership. First Platoon was not fractionalized by enemy fire; it was never collected in the first place. Its four squads held four separate positions roughly parallel to the axis on which the Chinese attacked; in this circumstance, none was in position to do much good for its neighbor, unless the line was redressed quickly. But this was not done.

No one took action to regroup men and weapons toward the line of danger. The LMG remained right where it was under the hands of its crew, looking down the draw, though there was no threat from that quarter. The one BAR with first squad was operating sluggishly and the gunner could get off only a few shots at a time: the other BARs remained in place, and so could not bear on the Chinese. Lieutenant Barbey, leader of First Platoon, remained with Fourth Squad, which was well over to the left of the line, holding a separate knoll. There was no early pressure on this ground. The squad as a whole was contributing nothing to the fight, except that under the hand of Sgt. Martin F. McCreary a 3.5 rocket launcher had gone into action to fire among the houses in the draw northeast of the position whence a 120-mm mortar was now firing into the command post area.

So for another hour or longer, First Squad just squatted there wearily and took it. The men fired, or heaved a grenade, whenever they saw a Chinese on the skyline trying to close in. But as the leader, Sergeant Roberts, expressed it: "We had no chance to run low on ammunition; we didn't fire enough. Their stuff was coming right in on top of us. To fire accurately down the slope, we would have had to stand in clear view. What was needed was a counter to their fire, which kept us pinned. But we didn't have it."

Counting the four who had drifted back from Bender's Third Squad, the machine-gun crew which was still in defilade, and a few extras, there were about twenty men in Roberts' position. By the end of an hour, there remained six who were still unwounded. The others had got it either from the machine gun or from grenades. Only one had been hard hit—a grenade had exploded against his side. But the others were suffering so badly that the force was less than half mobile. Pfc. Donald Kent had been blinded by a concussion grenade. Two of the ROKs were almost spent from loss of blood.

Roberts decided to get out. His party crawled away to the back slope of the hill, with the able-bodied packing some of the wounded. It was Roberts' intention to withdraw as far as the roadblock at the southwest corner. But he got a hail from Barbey, who told him to bring his squad up and form on Fourth Squad's knoll.

By then the Chinese were holding the foxhole line which Roberts had just vacated. They signaled it by playing a mournful blast on a bugle—a call that sounds somewhat like taps, though it is their signal for a consolidation.

For a few minutes after Roberts joined Barbey, all was quiet. Roberts was worried about his wounded; he was afraid that shock and exposure might finish Kent and several of the others unless they were helped. Barbey told him he'd find some blankets next to the machine gun on the cap of the knoll. They proved to be "gook" blankets, homespun, one-half inch thick, and white as fleece. Roberts held one up to admire it; machine-gun fire from the far hill ripped right through the blanket. These were the first bullets that had been turned against Fourth Squad's position. Roberts ran back to his men. He and a few other willing hands had just got well into the job of improvising litters from the blankets and a few M1s when the Chinese landed hard, right on the position.

The Chinese machine gun which had scored a bull's-eye on Roberts' blanket, and then quit, started clacking again, shifted its fire just a few feet, and hit square on the American machine gun, getting the weapon and the crew. At the same time, rifle and submachine gun fire began to strike among the foxholes in quite heavy volume. A few grenades sailed in among the wounded men whom Roberts was aiding; that meant the enemy skirmishers had come to within 20 yards or less, though no one had seen their advance. Lieutenant Barbey passed the word to his men: "Fall back on Second Squad's position."

McCreary didn't get the word as quickly as some of the others. He was partway down the knoll, trying to get a line on the Chinese machine gun so that he could let fly with a bazooka round. From above him he heard a yell: "Come on! Come on!" He was just raising the launcher, in readiness to fire. At that moment, two grenades came in on him. One hit him in the leg. The other went down the barrel of the launcher and exploded the round in it. It blew fragments into his legs, arms, side, and one hand. Roberts, who had come in behind McCreary to tell him of the withdrawal, had a fragment blown through his steel helmet. They didn't walk away from this one; they both ran.

By then, all hands were getting away from the hill as rapidly as the encumberment would permit; another half-dozen men had been hit by the Chinese fire. The Second Squad—final fingerhold of First Platoon—did its best for the column, pouring a steady covering fire toward the CCF until after

McCreary and the other tail-enders had closed on the last knoll. But Barbey decided not to halt again. He counted his wounded. Two of every three men were now in need of first aid; as he saw it, his group was no longer fit to fight. He directed the column to move along to Second Platoon's position beside the roadblock.

This occurred at approximately 0500. By then, the general position was already in dissolution. About one and one half hours earlier, the force around the Battalion Command Post had begun its withdrawal upon order of the commander. Its area had been pounded straight through the night by the Chinese mortars, and had taken many casualties. How many is beyond reckoning. The aid station was in the heart of the shelled area and its attendants were in no mood to count noses; men previously wounded elsewhere in the fray were hit again while awaiting attention. Kallmeyer was knocked down and stunned by a mortar WP round which landed almost on him; but Capt. John Welch took the worst of the burst, getting a hunk of phosphorus in one leg and bad burns on his back. It was about then that the order was given to withdraw.

The wounded were helped back by those who were still able-bodied. The two tanks which had been posted in the middle ground and the two squads of Third Platoon which had been designated as a "reserve," but had remained unemployed in the crisis, were used to protect the withdrawal, as the command post group took off to the southward. The men of Fourth Platoon were already out of it; having expended all their ammunition in fires directed to the north and east, whence the enemy pressure was coming, they became the target of CCF's 120-mm mortar fire just in the moment when they were without power to punch back. So, on their own initiative, they withdrew to the high ground southwest of the village.

Extricating the command post force was necessarily a slow and tortured movement because of the casualty burden and the need to get the covering force straightened around. The column became formed and ready to go at about the same time that Barbey, over on the left flank, decided to move back to the roadblock. Thus within a brief interval, the whole position was in flux. The Chinese infantry immediately rushed forward into the vacuum, threatening a disaster.

In that clutch, the salvation of the American infantry depended almost wholly on what could be done by the armor. The resolution and boldness of these few tank crews, fighting almost in isolation, was more than equal to the occasion.

Made careless by success, the Chinese tried to advance in column via the two footpaths which wound down into the low ground from the forward ridges. It was not necessary for the two tanks serving as backstop halfway between the two roadblocks to shift their positions. They had the marchers in dead line of sight, and they poured the fire to them, both with the machine guns and with the artillery pieces.

Over on the left flank, where Barbey was trying to get his wounded back to some kind of sanctuary, the results were not less spectacular. His remnants and the forward squads of Second Platoon had withdrawn from north of the road and begun a reorganization on the high ground which Second Platoon's left flank still held to the south of the road—the last vestige of the company position. A Chinese column came hard after them. At the roadblock, Lieutenant Lis saw this attack force as it came over the brow of the hill. The crew of the M26 waited until they had the head of the column on the low ground, right in their sights, not more than 150 yards away. The first round hit the lead files dead on, knocked the legs off the front man and wounded several others. Quickly the cannon spoke again, several times. Another twelve Chinese were killed—that number of dead men later was counted on the spot—before the living turned and fled back over the hill.

In the middle ground, the two tanks continued to shell the Chinese until shortly before daylight, while Love Company men made the shuttle to the aid station, bringing out the last of the wounded. The most serious cases were then loaded

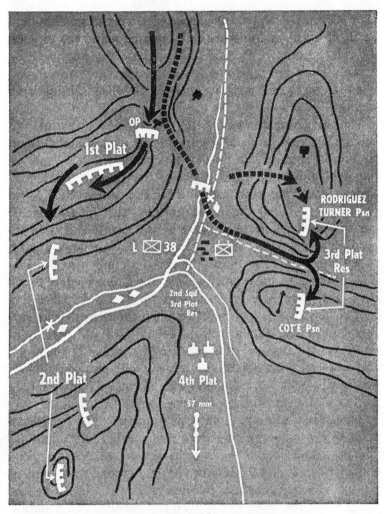

OP

1st Plat

RODRIGUEZ
TURNER Psn

3rd Plat
Res

L ⊠ 38

2nd Sqd
3rd Plat
Res

COTE Psn

2nd Plat

4th Plat

57 mm

LOVE COMPANY, 38TH REGIMENT

American dispositions at hour of attack and main CCF penetrations
which collapsed the position.

aboard the tanks for the carry to the regimental collecting
station near Yonghyon-dong. With that, what remained of
Love Company temporarily departed from the small valley.
Knots of enemy skirmishers had deployed along the caps of
the ridges rearward, in position to fire on the line of withdrawal. Their fire took further toll of the company. It finished the night with a 55 per cent loss in killed, missing, and
wounded in action.

That is about all, except for the further adventures of
Edsel Turner. We left him engaging in a lone-handed fight
on Third Platoon's hill. So did the company. For a time, as
the fight thickened in the valley, the pressure slackened
against him. Too, while Dill and his companions held forth
on the other side of the hill, Turner felt that his own niche
was snug enough. A small party of the enemy still tried to
push forward via the path in the gulley; but whenever a head
poked out, he fired at it, and he heard a number of his bullets hit home. In the moments when the Chinese effort slackened temporarily, he used his strength to build higher the
wall of loose rock which revetted his foxhole, so that at last
this parapet was shoulder high. Finally, his own M1 quit
firing. What happened to it, he didn't know, but it was probably a broken firing pin. Stucke was still with him, and Stucke
had a rifle which he couldn't use because of his wound.
Turner took over Stucke's and got back into action.

Then came pressure from a new quarter. The American
tanks in the valley, getting word that the hill was solidly in
Chinese hands, began shelling the slopes next Turner. Several of the infantry LMGs in the low ground swung their
fire in the same direction. Just above Turner's head, tracers
bounced off the rocks like a swarm of fireflies. But it didn't
unnerve him. He said to Stucke: "We've got good protection. They're less likely to hit us than to rattle the Chinese."
After a while the fire stopped and the valley grew quiet,
though Turner didn't know why.

It was shortly afterward that Stucke looked up and saw
Chinese coming over the rise behind them; the envelopment

which Dill had stalled temporarily was now resuming. At the same time, Turner saw a group dash out of the gulley and make for Cot'e's old position, apparently with the object of setting up another machine gun. He fired four or five quick shots at them and they went to ground.

Stucke asked: "What do we do now?"

Turner considered briefly. The Chinese on the path below him were about 30 yards away—a nice downhill throw. The Chinese approaching from upslope were perhaps a few yards more than that. He had left at this moment one grenade and five rounds for his M1.

He said to Stucke: "I'll throw the grenade at the people in the gulley; then I'll fire my five bullets at the people on the rise. As I begin fire, you jump from your foxhole and start rolling downhill. I'll follow you out and maybe we'll meet later."

That was what they did. As his last bullet was fired, Turner sprang from the hole, ran a few yards along the hill, then rolled more than halfway down the slope. In the darkness, he missed Stucke, and the Chinese missed them both.

Turner started running toward where he had last seen the Battalion Command Post. But as he ran, he heard nothing and the silence became terribly oppressive. At last he realized that of the American forces which had been holding this ground, he was now alone in the valley. Moving carefully, he worked his way down to the creek bed where he had last seen the tanks. There he found two large boulders side by side with just enough concealment between them to hide one man. He crawled into the hole and rested.

At dawn, Chinese parties of a dozen men or more began passing on both sides of his hideout, moving up to the hill where he had been and down again to the creek.

Finally, he understood the movement; these were first-aid men and burial detachments. Some of their number fashioned shallow graves by scraping sand away from the banks along the creek bed until there was a depression just deep enough to take a body.

The work went on only 75 feet from where Turner watched. It lasted for an hour, and he counted each body as it was placed in its bed of sand. When it was over he knew that twenty-nine Chinese—at least—had died on the hill which he had defended.

A little later, the enemy pulled away to the north. Turner could hear no sound of any kind in the valley. So he crawled from under the rocks and, weaponless, headed south to find and rejoin the battalion. As he started, he had no feeling of being a fugitive. He realized that the field was his alone, and that both friends and enemies had departed from it because of the bruises received during battle.

This was not an exaggeration of the fact. The armor, getting in its final punches, had actually routed the Chinese hitting columns from the valley. The detachments which came back into it in the early morning, while Turner watched, had been sent southward solely to execute the burial mission. This was competently proved when in the late afternoon the Americans, having reorganized, again entered the valley. They found their military stores exactly as they had left them. Not a weapon or a box of ammunition had been removed or damaged. The files at the command post and the stores at the aid station were intact. Nothing had been looted from the area except a few rations and personal possessions. The last of the Chinese had fled north upon completing the rude burial rite.

# 10

## Spots in a Big Picture

Early on 26 november, the turkish brigade (turkish Army Command Force) was committed by IX Corps to the right of 2nd Division with the mission of proceeding via the Kunuri road to Tokchon. The hope was that by regaining possession of this route they would temper the threat to 2nd Division's right flank arising from the collapse of ROK II Corps; it was like applying an aspirin bottle cork to the bunghole in a beer barrel.

On the march north there had been warnings that Tokchon might be the spot toward which the enemy would loose his thunderbolt. Air observers had reported seeing "hundreds of men" working on the Huichon-Tokchon road. Almost overnight it was transformed from a cart track to a broad highway. On receiving this intelligence, Maj. Gen. Laurence B. Keiser, commander of 2nd Infantry Division, said: "Goddamn it, that's where they're going to hit. That will be the main effort—off our flank and against ROK II Corps."

Still, at the hour when the TACF was given its longshot assignment, the extent of the disaster to ROK II Corps and the resultant jeopardy to Eighth Army's dangling flank were beyond full appraisal at higher headquarters. The enemy blow had landed with full speed, full surprise, and full shock. There is no need to speculate that some paralysis of thought derived from it. The physical damage to communications in the American sector was such as to prevent any immediate and accurate reckoning of the magnitude of the assault and of the wreckage. As to the ROK sector, it was practically a void. The Americans to the left of it had no news of its fate until late on 26 November, and even then the information was fragmentary. In fact, the first warning came not in the form of a message but from a tactical event. Shortly after midday, the ROK 3rd Regiment from ROK II Corps, retreating from its own sector, began to appear in driblets within 38th Regiment's lines. Colonel Peploe called Division and was told to collect the ROK regiment and employ it if possible. In this way came the first hint that the division's flank was dangling in air. On his own initiative, Peploe took steps to maneuver his own regiment so as to thwart the outflanking of Eighth Army.

Corps had sent the Turks forward as extra insurance against just such a happening. The mission, by its nature and by order, tied them to 2nd Division, though with none of the benefits which normally attend such a union. Keiser, overburdened by his own fighting problem, could not get down to visit his attachment. Neither his ADC, Brig. Gen. J. Sladen Bradley, nor any other senior officer managed to undertake this mission for him. In consequence, the Turkish Brigade, in its first engagement on Korean soil being tossed into the center of the caldron, was left alone, unhelped and friendless in a situation which was equally desperate and obscure. The results were not good.

The village of Wawon is but one third of the distance along the road between Kunuri and Tokchon. Reference to the map shows that Wawon is well to the southwest of the 38th Regiment position on 26 November, which is but another way of saying that it was in 2nd Division's rear area. But on the march to Tokchon the Turkish Brigade got only as far as Wawon and was there engaged.

No small fight ever won more impressive headlines around the world. The word was flashed that the Turks, meeting the Chinese for the first time, had dealt them a bloody repulse at bayonet point; it was the first stirring bit of news from the November battle. But what precisely happened in the first few hours at Wawon is still an open question. The bri-

gade also boasted the capture of several hundred enemy prisoners from among these first "Chinese" waves. The word gave
a lift to the neighbors. Lieut. Sukio Oji, a Nisei interpreter,
was sent by 2nd Division to interview the prisoners. Instead
of Chinese, he found 200 forlorn ROKs who had blundered
into the Turkish column while beating their way back from
the fight at Tokchon.

But if the first fight at Wawon, instead of being an epic,
was a grim tragedy of mistaken identity, it was still not the
Turks' fault. They were doing the best they could with very
little light to guide them.

Of what swiftly followed on the heels of this incident,
there is no detail, but only the fateful result in outline. The
first report from Wawon was taken at face value by the high
command; it was accepted as confirmation that the enemy-
turning movement was already embracing decisive ground.
The Turks' orders were changed; instead of advancing east
toward Tokchon against the Chinese flood, they should march
straight north along a cart track to the village of Tamgi,
where they could tie in to the 38th Regiment's right flank
and would be next an escape route to the west. But on 27
November they could not even get started on this maneuver.
While still astride the Wawon road, they were brought to
full battle. Only this time there was no doubt about it—they
were fighting Chinese. What happened thereafter toward the
shattering of the Turkish Brigade in the Chongchon action
is not reported. All that is known is that when on the following day its survivors at last linked with the 38th Regiment as both forces fell back to the southwest, the brigade
was no longer battle-worthy, though some of its small fractions still retained their fighting integrity and continued to
face the enemy.

In the meantime Peploe had regulated his dispositions as
if already knowing that no help would come. More quickly
than higher headquarters, he saw that, though the breakneck
plunge might be averted, at least the chasm was yawning.
Peploe had not underrated the blow dealt his front which

had cracked four company perimeters on the first night and had also mangled Baker Company when it was sent forward in the darkness to help shore up the position. If anything, he overrated it, and continued to think for some hours that he was standing off the main weight of the enemy, not knowing that the 9th Regiment along the river and the Koreans to his right were having an even worse time. These promptings gave him proper caution untinged by timidity. His initial moves looked to the re-establishing of his center. Fox Company went about restoring its hold on its nest of ridges. Love Company, plus elements of First Battalion, plus Charley Company of the Engineers, was sent north along the little valley to regain the high ground from which Love had been driven.

While these counteroffensive jabs were underway—and they took much of the day, being harassed by flanking fire from bands of snipers dug in along the ridge tops—Peploe undertook to learn if he still owned a right flank. It was a main question as news from Item and King Companies, and from the two-gun section from Charley Battery of the 38th Field which was supporting King, was a total black-out. In view of the melee elsewhere, that was enough reason to speculate that the worst might have happened.

Regiment sent one platoon of tanks along the road from Unbong-dong to the bend just north of Chon-dong to hunt the missing and explore the situation. Except for small-arms fire, they made the run unscathed, curiously enough to discover that Item and King were sound as a nut and had not been scratched. The information black-out was due either to enemy wire-cutting or to technical failures in their communications.

Tongchang was the coordinating point between King Company on 2nd Division's extreme right and ROK 3rd Regiment on ROK II Corps' left. It was from here that the bad news came. The 3rd ROKs had been as lucky on the first night as the two missing companies. The skin was still whole but the spirit was ebbing low. To their right, the ROK 5th and 8th Regiments had been hit and dispersed, and the 3rd

ROK was crowding westward, footloose and looking for something on which to anchor.

When Peploe got these tidings he saw their import. The hole on his right could undermine the division, if not the army. He made his decision to pull Item and King Companies back to the high ground west of the Somin-dong-Chon-dong road and put them in a blocking position facing directly east. First Battalion would be displaced to high ground backing up this same line and forming an arc to the northwest. By these dispositions Division would have the semblance of a front refused to the south and the 38th would still be protecting its gravity center. Whether it would work, and whether there was still time enough, would depend finally on how fast the Chinese could move on a southwest axis past Tokchon.

Peploe called up Keiser and told him what he proposed. This was Keiser's first knowledge of the ROK collapse on his right, and so far as he yet knew it involved only one or two regiments. Peploe told him that his situation was not good, and that if he did not pull his right back to protect the MSR, it would get much worse. Keiser said to him: "OK, go ahead and use your own judgment." He thought of it at the time as a local problem, necessary to the conserving of the right flank elements, but not directly related to the possibilities of any future large-scale withdrawal. The situation still did not seem hopeless. By his estimate at that hour, the 9th and 38th were held and could not advance farther without taking excessive losses, but he was not thinking of anything worse than that.

Much later, in retrospect, he came to value Peploe's initiative as a move which certainly firmed the general position temporarily and possibly saved the division.

There were other changes consequent to this maneuver. From its position between Somin-dong and Chon-dong the artillery was displaced to the Unbong-dong area to support the new line. A collecting point was established at that same village to reassemble the 3rd ROKs. One battalion was put in line forward of Unbong-dong. The other two remained in a reserve position not far from the artillery.

That day the 38th interrogated its prisoners; in the bag were men from the CCF 113th, 114th, and 119th Divisions. They responded freely but had almost no information of anything above platoon level; nothing was learned about the larger dispositions and intentions of the enemy. All of their units had crossed the Yalu River between 20 October and 10 November and had pushed south as rapidly as they could travel afoot, though they had marched only under the cover of dark. They said that their officers had frequently harangued the troops, the line being that UN forces would not stop at the Yalu but would continue into Manchuria. They had been told that China would furnish nothing but manpower; the North Korean government would provide the food and Russia would supply the weapons.

Yet they had come armed and also provisioned. Each man carried about ten rations on his back on crossing into Korea. It was partly a canned ration complemented with hard biscuits. Rice, millet, and corn were confiscated locally. The infantry companies did not have a general mess. Usually, groups of from five to eight men ate together. But they had not bothered to prepare food *because they had harbored in the villages,* where they had forced the local people to cook the grains previously stolen from them.

Other than the basic load of ammunition carried by the fighter, essential supply was transported by human bearers integral to the unit within the battle area; as far forward as the rear boundary of a division the hauling was done by truck, cart, and pack horse. Manchurian ponies were also used to carry heavy types of ammunition onto the battlefield.

Each combat soldier carried four grenades. The minimum load for the rifleman was 100 rounds. The light machine guns were supplied with 1,000 rounds prior to action; basic for the heavies was 1,500 to 2,000 rounds. The light mortar carry was thirty rounds; for the heavy mortar, fifty to sixty.

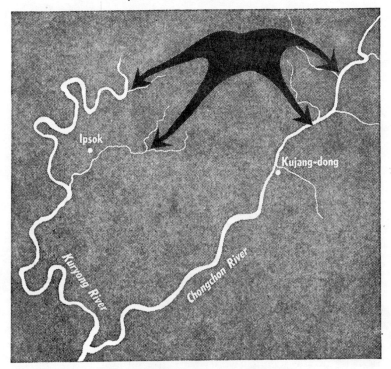

THE DECISIVE MANEUVER

This sketch shows the relationship of the CCF build-up and onfall against 2nd and 25th Divisions to the watershed of the Chongchon-Kuryong-gang.

Stale though this information of CCF may now seem in view of all that has been learned since, it is worthy of at least some emphasis, being the total of what the division learned of its enemy during the Battle of the Chongchon. If its knowledge of its own situation was not so scant, it was still running far behind the clock. Though its front was badly smitten and power from both directions was threatening to compress its regiments back into the narrow funnel of the Chongchon, there was no representation to Corps that the position and situation were becoming untenable. At the 2nd's command post it was believed that 25th Division on its left flank was still riding high, in relative aloofness from the storm. In this reflection there was a morsel of comfort, though the thought was contrary to the fact. The 25th had already felt the first hard blow, and it had stung enough to signal that there was more behind it. (This division's experience is described later in the journal.) Along with ROK II Corps and 2nd Division, the 25th was broadside to the Chinese area of greatest concentration. Those other divisions which composed the left flank of Eighth Army, while doing their part in the appointed hour, were but reaping the wind rather than the whirlwind. The battle belonged to the right and to the center.

These are among the considerations which gave the operations of the second twenty-four-hour period within 2nd Division and, for that matter, within 25th Division their particular significance. In the first twenty-four hours the position had suffered critical if not decisive hurt. But even those who were riding next to the fire did not know from how many deep wounds their front was already bleeding, nor did they sense the full meaning of the Chinese maneuver. After the fighting of the second twenty-four hours there was no longer room for doubt. The enemy's ultimate design was still not fully revealed, but the execution which had already come of it spelled death to the ill-timed MacArthur offensive and withdrawal for those whose personal fortune had enabled them to survive it. The ranks knew this as they counted their depleted numbers. Staff and command knew it as they scraped bottom in their search for oddments with which to plug gaping holes in the swaying line. Higher headquarters came to the realization somewhat more slowly because of the lag in communications more than because of ingrained military stubbornness; it is not always true that bad news travels on winged feet.

What happened to the units astride the Chongchon on the second night has already been set forth in some detail. The further adversity of the 38th Regiment on the right flank can be told only in broad outline. During the dark Decem-

ber in which the main problem was to get this division back
on its feet so that it could fight again, there was not time
to reconstruct the step-by-step battle experience of all these
men. The main object of search was to develop the pattern
by which the Chinese enemy fought, the better to know how
to fight him. Therefore the study embraced mainly those actions which were decisive or possessed some especial tactical
significance. The fighting of the 38th on the second night
did not have this character; the regiment was already rolling
with the punch and reacting to its own inspired estimate of
the general situation. It is nonetheless a pity that young
Americans have to die bravely but inconspicuously on a foreign hillside in a national cause and have no better words
than these spoken of them.

Love Company got back to the ridge of its defeat but did
not endure. At 2100 it was enveloped from the rear and
Regiment heard nothing more from it as a unit. Again the
attack had caught it unaware and the fight was lost before
its platoons could achieve unity. Lone individuals and little
groups of survivors got out and worked their way rearward.
They were still trickling back when daylight came.

Fox Company was again hit at the same hour. What was
left of George Company under command of the kid lieutenant Hollingsworth was rushed forward to help Fox. The
ground was held.

Hard after midnight, the Third Battalion command post,
the regimental aid station, and How Company (heavy weapons) were hit and smashed in their reserve position next the
road running westward from Somin-dong. Their broken parts
fell back on the regimental command post. Coincident with
their arrival, all communications between Regiment and Item
and King Companies went out.

There followed an hour or so of untold anxiety. Not long
before dawn outposts detected one battalion of the enemy
marching directly toward the command post from out of the
northeast. One Chinese platoon was moving along the high
ground while the main body advanced via the valley; this

flank guard was seen first and engaged. The battalion then revealed itself; it was headed straight toward Unbong-dong, where the command post stood.

In a draw to the southeast of Unbong-dong, the 38th Field and Able Battery of the 503rd came alert when the enemy flanker platoon stumbled bodily into the gun positions. Lieut. Col. Robert J. O'Donnell's gun crews killed them or drove them off with rifles, pistols, and grenades, losing only two or three men in so doing. The howitzers were then turned about in time to hit the enemy battalion point-blank as it advanced along the draw, a quite solid target not more than 300 to 400 yards distant. One Chinese, taken prisoner in the gun pits, said that a patrol had been sent back to bring forward the rest of the regiment. But its one engaging battalion was finished; later more than 100 Chinese dead were counted on the killing ground.

When daylight came, a liaison plane was sent to look for trace of Item and King. From the air, the pilot saw them standing steady with Chinese all around them, many of whom would not move again. King was foxholed on the crest of a steep-sided hill. When the fight cooled, King's men counted 173 Chinese on the slopes who had died in their last mountain climb. But there was only a handful of King survivors to make the count.

Later the air confirmed what the Chinese prisoner of war had reported. The other two enemy battalions were first seen advancing toward Unbong-dong. Bad news must have come to them, for they veered and were observed entering the shaft of a coal mine. An air strike was ordered. The works were first struck with napalm and then the shaft was sealed with 500-pound bombs. It is believed that about 600 Chinese perished belowground.

On that day seventy-two sorties were flown in support of the 38th. Another large enemy body was observed digging in along several ridges southeast of Chon-dong, "900 of them," the air report said. They were strafed and napalmed throughout the day. One group of fifty Chinese was caught by the air while crossing an open field; napalm was dropped and they were fried to the last man. All during the afternoon reports came in about other enemy groups being observed in motion toward 38th's front. Without exception, these troops were moving on a westward-running axis, as if emerging from the vacuum left by the collapse of ROK II Corps.

Baker Company was hit in midday and driven back along the main road. The battalion from 3rd ROK Regiment which had gone into line with 38th continued under sporadic attack but did not give ground. From the reserve position, the other two ROK battalions were given quick missions, one being sent eastward to tie in with Able Company on the right flank, and the other counterattacking northward toward the high ground which had been lost during the night. But these were not more than the motions of a boxer stiffening his guard while momentarily back-pedaling beyond closing distance from a powerful antagonist. Even as the ROKs went forward, Second and Third Battalions of the 38th withdrew through the First Battalion, Second Battalion going into a blocking position to west of Unbong-dong while Third Battalion closed next the 23rd Infantry. With this maneuver, which Division had sanctioned in the morning, the curtain was finally drawn on the overbuoyant hope with which Eighth Army had struck north with its sights on the Yalu. Thereafter the arrow on the road signs pointed southward.

Keiser had told Peploe to withdraw without further order when the hour came that he thought it was necessary to save his regiment. After the movement was underway there arrived an order from Corps authorizing Division to pull back as far as Won-ni, which was just a stride southward along the Chongchon. By its maneuver, the 38th simply stood on a right angle to the 23rd, which was anchored on high ground to the south of Sinhung-dong. Either could provide some protection for the further retirement of the other, depending on the direction from which the pressure came next.

That day the 23rd's position had been a little island of relative quiet in the general tumult of the battle. But on the west bank of the Chongchon, there had been no surcease from the struggle. The 2nd Engineers, which had been thrown in to strengthen the 9th's depleted left flank, had been over-run, along with the remnants of Lieutenant Colonel Mc-Mains' luckless Third Battalion. Second Battalion of the 9th, licking its wounds after the savage experience of the second night, was holding a blocking position west of the river opposite Kujang-dong; the left-flank survivors fell back into this ground.

But there is a bit more to the story than that and some back-tracking is required if the mounting desperation of the division's general situation is to be fully appreciated. That morning Colonel Sloane of the 9th had received the disturbing news that the Chinese had set up a roadblock behind his left flank. The enemy force was just west of the Chongchon opposite Kujang-dong, which was bounded on one side by the main road to the rear and on the other by the body of the division artillery.

Here again was an implied menace to the safety of the whole division, though, because it was in 9th's sector, Sloane fell heir to the problem. Southward he sent a strong infantry patrol, re-enforced by two tanks, under command of a colored soldier, Lieutenant Mallory. When the patrol got to seeing distance of the roadblock, the tanks couldn't maneuver to within clear sight of the target because of the roughness of the ground. Mallory called for artillery fires on the block, then under a covering fire by his own machine guns, charged in with his riflemen, and beat the enemy back from the road-way. But from his radio report to Sloane about the fire which had come against him from the ridge tops, Sloane judged that there was a Chinese swarm on his rear.

At noontime, Sloane told Major Barberis to move Second Battalion to the threatened spot, set it up as a block covering the westward approach to Kujang-dong, and strive to make contact on his left with 24th Regiment of 25th Division, which was wandering about somewhere in the wilderness. His ragtag companies had soon established their make-

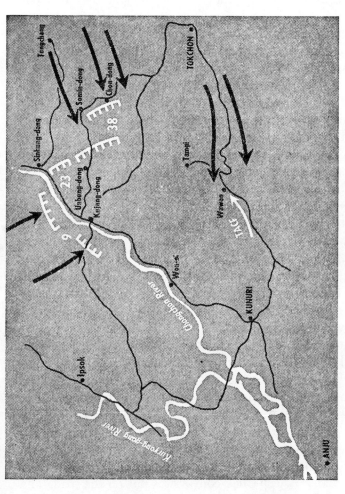

DEVELOPMENT OF CCF OFFENSIVE, 26-28 NOVEMBER

Showing advance of Turks on 26 November and contraction of 2nd Division position under enemy pressure from both flanks.

shift buffer, with George, How, and Fox in line and Easy in reserve. In late afternoon Barberis reported to Sloane that the major part of his mission was accomplished; his men had beaten back the enemy from the vicinity but they had not been able to find the loose flank of 24th Infantry. Sloane was convinced that his forces west of the Chongchon had about reached the point of final exhaustion. He called Division and said: "I must know my mission for the night. I can't keep troops going until dark, then give orders to consolidate ground and expect troops to execute them in a way which will give men a decent chance." By way of answer he was told: "Don't get your bowels in an uproar!"

Deciding then to act on his own, he directed his westward battalions to seek the best ground closest to hand, button up tight, and spend the rest of the day improving their positions. It was about one hour until dark.

A call came from Lieut. Col. John B. Hector of the 37th Field, which was directly supporting 9th. The battalion was practically out of ammunition, its trucks having been used during the day to shuttle infantry. Said Hector: "I propose to send trucks now for resupply." Already the night had come. Sloane answered: "Send as many as you can and tell them not to waste one minute."

The next few minutes proved Sloane's apprehensions fully justified. There came a frantic call from Lieut. Col. James Hill, who was having his first day as commander of First Battalion. Able Company had been hit in its position on the west bank opposite 23rd Regiment's left flank; its line had broken and the survivors were falling back on Regiment. So here it was again: another of Sloane's units was wading the icy Chongchon and would need resuscitation when it reached the east bank. A jeep-truck convoy was put on the road. The stragglers were rounded up and rushed to Kujang-dong for warm quarters and dry clothing. As quickly as their teeth quit chattering, they were put back into firing positions on the nigh side of the river—a dime's worth of insurance if the pressure on the far side at last became uncontainable.

Already it was building up at a tremendous rate. The engineers reported that they were being hit by CCF in "regimental" strength; Third Battalion's abbreviated line was strained to the limit. Still, at the beginning the engineer-infantry rifle team stood firm and replied steadily to the fire. Communications were working with a special charm and the fires from 37th Field were hitting exactly where needed. Shortly after midnight Sloane was told by telephone that the supply of 105-mm shells had run out. The close support job was swung over to the 17th Field, and under direction of the forward observers, the 8-inch guns began dropping their fires within 50 yards of the men in the foxholes. Enthusiastically, the observers reported that the big stuff was "accurate and very effective." Shells normally conserved for use against such targets as railheads and log-walled bunkers were being thrown against thinly deployed enemy riflemen as they snaked their way up and over the rock ledges. Even so, the big hows were powerless to change the end result. The engineers began to run out of small-arms ammunition; there were no men at hand to serve as carrying parties even had the way been open. Some of the engineers withdrew to the south, where they joined Barberis; others waded the river. Some of the infantry fractions were pulled along by this movement, but on the highest knob of the hill mass Item Company of 9th, along with Dog of 2nd Engineers and Easy and George of the 24th Infantry, which had broken off from their own command and at last found a precarious home on Sloane's flank, stuck their ground until daylight came. The enemy appears to have become exhausted by his own effort. At least his attack fell off sharply not long after the engineers had departed from their hill. From Barberis' battalion, Easy Company was pushed northward in the darkness to sit on a hill between the die-hard scratch battalion and the river, giving it such support as was possible. By the hour of its arrival (0300) the steam had already gone from the Chinese assault. After daylight there was only occasional rifle fire.

Thus the movements and actions in an affair to which the Division G3 Journal gives only this brief description, "The force was overrun." It hardly meets the occasion. Some men had held their ground; others had got out in orderly fashion for lack of bullets and grenades; and there were not a few who straggled. The footloose men were rounded up at Kujang-dong, given food and a brief rest, and formed into provisional units for dispatch to whatever spot was threatened next.

The division front was now bent like a sprung horseshoe with its one main avenue of withdrawal extending southward from the open end. On both flanks, its infantry was without friendly contact. All units were critically depleted by battle losses, and the survivors were worn down from lack of food and sleep. The enemy build-up pressed ever more strongly against both lower ends of the inverted U while almost ignoring its center part. Not only was the threat to the rear obvious; it was shaping like an attempt at double envelopment. Nothing remained but to withdraw and the hour was already quite late.

The artillery train was already pointed southward. Just before midnight of 27-28 November, the 15th Field had called from its position 5,000 yards north of Kujang-dong to say that, in consequence of the fallback by Able Company, 9th Regiment, the batteries were wholly exposed to attack from the Chongchon's west bank. The 15th was authorized to displace immediately to new ground 5,000 yards south of Kujang-dong. Subsequent action imposed a sufficient load on those battalions which remained in place. The 37th Field, which had lacked shells during the highest pitch of the engagement, still got resupplied in time to fire 2,951 rounds during the night. The 503rd, which was supporting the right flank, fired 600 rounds. The 17th used 406 8-inchers, helping to hold the northwest corner. The 38th Field got on the road about 0930, moving in the van of the combat team as it swung westward and onto the main road at Kujang-dong. At 1015 there came an order from the Division Commander: "Displace the 17th FA Bn to a point south of Kunuri." This was the first notice to the artillery command that Division was going back "all the way." Whereas Corps still insisted that the force, if it must displace, should reform on the next line of hills to the south, Keiser had about decided that nothing but a long jump could save the division from the meat grinder.

One minor event passed almost without notice that morning which later, as men looked back on it, was seen in a baleful light. The air reported seeing a ROK regiment, in solid column, marching around Peploe's flank from the northeast. Keiser could not believe that there were any ROK formations remaining solid in the neighborhood, three days having passed since ROK II Corps had dissolved. Members of 3rd ROK Regiment, with Peploe, when questioned said that it might be 6th ROK Regiment; but they were only guessing. Planes were sent out to buzz the column. They flew in low enough for the pilots to make sure that the ranks were wearing South Korean dress. But the marching men neither dispersed nor did they signal to the planes. As the planes dove, the column marched straight on. So no offensive action was taken. Subsequently this body vanished into thin air, and the mystery of its identity and disappearance was subject to but one logical explanation. This was a CCF column which had got reuniformed after breaking the front of the ROK Corps, and it was using this Trojan Horse trick to obtain free entry into the Eighth Army rear. Its tactics, however, were not more baffling than was the protest by Maj. Gen. Charles Willoughby, Chief of Intelligence in the Tokyo headquarters, that the enemy did not succeed in turning the Eighth Army flank.

The 38th Regiment shouldered its gear and started south while the phantom column was making the wide sweep around its end. The 9th was ordered to set up a new line near Pugwon except for its Second Battalion, which remained with 23rd Infantry in the hills serving to cover the retrogression of the main body.

There remained for all three regiments much hard fighting before they could depart from the valley of the Chongchon.

Their worst hours were reserved for the day on which they left the river behind.

On 2nd's left, 25th Division was also falling back toward the Kunuri junction, a defile which choked this army of its substance in the hour when it had to retreat. Twenty-fifth's four days had not run the same full scale of mad courage, abject misery, and crushing defeat as 2nd's. But they had been good and bad enough.

## 11

# Death of a Hero

On the morning of 25 november 1950, easy company of the 27th (Wolfhound) Infantry Regiment was a part of Task Force Dolvin, then serving as the spear of the attack by 25th Infantry Division under Maj. Gen. William B. Kean into enemy country.

The task force, advancing north to westward of the Chongchon River, was moving along with its left shoulder against the banks of the Kuryong-gang, a main tributary of the Chongchon, fordable by the men of the column but not by most of the vehicles.

The task force was commanded by Lieut. Col. Welborn G. Dolvin, a soldier not less able in his knowledge of armored maneuver than in his broad understanding of infantrymen and their combat problems.

Besides Easy Company, there were under him:

HQ, 89th Medium Tank Battalion
Co. B, 89th Medium Tank Battalion
8213th Ranger Company
Assault Gun Platoon, 89th Medium Tank Battalion
25th Reconnaissance Company
Reconnaissance Platoon, 89th Medium Tank Battalion
Co. C, 65th Engineer Battalion.

Dolvin's composite column had been in being for three days, and Baker Company, 35th Infantry Regiment, had come to it as a last re-enforcement. There had been no heavy action, however, and no untoward change in the enemy situation appeared to portend when the morning of the twenty-fifth dawned.

It is of the thought and action of Easy Company that this narrative speaks mainly. What happened elsewhere in the task force is highlighted only as it bears on the situation of this one unit. That is not to suggest that the others did any less well.

Lieut. William M. Otomo was already on the company objective with twelve men when Easy started forward. They had gone out as a patrol 2,000 yards in advance of the main body and had made the journey without serious interruption. At one point, however, bullets coming from far over on the right flank had droned dully past them as if almost spent. To the ear of Sgt. Jackie A. Lefler, it sounded like the work of a few irregulars somewhere far off in the bushes. The patrol did not stop to deploy or return fire.

When the company walked over the same ground, it got the same treatment and brushed it off just as casually. There were only a few shots from the distant ridges: no one slackened pace or hit the dirt. The company moved onto the hill, took over a few old diggings left on the crest by some prior military occupant, and proceeded to round out a perimeter with its own entrenching tools.

Through the chill of the November morning, the men had marched 6,000 yards airline along the road winding through the low ridges near the river to get to the position. They were still relatively fresh and they took actively to their spade work. However, M/S James B. Abernathy had noted that his men with the crew-served weapons had a "hell of a time" keeping pace with the column, and he had to prod them to keep closed up. The worst drag was in the mortar section; the ammo load wore men down and they had to change off. The other unequal burden was the 57-recoilless gun.

Initially, Third Platoon closed on the same peak as Second, and thereby spent some of its energy in what seemed to be useless digging since, too late, word came through that Easy was to outpost all the high ground covering the valley forward of Task Force Dolvin's position. This necessitated moving Third Platoon to the outpost line.

Its new position rested on three small peaks, almost cone-shaped, about 500 yards beyond the ridge where the company stood guard. Lieut. J. C. Burch looked this outwork over, then spread his three squads evenly over the crowns of the three peaks, except for putting one machine gun on the right-hand cone and adding a second machine gun and his personal weight to the center position.

Again the men dug. For the group with Burch, that task raised a special problem. The top of their cone had been sheared off. Earth mounds and crude monuments across its surface identified it as a Korean graveyard. That did not make for enthusiastic digging.

By 1730 as the sun went down, the position was as complete as it was ever to be. A few riflemen lay prone behind the monuments—rock cover—but most were in waist-deep pits. Through the late afternoon the men had strained to see some sign of the enemy. They had caught only fleeting glimpses of a few figures scurrying through the underbrush at great distance—Korean civilians possibly.

Burch had no time to look. He was intent on getting his squad positions linked by telephone, but finished by regretting that wire is nonelastic. What he had was too short by 50 yards.

Came the darkness. Then suddenly over on the right a machine gun chattered. The fire was close. The burst was prolonged. There were a few rifle shots. Fire flicked around the top of the righthand cone. But there was no other noise. Total silence followed. For a few minutes the whole thing seemed meaningless. Perhaps it had been a false alarm due to nerves unstrung by the sudden coming of the dark. Burch and the squad amid the gravestones wondered about it, though not for long.

The squad on the right-hand cone had been snuffed out in a twinkling. It happened this way. Pfc. Ackley had stepped out of his foxhole and downslope for a moment to relieve himself. That was the last thing ever seen of him; he vanished without a trace. Seconds afterwards a score of Chinese swarmed over the position. They were already manhandling the crew before the machine gun opened fire; aimlessly, the gunner continued fire until someone struck him down. Burch learned about this when Pfcs. Taylor and Fletcher staggered upslope into the graveyard position, dragging Pfcs. Melzer and Brinkman, both of whom were hard hit through the body. Melzer told the story as rapidly as he could catch his breath. He said he had last seen Pfc. Mays walking straight into a group of Chinese firing his BAR.

To the rear, the ridge where the company bivouacked was dead silent. Burch's two remaining squads had still felt nothing. But even as Melzer talked, Burch could hear foreign voices in a singsong jabber a few yards downslope. The noise continued but the men could see nothing.

That was how it was for about twenty minutes. To Burch it seemed much longer. He got on his SCR 300 with the intent of calling for mortar and artillery fire. But he couldn't get through. There were seventeen units on the one channel. Each time he got started someone else cut in. While he was still vainly trying, the jabbering ceased and his own hill became quiet. Then half a dozen grenades exploded all at once among the gravestones. The Chinese had crawled to within 10 yards of the foxhole line.

Easy, meanwhile, had made one move only dimly related to Burch's situation. The Ranger Company was holding a hill due east of the base of Capt. Reginald B. Desiderio's position, with its left flank in air. Desiderio's First Platoon was deployed among the tanks on the south slope of the main hill, and he figured that on that ground it wasn't doing the company much good. So Desiderio sent it forth to tie in with the Rangers and extend to Burch on the left. This happened at the time that Burch's first squad was overrun. M/S William D. Cox led the platoon out. In the darkness he somehow missed Burch's right flank and kept moving northeast, still looking for it. His directions had been incomplete; he had not been told the distance. Shortly he was 2,000 yards out in enemy country—one platoon surrounded by the Chinese Army.

In this manner—with only the best intentions—Easy Company became dangerously thinned and overextended just as the boom began to fall. It was wholly vulnerable, and the only remaining question was whether the enemy would collect the forfeit. Tom Dolvin, who commanded the task force defenses, hadn't been told about Cox's move; he continued on in blissful ignorance, not knowing that his tanks had been left unpicketed, and the force supposedly covering his rear was wandering aimlessly about far out to his front. For that was the truth about First Platoon at the moment. It was lost and didn't know how to get back.

Back in Third Platoon, Burch crouched in the shadow of a gravestone as the grenades fell, still working with his radio. At the explosion, he glanced up and realized what had given away the position. The landscape was now bathed by a full moon. Two of his ROKs had left the shadows and were standing clear in the light—conspicuous targets. A grenade exploded next them, and he heard them cry out. Then a dozen forms shining silver in the moonlight broke from the underbrush and came over the rise. Pfc. Navarro met them with machine-gun fire but got off only one short burst. They went straight for the gun. Navarro and his assistant, Pfc. Beverly, were shot to death by a Chinese with a tommy gun, standing directly over them. A grenade landed hard against Sergeant Hawkins, lying in the shadow beside Burch. The explosion lifted him bodily and blew him across Burch; his leg was shattered. Pfc. Brinkman, already wounded in the skirmish on the right, was struck by a second bullet. Corporal Barry, who had been trying to dress his wound, was also shot down. Someone yelled: "The BAR's jammed!"

These things happened as fast as the next second. Burch shook loose from Hawkins and jumped to his feet. Now he

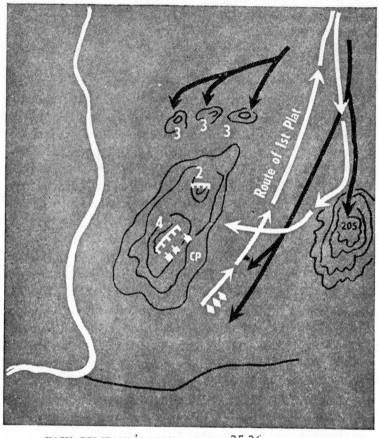

EASY COMPANY'S FIRST NIGHT, 25-26 NOVEMBER

could see from seventy-five to a hundred Chinese in a wide semicircle so close upon him that he could have dented any part of the line with a well-thrown rock.

He knew that his own position was no good. From the higher cone on the right, the Chinese could look right into the graveyard, and their fire would take him in flank even if he could beat back the line closing around his front. He shouted the order: "Fall back on the company!" and as his survivors took off at a run, he stood his ground—one man, covering their retreat with the fire of his carbine.

It worked beautifully—full automatic as long as he continued to press the trigger. At less than five yards' range he killed two Chinese who tried to take him in a rush. The rest hesitated just long enough. He turned his back and followed his men down the path. Had the enemy charged, or run to the rear slope and volley-fired at that moment, he couldn't have saved a man.

But not a shot was fired. The Chinese, as if struck by moon madness, sauntered around the burial mounds yelling derisively: "Come on back, GI! Afraid, GI?" over and over. They were still chanting it when the little party passed onto the big ridge.

Burch could not get hold of his Third Squad on the leftward cone. It was hit just as he quit the middle hill. Pfc. Fletcher, crouching in his foxhole, was startled to see a man standing downslope just 10 yards from him.

In perfect English, the man said: "I'm an FO."

Fletcher said: "From where?"

The man said: "How many men you got up there?"

Fletcher yelled: "Who in hell are you?" and fired.

The man ran back into the underbrush. Then the attack started and rifle and tommy-gun fire blazed from the growth all around. As time went on, single skirmishers, wiggling along the little gullies, tried to close upon the squad position around the crest.

But the last 20 yards of the cone rose very sharply, and the defenders had a clear view all around. By rolling grenades down the slope and interspersing rifle and grenade fire, the squad kept the upper hand despite its being outnumbered ten to one.

Back in the company position, Burch called for artillery fire to cover Third Squad. For about forty-five minutes, a baby barrage was dropped in front of the cone by one battery of 155s. Three rounds went wrong and fell within the squad perimeter, but by a miracle no one was hurt. The effect on the Chinese seemed to be thoroughly discouraging.

About 0200 the squad withdrew from the position, dropping back toward the company just after the last 155 round had fallen. Sgt. Henry Pertee made the decision after weighing his situation. So far he had not lost a man. But the grenades were gone, the BAR had run dry, and some of the M1s were low on ammunition.

What remained of Third Platoon was redistributed to all points where it could re-enforce Second's general position. The perimeter sweated out the small hours, wondering where the next blow would fall and whether First Platoon would ever get back.

Though the men on the big hill had need to be concerned, Sergeant Cox and his platoon that night were walking knee-deep in horseshoes and rabbit's feet. Missing the key ridge which the Rangers were holding, they debouched into a fairly wide valley (by Korean standards) and, just as the moon lighted the scene, found themselves in a maze of iced-over paddies. Cox heard the sounds of distant fire on his right rear, and just in time his men, moving single file, froze back into the shadow of a high dike. Along the embankments at both ends of the dike, moving past his flanks, two columns of Chinese headed south. They were jabbering excitedly as they went past at a half run. Boxed in, the platoon held its breath, not daring to talk, fire, or dig. In a few minutes they were out of earshot.

But it had been too close a thing, and Cox knew he had to get out of the paddy area as quickly as possible. The nearest high ground was a small hill several hundred yards yet farther north. SFC Maynard K. Bryers suggested that they head for it and move to within the shadow at the base. There they had got just barely tucked in when they saw another column come around the hill and strike southward. The silvery sheen of their uniforms identified them as enemy.

It was after they had disappeared that Cox raised Desiderio on his radio and told him that the platoon was in the middle of the Chinese Army. He described the ground. Desiderio told him to march directly southward 2,000 yards. He would come to a big ridge. The Rangers were on it. The platoon was to join them.

They marched, and they got almost to the forward slope of the ridge which had been held by their friends. But the Chinese had beaten them to the target. The Ranger Company had been cracked twice and finally had met disaster at the close of a terrible day. To win Objective 8, they had had to fight for every yard of ground in the late afternoon. The defenders were part of the tough, unyielding screen which the enemy had set to contain our northward advance while unloosing their own counterattack along both sides of the Chongchon. This solidifying, had all information along the general front been promptly correlated, would have been read as a warning that the situation had diametrically changed. But that did not happen, and the hand-to-hand fight by which the Rangers carried the hill just before dusk was seen only as an isolated incident. In the final clutch, the enemy had been beaten down by heavy fires from the 77th Field Artillery Battalion.

In the hours while Burch had been fighting, the Ranger hill was quiet. At 2350, Dolvin in his command post got word that the Ranger Company was under attack by a Chinese battalion. One hour later came the cheering news that the Chinese had been beaten off, though Lieutenant Puckett, the commander, had been shot through the arm and there were other losses. At 0245 came the brief message that the company was being enveloped from two sides by a greatly superior force. Then there was silence.

Cox's men, threading their way softly through enemy country, got their first warning of the untoward development on Objective 8 as they left the little valley and started to climb the ridge. It came when six rounds of 155-mm HE landed right among them. Four men were knocked down by the blasts, but though shaken were otherwise unhurt. The Rangers had called for these fires along the north slope of their hill, but they came too late to have any effect save the stunning of the platoon which might have helped them had it arrived earlier.

Since the barrage was breaking between Cox's men and the crest, there was nothing to do but sit and wait it out. It was an uneasy period. While they were still sitting, three Rangers came into their lines under Lieutenant Puckett. He was now bleeding hard from two places; a second bullet had got him through the chest. Puckett told Cox he thought the four of them were the only survivors. But he was wrong about that. In all, twenty-two men managed to find their way back out of a command of eighty men and three officers.

Again Cox called Desiderio on his SCR 300. The Captain told him to rejoin the company on the main hill. It was easier said than done. Cox and Bryers went around giving whispered instructions to the men. Once started, they were not to fire a shot or say a word. They would move single file, stay closed up, and join hands if necessary when they came to the dark spots. Instead of taking the straight line, they would move from one patch of underbrush to another, always taking advantage of shadow. If they encountered any Chinese, they would freeze and take no action unless otherwise ordered.

These instructions were observed to the letter. At 0430 First Platoon got back to the company. Not a man had been lost during the maneuver. They had passed Chinese on the way but had remained unobserved. The discipline could not have been better preserved by a band of forest-bred Indians. True enough, Cox's men had not engaged. Even so, the control and response by which this group of enlisted men extricated themselves from a wholly formidable situation is one of the highlights of the task force's action.

The Chinese drew off before dawn from in front of Easy Company. The fight over on the right had not stopped when the Rangers lost the hill. Dolvin, when he knew that the enemy held it, had the artillery concentrate its fires against the crest, with heavy shoots of white phosphorus. The ridge danced with fire for the rest of the night. After daylight the bombers came over and in repeated waves struck against Objective 8. Dolvin, worrying about how he would win the ridge back, decided tentatively that he would put Baker of the 35th Regiment into the attack. The beaten-up remnant of the Ranger Company had already been passed back to Division.

As he saw the situation, things were getting pretty tight. The 35th Regiment had not come up abreast of the task force on the west side of the river. He had no contact with the 24th Regiment along his boundary on the right. Looking back over his right shoulder, he could see an enemy-held ridge within the 24th's zone which menaced his own rear. His one gate southward was held open by Baker of the 35th, which was perched on Objective 7, a small ridge next the river on Dolvin's rear. The Chinese had given Baker a tussle during the night, at the same time plastering Dolvin's command post with mortar and machine-gun fire. In the end, Baker had emerged not too badly bruised. But the loss of the Ranger Company created a hole which could not be filled. If Baker was swung over to retake the ridge lost on the right, the task force would be sailing into shoal water with no anchor. Adding one thing to another, Dolvin reluctantly concluded that unless the 24th should come abreast, he was hardly in business.

Though obscure to Dolvin, 24th Regiment's situation during the advance is no mystery; it was lost and muted by the vastness and perversity of the ridge-ribbed countryside. Commanding it was Col. John Corley, one of the boldest young fighters in the army. His battalions—deployed One-Three-Two in that order from left to right—were trying to embrace all of the badland lying between Dolvin's force and the left flank of 9th Infantry. In that heavy assignment lay their tribulation, but their salvation, also. Getting across the ridges was more exhausting, more time-consuming, more confounding to communications than threading the river valleys. But a bonus which Corley could not see at the time went with it. Unknowing, 24th Regiment was marching straight toward the heart of the Chinese build-up area. But because the enemy was rolling down the tributary streambeds toward the main valleys, this deployment of itself carried the main Chinese forces obliquely away from Corley's front. Thus it happened that his Third Battalion, under Lieut. Col. Melvin R. Blair in the central position, though physically closer to the enemy mass than any other American unit, remained virtually non-engaged during the two-day battle crisis. On the morning of 26 November, Corley was still unaware that Dolvin had been cracked hard, and though he had heard that Third Battalion of the 9th Regiment was "having trouble," he had no idea that its situation was desperate. Because of the tactical vacuum, his own regiment remained temporarily unscathed, though highly vulnerable because of the stretch-out. He spent the day prodding it farther forward and during a personal visit with Dolvin gained a little clearer view of the situation's realities. If he was to help Dolvin and Easy Company, his First Battalion obviously had to come abreast. It was simple enough to see that, and Corley's Baker Company was plodding in the required direction, but it was a long, long trail.

On Easy's hill the morning was promisingly quiet. The company breakfasted on cold C-rations. No enemy was seen. Burch led a party of his men out to his position of the night before. They retrieved one machine gun and one BAR, and came back carrying their dead in rifle-blanket slings. There were a few Chinese bodies strewn around the cones but the enemy had removed most of his dead.

In midmorning a party of Korean bearers came up carrying ammunition. The cargo was long on grenades and machine-gun boxes. Sergeant Abernathy, in passing out supply, noted that whereas on the preceding day the men were reluctant to carry more than one grenade, now they were demanding from three to five.

Easy spent the day digging deeper and trying to free the weapons which had jammed during the fight. But there was no general policing of weapons; the company was totally without cleaning materials. For all their extra labor, however, the men were not destined to fight again on this same ground.

Division had taken quick thought of its general situation. Brig. Gen. Vennard Wilson, assistant division commander, came up to take command of the forward situation, and the left battalion of the 24th Regiment, though not yet in contact, was put under the task force command. Wilson told Dolvin to fall back to better defensive ground, which movement would in any case put him into better adjustment with the support which was expected to come up on his right. When the combined force was solid, it would attack again. On the new ground, the task force would be just north of the ridge held by Second Battalion, 27th Regiment (minus Easy Company), under Lieut. Col. Gordon Murch, which was part of the division reserve.

The companies did a staggered retrograde to the new bivouac area, which was anchored upon Objectives 6 and 7, two lesser ridges which the task force had prowled during its advance north. Baker of the 35th pulled out first and took position just to the west of Hill 234. Charley of the Engineers set up on Objective 6. The Reconnaissance Company, which had been screening the whole river line west of the task force, set up a defensive just south of the big bend in the Kuryong-gang. Easy Company was last. Dolvin had purposefully assigned it to a reserve position in rear of the force, figuring that it was spoiling for a night's sleep.

Though these arrangements had been evolved during the midday, it was 1630 before Easy got word that it was to move. The sun had already set by the time it had loaded and started off the hill, heading south. But Easy's cheer about the new development was unalloyed. Hot chow was waiting at the new position. The company bedrolls had been brought up. Some of the men ate hastily and then got into the sack. Nobody bothered to dig a foxhole. Though the ground was weak, the company having been spread in a semicircular perimeter over two squat hills, Desiderio and his men all took it for granted they were so far back there was no danger of being hit. A guard was posted and the remainder of the company turned to for a night's sleep.

At some time during these hours, Baker Company of the 24th came abreast on Dolvin's right and, without making its presence known, pushed deeper into enemy country. When dark fell, it was about 1,000 yards northeast of the main position. Thus it was already a castaway and its main chance for survival was that its presence would go undetected.

Easy was just well bedded down, and the hill had become soundless save for snoring, when the Chinese hit again. The men felt no fire, but heard the sounds of battle north and south of them. The enemy attack had closed almost simultaneously against the main body of the task force, forward of the company, and on Murch's battalion, along its rear.

At the half hour past midnight Desiderio got a telephone call from Dolvin: he was to have Easy at the base of the hill and ready to move within fifteen minutes. Still unscathed, Easy loaded on five tanks of HQ Company, 89th Tank Battalion. The armor rolled forward into Dolvin's command post during a lull; not a shot was being fired. The men dismounted. Dolvin told Desiderio he wanted Easy to secure the small L-shaped hill about 150 yards forward of the command post. The company advanced to its base still without sensing anything of the presence of an enemy. It looked like a wild-goose chase.

They started the climb in squad column, Cox leading with First Platoon, followed by Third, Second, and Fourth in that order. Cox had not advanced three strides when small arms and machine-gun fire broke all around his men. They went flat among the rocks, and no one was hurt.

This volley had come from the left flank. The enemy was holding the peak of a connecting ridge not more than 200 yards away. Taking cover behind brush, rocks, and earth embankments, some of the men began to return fire. A few started to dig in. Still others worked their way to the crest, alternately firing and moving.

Cox continued his prodding until the body of his platoon had moved up to the skyline and deployed. Under cover of their fire, Burch brought his men up and over the crest. Third

Platoon followed, and with Desiderio directing the men dug their fire positions around the top, facing toward the sound of the enemy fire.

At first Lieut. Dell G. Evans of weapons platoon could get no accurate sense of the enemy location. So he had the mortars carried to the hilltop so that his men could get a good look. Then as the Chinese fire continued to search the crest, he followed the tracers and could see enemy soldiers in silhouette as they worked their weapons.

This was it: the Chinese were holding a parallel hill linked by a saddle to Easy's own position. Reading from left to right, the Chinese were 150 to 200 yards from Easy's foxhole line.

Having made his calculation, Evans led the mortars down into the angle on the L on the far slope of his own hill. He had lost no men to fire but was already short-handed, one squad having split off the company and missed its way when dismounting from the tanks. Evans got the mortars going immediately, shelling the crest where he had seen the Chinese machine guns firing.

Meanwhile, Desiderio had quit the hill and gone back to the task force command post. The five tanks were still there. He told Dolvin that he had to have them, and that the armor could climb the hill as easily as his own infantry. Artillery help was out of the question; the artillery was fighting for its life at its own gun position. Fifteen minutes later Desiderio led the tanks up to his perimeter. They had just topped the rise when the first Chinese charge broke against the position.

Sergeant Bryers was on a machine gun at the extreme left flank of the company. He had watched the section of 81s, set up behind Evans' 60s, shell some of the intervening low ground and the forward slope of the enemy hill.

There had been a liberal dousing with white phosphorus and some of it had started a grass fire. A sharp wind whipped it up and the blaze was soon going strong.

Then Bryers saw about 100 of the enemy rush forward into the fire circle and try to stomp out the flames with their feet.

They scarcely paused in so doing. The body suddenly broke in half. One half came charging across the saddle on the left. The others dashed for the open end of the little valley as if to turn Easy's right flank.

The saddle was bare ground, and Bryers' gun mowed them down, supported by rifle and BAR fire in good volume from Cox's men. The Chinese attack on the left faltered and stopped. Then some men could be seen running back while other skirmishers came forward singly and stealthily, crawling via the slopes of the saddle.

Simultaneously, the first two tanks coming into the perimeter centered their .50 fire on the Chinese attacking across the valley. Some fell from the fire. Others scattered and advanced to the slope of Easy's hill.

Bugles were now blowing from both ends of the Chinese line. In the flicker of the dying grassfire, Easy could see a steady flow of skirmishers working across the intermediate ground.

The armor drew bullets like a magnet. Burch's platoon, put out on a limb the night before, were now spotlighted by being next the tanks. Eight of his men were cut down, four of them ROK soldiers.

As the third tank drew into Third Platoon's position, it drew mortar fire. The tanks were deployed 25 yards apart, all facing northward, with riflemen spaced in between them. So placed, the armor could use its artillery against the enemy base on the opposite hill, while the .50 machine guns, firing downward, swept the gentler slopes of Easy's own hill, along which the Chinese skirmishers were trying to press forward.

Thereby they partly dampered the Chinese bullet fire, but could do nothing to stop the mortars. They fired in salvos, four tubes at a time, and altogether about forty rounds landed within the perimeter. Evans, at the mortar position, was in a sweat because no one on the hilltop could give him any idea where the enemy battery was located. Dolvin's command post was also drawing a heavy share of their fire. The enemy fire pattern was consistently two salvos of four each, followed by a prolonged break, as if a displacement had occurred.

Evans adjusted to the back slope of the enemy hill and kept searching vainly until he had exhausted his ninety rounds.

These were the terms of the fight for the next two hours. The Chinese kept walking into it, and with the armor and all infantry weapons firing, Easy continued killing.

Finally, from beyond the other hill, an enemy bugle sounded recall. At that moment, by their own account, there was no question in the mind of any infantryman present but that the tanks had saved the position. On the left, Bryers had spent six boxes of machine-gun ammunition, most of it against live targets. The gunners in center and on the right had used the same amount. But the five tanks together, firing from a superior height, had burned up forty-five boxes of .50 caliber. Out along the saddle and in the valley the men could see Chinese bodies lying in windrows.

In the quiet, Easy looked itself over. Another fourteen men had fallen, most of them from mortar wounds. But as a partial offset, three unexpected replacements had arrived. Dolvin during this time had been busy building a secondary defense line around his command post, using all administrative personnel except his switchboard operator. Returning to his command post, he saw three men apparently loafing nearby. They were armed with carbines. Dolvin said: "What are you doing?" Their spokesman said: "Nothing." Dolvin then ordered: "Get up to Easy Company's hill and join the fight." They took off without a murmur and fought with Burch's platoon. On the next morning Dolvin learned that the three unknowns were an Air Force fighter pilot and two enlisted men, who were in the vicinity on official business.

During the lull the wounded were taken to the task force command post for first aid. Easy looked to its ammunition; except for the M1 firers, the company was scraping the bottom. But there was a plentiful resupply at the command post. Cooks and clerks were rounded up as bearers to get it forward.

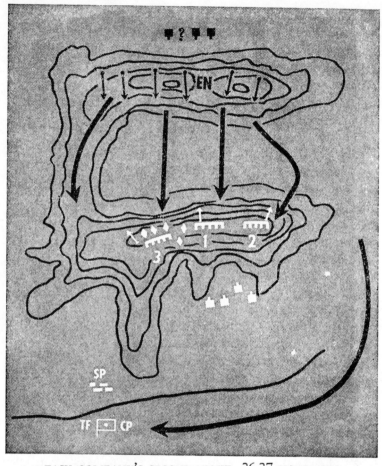

EASY COMPANY'S SECOND NIGHT, 26-27 NOVEMBER

Evans, having spent ninety mortar rounds, now called for a resupply of 400 and got it. Before daybreak, he was to use it all, though the tubes and base plates stood up beautifully under the pounding. Not so the men! The battery had no night-sighting devices. The gunners had to smoke up about two packages of cigarettes apiece so that by the glow they could follow the hairline. Their coughing grew steadily worse as the night wore along.

Desiderio had taken the first encounter with a workman-like calm. Much of the time he was with the tanks, pointing out targets and helping adjust fire so that the tankers could make the best use of their protective metal. For the rest of it, he was moving about among his own men, encouraging the junior leaders and checking on the output of his heavy weapons. He said little but the men felt his presence.

True to proverb, the darkest hour came just before dawn. The night had been overcast; the overcast thickened. A ground murk hung like a shroud around the fringes of the little valley. There was still no fire or sound from the other side. But under the full cloak of dark a line of Chinese grenadiers crept silently along the low ground and, still unperceived, crawled up the slope and to within 15 yards of the foxhole line. There they went to earth and lay quiet. On the top of their base hill, four more machine guns were readied, making six in all.

In an instant, the new setting exploded. From flank to flank, the machine guns blazed in unremitting fire. The barrage was dead on the target, pinning men to their foxholes. At the same instant, a shower of exploding potato mashers dropped inside the perimeter—the first signal that these skirmishers were right at hand. Some of the grenadiers were on top of the foxholes almost as their grenades burst. A few took bullets in the back of the head from their own machine-gun fire. Others were brained with rifle butts.

Beyond the grenadiers, other Chinese came on at a charge, some trying by the saddle again and others streaming across the little valley. They moved at a run, firing rifles and burp guns wildly toward the hill.

One team of bazooka men broke into the perimeter, got off one round and knocked a tread from a tank before a BAR man shot them down. Another bazooka team was caught by Cox's men while crossing the little valley; its three members were riddled by rifle fire.

A grenade landed on a tank turret and felled the gunner. M/S Elmo L. Fuller of Easy jumped onto the tank and resumed fire with the gun. Minutes later, an American fragmentation grenade hurled by a Chinese bounced off the tank and exploded in air. Pfc. Copeland was standing beside the tank, in the act of firing his carbine. The explosion blew his arm off and opened his side; he died within a few minutes. Lieut. John J. Finnegan was hit in the back and jaw by the same bomb. A fragment hit Fuller under the chin and lifted him from the tank; he fell to earth groggy and blinded, like a boxer nailed on the button.

Then a mortar round exploded next the tank on the extreme right, scoring heavily. Desiderio went down with a shard through his right shoulder. Capt. J. C. Bayliss, the company executive, Sergeant Yurick, in charge of communications, Sergeant Pelphrey and Corporal Swan were all wounded by the same round. The two captains continued in the fight; the NCOs were bleeding so hard they had to be evacuated to the base of the hill.

In the confusion coming of that one blow, the enemy found a new opening. Possibly a dozen Chinese crashed through where First and Third Platoons joined flanks and made straight for the tanks. A few were shot down as they ran. Seven flung themselves on the hulls and started scrambling upward. Cox and his men vacated their ground a moment, came on the run, and shot them from the tanks with rifle and BAR fire. They were so close that the Chinese fell at their feet.

It was a lucky break doubly. In that brief interlude, six rounds of artillery—the only ones fired by CCF in its engagement with Easy—exploded into the ground which Cox and his group had vacated for the minute. The gun was never located, but it sounded like 105-mm fire.

On the left flank, the situation was in hand. Bryers and his machine gun, with a half-dozen riflemen supporting him, had stopped cold the Chinese effort to advance via the saddle. In the center things were getting a little better, though the grenade fight had not slacked a trifle. Fifteen of the men around

Burch and Fuller were now bleeding from grenade shards. Still others had been carried out by the stretcher bearers.

Desiderio, reeling from his own wound, sensed the weariness of the others. At the top of his voice he began calling out over the hill what he had been saying to his men throughout the night: "Hold till daylight and you've got it made! Hold till daylight and you've got it made!" The others picked up the call. They could hear Second Platoon yelling it back from the far end of the line.

But Second's heavy ordeal was just in the making. At the extreme right, the hill tapered off into thick brush, now shrouded in heavy mist. There Sergeant Lefler had placed his machine gun and BAR. It was a blind spot and the enemy soon found it, gathering among the scrub pine in heavy numbers. They were on top of the gun almost before Lefler knew it, walking at a crouch and heaving potato mashers as they came. There was time only for a scattering rifle fire in answer. Then a grenade landed on the machine gun, knocking it over and killing a ROK soldier beside it. Corporal Savage tried to fire the BAR; it went out completely. The gun had already fired 2,000 rounds that night. Savage was shot and killed by a bullet. Sergeant Delotoba met death a few yards from him at the hands of a burp gunner. Ten other men were hit by grenades and bullets within a few seconds. Lefler sized it up that with his two guns gone, so was his ground for the moment. He yelled to the platoon: "Follow me to the back slope!"

Evans once again had run his mortars dry. The last of his 400 rounds gone in firing against the enemy base, he scrambled up to the tank position to see what further help could be given. His arrival coincided with the cracking of Lefler's position. He could see burp guns and rifles firing toward the tanks from within the perimeter line.

The wounded men crouching within the relative shelter of the armor could see and hear it also. They started to cry: "The line's cracked! The position's going! Get the hell out!"

The tankers heard and took alarm. Two of them got in motion and started to leave the hill.

Running from one to the other, Desiderio beat on their armor with a rifle butt, yelling: "Goddamn it, you've got to stay and fight! Goddamn it, we're not quitting!" Otomo joined him, alternately beating at the hulls and cursing. By sheer audacity and anger, the two men dancing around the hulls kept the armor tied to its task.

Then Desiderio turned back toward his own men. Otomo was still with him. He said to his lieutenant: "They're coming on us now. You take one side and I'll take the other, and we'll stop them."

Those were his last words. As he started toward his broken flank, fire from a burp gun ripped him up the side and through the heart. He pitched face forward and rolled on his side, raising his hand to his wound as he fell. Within a few seconds he was dead.

To all who watched at that moment it looked as if the cause was gone with its captain. His men had loved Desiderio like a brother; to them, he had seemed totally without fear. A few yards beyond him Otomo had been struck down by a grenade which had landed against his parka, tearing it to shreds and driving splinters into his back and arms. The two-man rally had died and the enemy still held the right flank of the perimeter.

But Lefler and his men were already on their way back. They had moved 40 yards down the back slope and had stopped there to reorganize. Lefler got grenades for all hands. In ten minutes they were ready to go again. He told them that they would march straight back to the same ground, grenading as they went. That was what they did. As the grenade wave came on, the enemy survivors broke and ran for the undergrowth.

At that moment the pressure ended. A few Chinese snipers remained in the little valley keeping up a desultory fire for the next half-hour. But the main force began its withdrawal when Second Platoon restored its lines. The fight had been won in the very moment when it looked lost.

Evans walked to where Desiderio had fallen and glanced down. Then it came to him that he could see the features clearly and he realized for the first time that the morning had come. That was the irony of it. He repeated to himself: "Hold till daylight and we've got it made."

Some of the statistics of this fight may be worth mention.

Of the sixty Easy Company men hit by Chinese fire that night, eight were killed in action.

All nine BARs within the company went out in the course of the action. One had been hit by a bullet. The others had jammed or otherwise become unworkable because of excessive fires. Even so, the men all swore that the weapon was the mainstay of their rifle action.

Task Force Dolvin had gone into position with five days' basic ammunition supply for all weapons. The total had been consumed in one night's action, except for the rounds meant for the 3.5 bazooka, the 57-recoilless and part of the M1 supply.

Desiderio was awarded the Congressional Medal posthumously.

Easy won a Distinguished Unit Citation.

There was never any opportunity to evaluate the killing power of the defensive weapons by counting the enemy dead. Dolvin, who had fought off Chinese grenadiers attacking his command post in the last strong surge which had almost swept Easy Company from its hill, called soon after daylight and told Lieut. Richard D. Boyd, the new commander, to march the company back the way it had come. The men collected their weapons and took the road out. That afternoon the task force fell back toward the division. The enemy still pursued. The long fight with the Chinese was only just beginning.

Amid the company, as it passed the command post, was the air fighter pilot whom Dolvin had ordered to Easy's hill in the crisis of the fight.

He said to Dolvin: "I got my Chinaman. I will return to being an air pilot. I have done my share of ground combat."

Even so, the pilot could have had a harder fate than sharing with Easy Company on that particular night. To Easy Company had come the power and the glory, and much of the pain, of the task force's first grapple with the Chinese. But in the same way that the Ranger Company had paid the full price for the first night, Baker Company of the 35th Regiment with an attached mortar section from Dog Company became the sacrifice to the task force's survival during the second night. It was swamped by a yellow tide which moved upon it from all sides. When morning dawned, only twenty-six men survived whole-bodied of a committed strength of 203 men. Baker's heroic remnant still held a portion of its ground, defending with weapons which had been physically wrested from the Chinese after its own arms had been shot away or fired until empty.

Nothing else as doubly perverse as the destruction of this company while orphaned from its regiment occurred during the entire battle. For the main body of the 35th had been launched on what was seemingly a more hazardous mission. Forming the division left flank, it advanced north hugging the Kuryong-gang straight toward Unsan, which Eighth Army had reckoned was the probable heart of the Chinese build-up area.

But nothing happened. The 35th met no Chinese. Quickly, the greater part of the regiment was standing on the ridges dominating Unsan from the south. One rifle platoon got to the bridge just short of the town. Col. Henry G. Fisher's men could look into the Unsan schoolyard and see a dozen or so trucks and jeeps which had been abandoned one month earlier by Eighth cavalrymen ambushed at this same point.

Fisher planned to have his Second Battalion circle Unsan to the east and then stand on a hill mass northwest of it. That done, he would put his other battalions through and continue the plunge north. "Not knowing what was happening to TF Dolvin at this time," he said, "I was confident I could get to the Yalu in a breeze or, if need be, stand at Unsan until hell froze over."

This perfect illusion and Fisher's plan along with it were shattered by a telephone call from General Wilson, the ADC, who told Fisher to stand fast where he was and get his guard up on his left flank—the first intimation to 35th Regiment that 1st ROK Division to their westward was in heavy trouble. They were still in the dark as to how Task Force Dolvin was faring on their right.

When next Fisher got orders to retire southward, he still didn't know that Dolvin had been hard hit. The 35th's main body was as yet whole and unhurt. But it hadn't set foot in Unsan, and as the withdrawal got started, its outpost was mocked by the sight of the abandoned American vehicles laagered next Unsan's schoolhouse.

Having marked time in a tactical vacuum during the crisis of the battle, the 35th got its baptism of Chinese fire as its road columns moved back toward Yonsang-dong. It was a bushwhacking effort. The enemy mass, which had been concealed along the divide of the Chongchon-Kuryong watershed, having broken the defensive crust, was by now deploying into the abounding valleys, seeking to put a death grip on the main roads. This flow struck Fisher from the east while other enemy groups drove at him from the west. The cross buck did not get him off balance. His team—the 35th and the 64th Field Artillery Battalion—faced about and squared away for a fight whenever the Chinese grew too bold. Its retirement was a series of blocking and turning actions. Fisher lost men. Probably he saved more than he lost by ordering vehicles abandoned when the tail end of his column became trapped while in march.

But the Chinese attack continued to be of such low order that Fisher felt certain he would shortly be told to resume the march on Unsan. For a little while longer, he was spared the sweat of knowing that the roof had fallen in.

It was different with the 24th Regiment on the division right flank. Along the fringes of their ridge-ribbed sector,

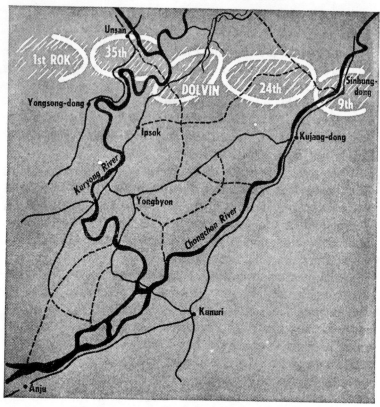

25TH DIVISION FRONT ON 25 NOVEMBER

The 35th Regiment's left flank extended somewhat farther to the westward; 27th Regiment was in a reserve position.

Colonel Corley's colored soldiers were getting the spillover of the Chinese attack into the main valleys against 9th Regiment on their right and Task Force Dolvin on their left.

They had been spared during the night of 25 November. The first enemy tide had not risen very high. It came full in the second effort.

On the night of 26 November, Corley's Second Battalion on the regimental right was hit from the northeast and west. Becoming cut off, two of the rifle companies, George and

Easy, took a road leading northeast through enemy country, gained the flank of 9th Infantry, and continued to fight with that regiment.

Among First Battalion, which was supposed to have its shoulder next Task Force Dolvin, fortunes were ironically mixed. Baker Company, which had gone on past Dolvin, should have been slaughtered. But the enemy charged past this small island of resistance, missing it wholly. When morning came, Baker's commander, Lieutenant Green, saw Chinese troops laying wire along the trails off his flanks. Checking the nearby villages, he found that Chinese troops had slept in the huts until dawn. Quite suddenly it came to him that his company had spent the night in the enemy rear area. Charley Company, holding a ridge some distance to the rear of Baker, had not been touched. Corley sent it forward to help extricate Baker. On the way up, Charley blundered into a position manned by Chinese and was surrendered in a body. Baker Company made to the rear under its own power.

But the quiet in the center of 24th Regiment's sector still continued. Lieut. Colonel Blair, commanding the Third Battalion, had sent his rifle companies cross-country, remaining farther to the rear with his headquarters elements, heavy weapons company, and platoon of tanks. Closer to the heart of the enemy mass than any other American unit, the rifle companies endured untouched because of the tactical vacuum. On the morning of 27 November, the rear force around Blair was hit by Chinese skirmishers deflected east by the multi-layered strength in the division center. Blair counterattacked with his tanks and weapons company and the enemy force was liquidated. After taking a long detour toward the southwest, he then rode his armor forward to the three rifle companies. The battalion was shifted east closer to the Kunuri road to fill the spot which Second Battalion had left empty. But the small tank action of that morning was its only fight.

While Blair was maneuvering, Colonel Corley had laid on an air drop to come in next his command post with ammunition, food, and water for the regiment. The drop was just a little off. Chinese came pouring from the ridges to grab the supply. Ultimately they were beaten back by fire, but they did not go empty-handed.

These several eruptions had given the situation on the division right an unhealthy look, and concern over it was deepened by the fact that it was through this flank that the columns farther west must perforce retire. So 27th Regiment, under Col. John H. Michaelis, was committed to the ground on a backstopping mission with Corley's First Battalion attached. That made Corley temporarily almost a pauper, since most of his Second Battalion had decamped to the 9th Infantry.

Michaelis is a soldier with an affinity for heavy trouble. But for once his luck ran out. The situation he took over never developed into a real fight.

## 12

## Murch's Battalion

D URING THE HOURS IN WHICH THE FORWARD ELEMENTS
of 25th Infantry Division pushed northward from Ipsok in
the large-scale reconnaissance undertaken by Task Force
Dolvin, Second Battalion of the 27th Infantry Regiment (except for Easy Company which was carrying the mail for
Dolvin) anticipated that it would remain unengaged.

The regiment was in divisional reserve and the battalion
was reserve for the regiment. To all hands, from the commander, Lieut. Col. Gordon E. Murch, on down, this had
the look of a free ride, and they were quite content with it.

Dolvin's force, with its left shoulder on the bank of the
Kuryong River, occupied the central sector in the divisional
front, the 35th Regiment being westward of the stream, while
the 24th Regiment, on the extreme right of the line, was trying to fill the gap between Dolvin and the 9th Regiment of
2nd Infantry Division. Such were the distances and the roughness of the country that the 24th Regiment became frayed
by this stretching effort without gaining firm contact on
either flank.

The most negotiable roads and trails followed via Ipsok
the main thread of the valley, which meant that most of the
division's heavy stuff trailed in the wake of Task Force
Dolvin. The artillery was grouped around that town. The
ammunition trains had moved into it by the afternoon of 25
November. It was just after dark that Murch, still on the
road rearward, got word that the battalion was to go that far
by truck convoy, march from Ipsok two miles northward to

an assembly area, and be ready to answer the bell if Task Force Dolvin met any fires it couldn't put out.

Division's ears had also heard the story about the column of Chinese "2,000 strong" moving upon the American front. This embellished version had it that the enemy brigade was moving on a line between the 24th and 9th Regiments. That was one reason why the backstop was put behind Dolvin. The whole division would be in trouble if the CCF column got into the 24th's rear.

Murch's outfit was numerically strong and averagely well armed. Most of the men had one or two grenades; the riflemen were carrying between 80 and 160 rounds apiece; the men with carbines were toting 90 rounds.

By approximately 2300, the battalion had closed on the assembly area and set up a fairly tight perimeter defense, embracing all companies, on one hill mass. During the hours in which it moved up and dug in, Task Force Dolvin—only 2,500 yards to the north—was having its first heavy encounter with the Chinese. But of the sounds of this encounter, Murch and his men heard almost nothing. Their night passed quietly, except for the nocturnal sweat and cursing which went into the digging of foxholes. One platoon of tanks from Charley of the 89th Tank Battalion had been attached to Murch. He put two of the vehicles on the east end of the perimeter where they had a good sector of fire toward the northeast; the other section outposted on the west, with a limited field of fire toward the river. Two infantry outposts of squad strength and drawn from Fox Company dug in on two low-lying hills 400 yards to the north of the battalion circle. With the build-up of enemy pressure against Task Force Dolvin after midnight, there came a request from that command post that at least one platoon from Murch's force be swung northwest to tie in with the task force perimeter. Since Fox Company was fronted along the north side of the hill mass, Murch gave one of its platoons the mission, then filled in the outpost line with his own headquarters people.

He was worried about his northwest corner, reckoning that the worst threat was that the Chinese would move on him from the river bottom—an open thoroughfare into his position. But nothing stirred.

They were still on this same ground the second night (26 November) when just prior to midnight the Chinese attack broke over the task force to their north with full weight, and Easy Company moved directly under the hammer. In the battalion position at first there was plenty of strain, but almost no action. How Company stood steady at its two roadblocks, one at the north and the other at the south end of the perimeter, where the roadway skirted the eastern edges of the hill mass. George Company was on the western facing, extended north and south. Fox guarded northward, whence came the sounds of the fighting.

By 0100, the mêlée around Leader (TF Dolvin) command post already threatened to strangle its command. Brig. Gen. Vennard Wilson, ADC, was under sniper fire from Chinese who had pushed to within 20 yards of his post and were threatening Easy Company's supply point. Wilson's operations officer, Maj. Leon F. Morand, Jr., was killed by a bullet. Wilson got Murch on radio and asked him to send another Fox platoon to restore the command post area. Even as it started forward, Murch's own lines were already under small-arms fire, with the Fox position drawing most of it. The platoon got there in time, and according to General Wilson, its prompt mop-up was a major contribution to the steadying of the task force's position.

Murch's own immediate problem was to get himself better set for in-fighting. The battalion was still in assembly when hit, a grouping of rifle companies properly foxholed, but enclosing along the low ground at their rear their medical section, the trains, and other vulnerable installations; they had not expected to engage so far back. About one hour after receiving the call from Wilson, Murch decided to send these components 2,000 yards to the south, for safety's sake. They took off but they didn't go far. Though the battalion was totally unaware of it, the Chinese had already made a long left hook around the hill position and were partly dug in on both sides of the road, 600 yards southward of the battalion. How this ambush was weaponed, or what strength force manned it, is beyond saying. The medical section, in the van of the column, got full-length into the gauntlet and then drew fire from both sides. The section was destroyed; the vehicles which followed it were all knocked out. Four American wounded, captured by the Chinese as they closed on the road, managed to break away and get back to the battalion before dawn. They told Murch that the medical officer, who had joined the battalion only that morning, had pleaded with his captors for a chance to treat his own wounded, but they had cuffed him for so doing and then hauled him away. This enemy block remained tight on Murch's rear until well after first light; in the circumstances, there was nothing Murch could do about it. His situation is best understood in the light of what was happening to the two companies—George and Fox—in his rifle line.

The character of both of these units is well attested by certain incidents which attended the establishing of the perimeter, hours prior to the start of battle. Fox Company numbered 177 men under Capt. Robert B. Gough, twenty-seven of whom were ROK soldiers. Gough had inspected all of his foxholes in early morning and found that all of the men were dug in; but, judging that the diggings were still too shallow, he had put the men to work again until by mid-afternoon he was at last content that the position was as it should be. Meanwhile, the company had sent two small patrols out to prowl the country eastward and westward to about 1,000 yards beyond the foxhole line. In midday, Second Platoon, re-enforced with a 60-mm mortar squad, was sent northward to patrol the river bend around the village of Sangchon-dong—approximately six miles via the road—during which journey the patrol kept constant contact via the SCR 300. The results of all three excursions were negative. On its return journey, Second Platoon tied in as the link between Task Force Dolvin and Murch. That adjustment was completed by dark, when SFC Edwin F. Mahoney moved the mortars into a draw just southward of Dolvin's hill. Gough and all of his men had concluded that the events of the preceding night were fully ominous, that the real show was about to start and would engage them on present ground. One thing worried them: their hill was thickly wooded; the enemy could move unseen to within 100 yards or less of their rifle pits. But nothing could be done about that. Third Platoon held the right flank and First Platoon, the left. The stretching out of Second Platoon to give Task Force Dolvin a line to the rear had quashed Gough's intention to use it as a support force even as it had stripped Murch of his final reserve within the battalion position.

In the bowl-shaped extension of the ridge where George Company had set up, it was practically back-to-back and bottom-to-bottom with Gough's two remaining rifle platoons. The bowl was open on one end in the manner of a horseshoe, that side facing toward the main road. Capt. Jack Michaely and his men (the strength was 116, including fourteen ROKs), on first taking over the ground, had done a little imaginative scouting and convinced themselves that they were not far from a considerable enemy force. The crest was already pocked with rifle pits when they gained it—and in the spoil around the pits were blurred footprints. The holes were deep, but not as wide as a GI digs them. Lieut. John F. Land concluded from these signs that the hill had but recently been held by Chinese. The ridge top was only about 60 to 70 feet above the valley floor, and the gradual facings of the ridge were well covered with densely grown screw pine and scrub oak. Several of the men prowled this forest on the lower slope and found numerous piles of horse dung—enough to suggest that upwards of twenty pack animals had been picketed there. The dung was still fairly fresh—about two days, they figured. In front of First Platoon's position, SFC Marvin P. Martin investigated a small frame house, carefully camouflaged and well bunkered in: it looked like a command post. SFC John W. Kennedy drew his attention to a dozen split gourds scattered about the main room. Bits of cooked rice—perhaps fifteen or twenty grains in all—clung to the sides. Kennedy pressed them with his fingertips; they were still soft to the touch. Adding all these things together, Michaely speculated that an enemy force, of approximately battalion strength, had held the same ground not more than forty-eight hours before.

George Company spent its day cutting the Chinese foxholes broader and deeper. Its line, extended around the horseshoe-shaped hill, was about 1,500 yards long from end to end. But there were compensating factors. Two tanks and two HMGs from How Company had been positioned on the flat ground, covering the open side of the bowl and pointing toward the road. Michaely's three 60-mm mortars were right down in the bowl, whence they could fire in any direction. Of his four LMGs, two were on the high ground with First Platoon, where they could fire northward toward an enemy coming through or around Fox. The other two were spaced along the ridge so as to fire toward the river, though because of the scrub forest, their fields were limited. Each platoon enclosed one 57-recoilless within its area. In this way, a circle of weapons was formed up around the battalion command post.

The fight started as a rumble from northward, and the only word which at first came back was that Task Force Dolvin was being hit by "many" Chinese. That was all that Michaely could learn of the situation when he went to Murch to get the score. But Murch added that he would be sending more of Fox forward to help the task force, and he would want Michaely to swing Third Platoon around to the opposite flank, prepared to take up the ground which Fox was holding.

Already Fox was under small-arms fire, but the fight was developing in such an eccentric manner that the men could scarcely believe what they heard and saw. Only a few bullets had struck among the rocks, and the men along the crest were still withholding fire for lack of targets. Then there arose from the valley below a furious jabbering and yelling, the notes of which were indistinguishable. To Sergeant Mahoney's ears, it sounded as if this chorus was arising from almost the spot where he had placed Cpl. Lonzo Mosier and an LMG some hours before—in what approximated an outpost position in relation to the company's right. Mahoney went running down to the gun. Mosier was still safe. Off in the distance, Mahoney could hear the rising clamor of battle from the direction of Dolvin's hill; the volume was building up, up, up. Right at hand, in the trees just beyond Mosier, he heard a wailing chorus of voices, men chanting over and over: "GI, how many people you got up there? GI, how many people you got up there?" Mahoney said to Mosier: "Hold fire." Then he listened again for a moment, and this time he heard the same chant coming from his flank and rear. He told Mosier to take the gun and run back up the hill. So far, not a shot had been fired by the company; the men hadn't seen a thing.

In front of Third Platoon, they heard the enemy force yell: "Yea beau, yea beau, yea beau," quite lustily, followed by a prolonged tooting from shepherd's pipes. From among the trees came a scattering fire—rifles and tommy guns, all of it going high. One of Fox's LMGs joined the clatter, and a few of the riflemen also cut loose. The men could see their own tracer fire winking out among the trees on the downslope, but other than that, the whole situation was phantasmagoric; the enemy was like a disembodied spirit, and their own fire was just so much punching into wind.

At the tip of First Platoon's position, however, the Chinese had made a quick pounce and almost bagged a fire team. Three men broke from their clutches and got away toward George Company's position. The Chinese bagged the fourth man, Cpl. George Barber, rushed him to the base of the hill, and put him to work carrying machine-gun ammunition.

On the ground where Barber had been, the grass blazed suddenly, and the flames, fanned by a strong wind, raced toward the hillcrest. The fire—hand-set by the Chinese—spread to the stunted trees and leaped upward at a terrific rate. As the glare increased, and the smoke with it, Gough's infantry-men could see a few of the enemy in fleeting outline as they darted among the trees. They snap-fired at these targets and saw one or two fall, but there was no time for a concentrated fire. The conflagration had already reached the foxhole line, and Mahoney was leading his men in an attempt to stem it. Working on their knees to keep from being silhouetted against the skyline, they beat at it with blankets, bedrolls, and their bare hands.

Just at the line of foxholes there was a broad footpath which served as a partial firebreak. That helped momentarily, but even so, the greater part of First Platoon had to displace rearward to avoid incineration, while a few hands around Mahoney and Pfc. Dean K. Gibb fought to damper the blaze in the center, so that at least one BAR could hold its ground. But as the group in this small salient got the ground fire under control, the dying flames spotlighted them neatly for the benefit of the enemy weapons. Initially, there was noth-ing against them but rifle and tommy gun fire, and at 75 yards' distance, it was wild as a hare. Then the Chinese bore on the hillcrest with two heavy machine guns, firing Amer-ican ammunition, as Gough and his men could judge by the sound and the look of the tracers. Gough called Murch and said: "I can whip Chinamen all night long, but this damned grass fire is about to chase me from the hill." Still, the enemy did not thrust home. His forces could be heard jabbering and yelling as they flowed on around the company flanks; they made no effort to storm the face of the hill, de-spite the dissolution resulting from the grass fire.

Gough made a quick decision, abandoned his line, and regrouped his platoons in a tight circle covering the high ground on his left flank. Almost coincidentally the Chinese hit, but in such bizarre fashion as to make it appear an act of mass madness. A column of about seventy marched right up the hill in even fours just off Fox's left end, where the latter's ground joined George Company. They overran one

57-recoilless rifle, killed the crew, picked the gun up, and then tossed it away. In the next minute or so, still marching in fours, they physically overran Gough's command post, but paid it no heed. Gough watched them almost transfixed from a distance of less than 15 yards, scarcely believing what his eyes told him. They were armed, but were not holding their weapons ready; they stared and strained straight forward, never once breaking stride. It made him think of a "steamroller on the loose." As they passed, they were in arm's length also of two jeeps and a pile of equipment. But they didn't give it a passing look.

In the middle of this march-past, Gough's telephone rang. It scared hell out of him. He tried to muffle it, but couldn't. So he answered. Lieut. James F. Gallagher was on the other end, saying: "Captain, they're all around me." Gough replied: "I know it; seventy of them are going by my door," and put down the phone. Gough was carrying a carbine; something told him this wasn't the time to use it.

The mortar section behind the command post saw the column approach just in time. The men picked up the tubes and ran for a draw alongside the road about 400 yards to the southeast. The enemy must have seen this movement, but no attempt was made to fire or to follow.

This robot column, instead of turning against George Company on Fox's rear, marched straight for a hill to the east, temporarily removing itself from the fight. Other smaller groups, moving in their wake, peeled off to the south and took up positions along the nose of the hill. That split Gough and his command post group from Gallagher, who amidst these trials had succeeded in making a tight circle of the two platoons. For the time being, Fox was surrounded, with no place to go. The key to the riddle of the eccentric action by the column which bucked through tackle and kept going lies probably in the subsequent ambushing of Murch's trains and medical section. The body had been given a set mission and was going for it, do or die.

Gallagher's force was still under a steady automatic fire, more harassing than accurate. (The losses on the hill that night were only seven killed and eleven wounded in action.) What bothered them most, however, was that they could hear the Chinese downslope yelling shrilly, as if cursing an individual. Then they heard an American voice cursing back at the Chinese, and somebody said: "That's Corporal Barber." Gallagher's riflemen centered fire in the direction of the voices, taking a chance on killing Barber. By rare luck, they knocked down several of the Chinese, and in that moment, Barber broke away. Seconds later, after three hours of captivity, he was being challenged by a Fox outpost. Mahoney talked to him. He was so confused that at first he could not believe this was his company and the same hill position. His captors had moved him around a great deal, and he was under the impression that he was miles from the scene. Close on Barber's heels, the same outpost challenged another man; it was a Chinese, surrendering on a safe-conduct pass. Nobody at the time thought it particularly comic that an enemy soldier would surrender to a force which was itself surrounded.

Gough called Murch and asked that two tanks be sent along the road to the east of the hill where they could mop up the groups on his own rear and relieve the pressure inside the battalion position. Murch came along with the tanks. The commanders together were reconnoitering the ground to see where the armor could best serve when down the road from the north they saw coming toward them a column of men. Gough at first thought they were Chinese, but he told the tanks to hold fire, wishing to be sure. They proved to be the party of Korean bearers which had served Task Force Dolvin. So Gough passed them on southward, not knowing that How Company had set up a machine-gun roadblock farther down the road. The Korean friends headed right into it. The men on the block mistook them for a Chinese party, and they were killed to the last man. It was then within a few minutes of dawn and the enemy pressure was rapidly diminishing.

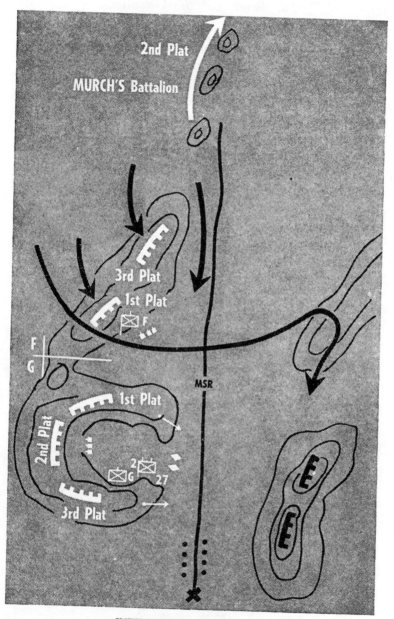

**INFILTRATION MANEUVER**

CCF movements on night of 26-27 November against Second Battalion, 27th Infantry Regiment.

That was the condition also at Dolvin's command post, where Second Platoon of Fox had fought an engagement almost unrelated to the affair on the company hill. To review briefly why this was so: Second Platoon had gone out on a long patrol the prior afternoon; on returning, it had filled in on Gough's right, stretching far enough to connect with Dolvin's back door; then when the command post came under sniper fire in the crisis of the fight, the platoon had cut loose from the company and gone forward to help Dolvin.

Before the movement was well underway, bullets whined and thickened overhead. Most of this fire was "overs" from the stuff being thrown at Easy Company and did no hurt. But the platoon was tired from its mission of the afternoon and the fire was an excuse to hit the ditches and gulleys, where the men remained for about thirty minutes. During a respite in the attack, they collected and went forward again. At the command post, Lieut. Melvin Anderson, the leader, was told to move the platoon into a dry creek bed a few rods distant, which seemed to be the source of the sniper attack. Anderson was in the act of complying when, taking second thought of his situation, he decided to go on alone and get an idea of the ground.

A few minutes later, he halloed from out of the darkness and told SFC Ray W. Henderson to get his squad in on the left of what was to be the platoon's general position. Having given the order, Anderson walked on beyond the creek bed and was not there when Henderson brought his men up. Henderson saw a shallow gulley running off to the left from the creek bed and guessed this was where he was supposed to deploy. He got three riflemen set and was just ready to station the BAR gunner, Pfc. Walter Hrycyna. Before he could move, a squad of about six Chinese reared up from the rocks just ahead of him and opened fire with rifles and a tommy gun. One of Henderson's ROKs was killed. The man next him yelled: "Medic, medic!"

Then Henderson saw Anderson—he was standing clear in the moonlight, on beyond the Chinese who had fired, and looking in the opposite direction. Henderson yelled: "They've stopped us!" but Anderson didn't seem to hear. Then Henderson called to Hrycyna to open fire. He shouted back: "They shot up the BAR!" At that moment a bullet got Henderson through the shoulder. He yelled to Hrycyna to stay flat and he would try to get the Chinese with his M1. But he got off only one round, and missed. Suddenly Anderson, appearing out of nowhere, tried to walk around Henderson, bound straight for the enemy pocket. He was like a man moving in a trance, and Henderson had no chance to yell. The Chinese tommy gunner got Anderson right between the eyes. That stopped the squad action absolutely. Henderson pulled back into the creek bed and went looking for a first-aid station. It wasn't until morning that he learned that the first volley which had killed the ROK had also killed M/S William Stephens, though Stephens had not been more than five yards from him.

The loss of the BAR at that point came near to folding the whole platoon position. When Henderson's survivors crawled back toward the center, their withdrawal left naked the ground around the platoon machine gun. The gun had been busy; Sgt. Allan D. Snider had been trying to eliminate the enemy pocket, but whereas the snipers could rise up from the rocks and pop away at the gun, their own cover seemed invulnerable to its fire. Now other small enemy groups were working forward toward the gun around both sides of the gulley. This movement went unseen; grenades exploding into the American line were the first warning that it had occurred. Pfc. Burke was wounded. Pfc. Esser was killed. Then the machine gun went out of action. The survivors nearest the crippled gun backed away, dragging it with them.

SFC Edward E. Mash talked it over with Snider. They agreed that someone had to get back into the gulley with a BAR and wipe out the pocket, or the platoon would be finished. So Snider volunteered for the job and led Third Squad's BAR team into the gulley. The platoon had already won the skirmish without knowing it. Bullets—probably from the M1 firers in the platoon line—had killed the tommy gunner and several other Chinese. To Snider's surprise, the gulley was quiet, and the BAR team took over without receiving an answering shot. Mash joined them there within a few minutes. Perhaps one hour later, the platoon was told to leave the creek bed and move back to Dolvin's command post. As Snider's group left the gulley, a machine-gun bullet got Mash through the legs. The column moved along with Mash crawling behind it to the aid station.

With fire breaking over all other portions of the front, George Company had survived the night with little stress. In the midst of Fox's distress, Michaely had broken his own perimeter to move Third Platoon from the far left of the bowl position northward into ground where it could fire upon the Chinese which had swung around Fox's lower flank, but nothing untoward came of the gap in his own line. First Platoon braced itself at one point for an attack. It could hear Chinese milling around and chattering to one another in the thicket a few yards downslope from the foxholes. Sergeant Martin judged from the noise that about one platoon of enemy was opposite him. But he walked up and down his line, telling his men: "Hold fire! Hold fire!" which they did— perfectly. There was one small incident at Third Platoon— chicken feed, but interesting. Two Chinese came along a trail which led directly into the platoon's ground. Lieut. John F. Land thought it might be a point for a larger group and told his machine gunners not to fire. Both men were armed with grenades. Cpl. Julian Castorina, one of the gunners, let them get right up to the earthbank of his position. Then he shot them both with his .45 pistol. The seeming threat was dissolved by two bullets. As the night wore along, Michaely, sensing that the country round about was swarming with Chinese, attributed his own immunity to the good discipline of the company. There had been no loose fire; the enemy didn't know the company was there.

Having moved three of How Company's HMGs to the lower shank of George's ridge to cover the space vacated by

Land's Platoon, Murch at 0400 called Land to his command post and told him that if the Chinese threatened to overrun the guns, he should get his men back to that ground immediately. Daylight was only two hours off, and from the events of the night, Murch was apprehensive that the enemy was building up for a main attack against his rear. Land went back to the old position, along with Captain Eddington, How's commander. From the high ground, they could hear the Chinese talking and yelling as they dug in along the ridgeline southeast of the battalion position. They passed the word to Murch and he joined them to observe the height opposite. At first, they could judge only by sound; then as the first streak of dawn appeared, they could see large numbers of the enemy digging rifle pits along the top of the ridge. So sited, they were looking right into the opening of George's bowl-shaped position, and their weapons dominated the one road by which Task Force Dolvin could fall back upon the division.

The threat materialized rapidly. Mortar, machine-gun, and rifle fire came down on Michaely's ridge immediately and thickened as the light grew. Along the foxhole line, three men were hit by mortar fragments and two by bullets in the first few minutes. Major Haguey, the battalion executive, was hit in the chest by a bullet and paralyzed from the waist down. Lieutenant Thompson was struck down by a sniper's bullet. (There seemed to be one good Chinese sniper posted just across from the open end of the bowl; he fired at anyone who moved in the open, and was never located.) Captain Hone of Headquarters Company was killed by a ricochet off the tanks. At this stage, the armor was pulled tight together across the entrance to the bowl to serve as a shield behind which medics could aid the battalion wounded.

The two command posts perforce displaced to the opposite side of the bowl to remove themselves from line of sight. All hands returned fire, as did the tanks, using chiefly their machine guns. Also, a 75-recoilless, posted with the HMGs on the lower end of the bowl, kept banging away. But there was a dearth of pin-point targets, and though the exchange lasted for five hours, there was no way to judge the effect on the enemy.

Shortly before noon, a tank was sent south along the road to feel out the situation. It got about 1,000 yards. Then the Chinese got in close, exploded a bazooka round into the tank's ammunition, and blew it up.

That blow underscored the complexities of Murch's problem. Much earlier the decision had been taken to withdraw Task Force Dolvin, and its elements were already preparing to hit the road back. But unless Murch cleared the road and the covering ridges to the southeast before Dolvin came along, there might be a pile-up which would trap the force into another night of disadvantageous action. Of the two rifle companies available, George was still relatively fresh and unhurt; it was also closer to the scene. On the other hand, it was already operating as a defensive and covering base, and in the situation, it could not regroup its men in the open without taking hard punishment. Fox's two platoons were more distant from the scene, and their men were more used up, but Fox was no longer under fire, and it possessed initial freedom of maneuver.

Murch had long since added these things up, reached definite conclusions, and taken positive action. He estimated that one CCF regiment had gone around his flank and closed generally upon his rear. At Ipsok, the artillery and trains had been hit by a mobile infantry column at about 0300, and some of the batteries had been forced to displace. Other enemy groups were set up as roadblocks within 30 to 50 yards of the MSR southward of him. The force which had emplaced along the ridgeline east of the road was in the 24th Regiment's sector. But the 24th had not appeared, and Murch knew not only that he had taken on the mission by default, but that a sound execution of it was the key move in clearing the road all the way. He called for supporting fires from the 8th Field Artillery Battalion, and two batteries went to work against the enemy's main ridge. Combined with the tank fires delivered by Lieutenant Benson's men, that considerably reduced the outward showing of Chinese activity on the ridge top.

At about 0900, the whole problem was suddenly put in Murch's lap. By telephone, General Wilson told him he was recommending to General Kean that the task force be dissolved and that all elements be put for the time being under Murch's command; the task force simply no longer possessed fighting power. This grim state of things is noted in a few moderate words in Dolvin's after-action report: "With the road already cut to the rear the TF Commander felt he did not have sufficient forces to clear the enemy roadblock, eliminate a possible second roadblock, and engage the enemy to the front." The one sensible tactical alternative was to get out, with the help of God and a few friends. General Kean approved this course by radio.

Wilson then asked: "Can you extricate the force?"

Murch said: "Yes, sir."

That left it to him to pick up the pieces.

Shortly thereafter, he called Gough and told him to get ready to fight again. For the mission in hand, Fox Company would be re-enforced by one platoon of George, one tank section, two 75-recoilless rifles, one section of HMGs from How, and the battalion 81-mm and 4.2 mortars. It would attack south and southeast from the perimeter and eliminate the Chinese east of the MSR—mainly on Hill 216.

With First and Third Platoons moving abreast, Fox Company jumped off at about 1130, one tank moving apace with the infantry left flank and the other following at a distance of about 50 yards so as to get fire higher up the hill. Almost immediately, the tank on the left was hit by a rocket which killed the driver; it went out of action. Lieutenant Gallagher was hit by a bullet while leading Third Platoon; Mahoney took over. Lieut. Clyde Force, leading First Platoon, was knocked out by a mortar round; M/S Samuel A. Cosman took over.

These losses had come from a fusillade which swept the line just as it crossed the road. Twenty yards beyond it, by good luck, was a ledge of rimrock just high enough to give cover to a crouching man. Mahoney yelled to the men: "Make for the ledge and then hold steady!" That was what they did, and Mahoney kept them there for about ten minutes while he moved along the line, making a few shifts here and there and telling the others what they would do in the next stage. When they again bounded forward, it was behind a steady curtain of their own marching fire, which continued throughout the ascent. Fifty yards above the ledge, they ran a Chinese crew off a .50 machine gun, still in good firing condition. Gough, who had at last overtaken his line, after spending the first minutes helping to coordinate the supporting fires, sent a runner back with word to "send forward all the .50 ammunition that can be lugged." Five cases were rushed forward and the gun was turned against the Chinese on the crest. The line then moved upward again, firing as it marched. Said Gough: "There was only one word for it—beautiful." Cpl. Mosier was firing the captured gun.

Numbers of the Chinese along the ridge top were peeling off to the north, where they collected in a deep ravine midway to the next knob. Gough dispatched a tank along the road to enfilade this pocket. Mosier and several other men had run over to that part of the ridge from which they could aim directly into the declivity. Mosier yelled: "Come on over! It's like a shooting gallery," and Gough answered back: "I'm too busy showing the mortars where to fire." One Chinese in the ravine saw the tank draw abreast of it and started running for the tank, carrying a satchel charge, which was fitted with a short fuse, already fizzing. Mosier shot him down just as he got to the tank. The charge exploded in that split second and the man disappeared as if by magic; not a shred of him was to be found.

Second Platoon of George Company, which was helping Fox, had been slightly delayed by a similar occurrence. As it started across the road, an American jeep, two men aboard, came barreling along. Directly in front of the platoon, the jeep and its occupants exploded—probably from detonating an enemy mine. Blood and brains and flesh spattered over George's twenty-eight men; the motor, blown right out of the jeep, struck one of the platoon's ROKs and broke his leg. But the others gathered themselves and quickly joined Mosier at his killing perch above the ravine, helping to dispatch the last dozen or so of the enemy as they tried to climb out of the trap. The George Platoon then turned its weapons against the hilltop as Fox's line continued its climb. They had the crest in a few minutes, but no sooner was it won than the Chinese came down on it with a steady and amazingly accurate mortar fire. Fox had lost only six men during the uphill charge; it lost twelve others to mortar fire before it had time to take over the diggings on the skyline. Gough guessed these enemy tubes were positioned on the backslope of the next ridge to the east. He called his own 81s to the crest and worked over the top and far slope of that ridge for about one quarter hour. The barrage quieted things temporarily.

What remained of Task Force Dolvin had loaded up and started its move south about the time that Fox Company jumped off. The head of the column came even with Murch's position while Gough was subduing the Chinese mortar battery. But it was tough going all the way; enemy snipers had taken position within the brush and behind rock outcroppings on both sides of the road. That losses during the outward march were not prohibitive was due mainly to the bad quality of Chinese marksmanship. Murch loaded his casualties on the remaining tanks and cleared them just ahead of Dolvin's command elements.

Gough and his men stayed on Hill 216 until Dolvin's remnants had passed through and the battalion's main body was on the road and rolling. The extrication of this rearguard was greatly assisted by the air, which hit the next ridge with napalm, rockets, and .50 fire as Fox Company prepared to depart from its ground. The planes returned to give Hill 216 a going over with napalm about ten minutes after the company had hit the road.

Fox Company went southward at a trot to keep pace with the tanks which were carrying some of its wounded. The Chinese were given no chance to close in behind, and the rearguard got into Ipsok without further difficulty.

The mission, however, did not end at that point. On passing through, General Wilson had told Murch that he would collect the fighting elements of his command as quickly as possible, take up a new position on the high ground south of Ipsok, and prepare to fight a delaying action.

Gough heard of the order and reflected that the average strength of his platoons was already reduced to seventeen men. Even so, Murch realized that in taking over what was left of Task Force Dolvin, he had scarcely fleshed out his own command or increased its moral power. The increment might have seemed impressive had the units been listed on an order, but the real story was to be told only in numbers of men available for duty. Baker of the 35th—now eighteen men; the Ranger Company—now twenty-two men; and Baker of 89th Tank Battalion, with more than half of its metal gone. If Ipsok was to be held for long enough to permit the 35th Regiment to pull back across the Kuryong River and tie in with the division, it would be done by the fight remaining in Murch's already hard-hit battalion.

Division's trains were already en route back to their original position southward of Yongbyon.

By 1800, the first arriving troops from Murch's column had begun to entrench in the hills next Ipsok. by two hours later, the tail end of the column—Fox Company—closed to within the new position. Murch got the word and went out personally to make a size-up of his own lines. It was right then that the Chinese hit again—they had trailed behind the withdrawing column like tired hounds after a worn fox.

The enemy came on with his full bag of tricks—not yet old and familiar to the American side. There was strident blowing of bugles, shepherd's horns, and bronze whistles—the noise-making feature of a preliminary tactical reconnaissance purposed to draw fire. Long before there was any intense fire,

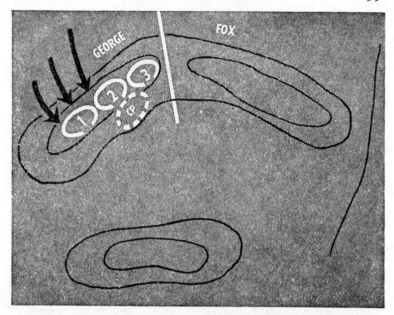

GEORGE COMPANY, 27-28 NOVEMBER

The outline around the command post shows the secondary perimeter.

many red and purple flares from enemy lines partly illuminated the night. Murch's men fired back at what they saw and heard, not yet having fathomed that this was playing the Chinese game the way the Chinese liked it.

The battalion was set up as two companies in line, Fox on the right of the ridge and George on the left. (The location of the various platoons is as shown on the diagrams.) The ridge bumped the river and ran at approximately right angles to it, though it was bent boomerang fashion, with the bend pointing northward. The bend was the boundary between companies. As to the top contour, the ridge was quite even for the greater part of its length, but the horizontal outline was most irregular, with multiple fingers extending outward from the main mass along both front and rear slopes. By average standards, it was a critically weak position for defense. The fingers made it approachable from such a number of points that the automatic weapons could not hope to canalize the enemy attack. Too, the ridge was covered with thick pine scrub which denied any real advantage to the high ground. Over all, the battalion front was about 4,000 yards long—an excessive line for two fresh, full-strength companies; an impossible one for Fox and George in their reduced state. The men were battered and weary, having had no sleep the night before and no food during the day; the Chinese road-block had kept them on a fresh air diet. The ground was hard for digging, rocky and filled with roots. The diggers quit work before completing their positions. They solaced themselves with the thought that the noise of their labor would give away their positions. Truth was that they were too tired for a further try.

Michaely felt that he was putting George in a wringer by letting it be committed to this ground. He had found a smaller ridge to the rear which was not tree-covered and had fairly regular slopes. He asked the operations officer to let him fight there. But Fox was already camped on the right flank of the boomerang, and the command was fearful that if it switched arrangements, it might be hit right in the middle of a move.

At exactly 2330, after three hours of clacking and fluttering around, the Chinese cracked down on Michaely's perimeter. At the left, there was an irregular knob enclosed within First Platoon's position. It had to be covered to deprive the enemy of a perch made to order for an enfilade, but for defensive use, it was valueless because of the thick foliage forward. Sergeant Martin had an LMG on the knob, with one rifle squad to the left on it, and one on the right. A second LMG was sited just beyond the left-hand squad.

That was where the first action came. There was almost no warning except a sharp crackling of brushwood just outside the rifle line, and that only for a few seconds. The Chinese skirmishers must have wiggled on their bellies up the ridge fingers leading into Martin's ground. The defenders saw nothing, and had no reason for firing a shot, until the Chinese opened on them with grenades from a distance of not more than 10 to 15 yards. There was perhaps a score of them, all grenade-loaded. After the first heave, in which they achieved surprise, they made no effort to conceal themselves but advanced boldly on Martin's men, standing up and grenading as they marched. A few riflemen opened fire. So did the machine gun on the far left. The LMG on the knob froze immediately; there was an excess of oil on it, and the cold had hardened it. Four grenadiers were shot down, and the others wavered. Machine-gun tracers set the grass afire 20 yards down the hill. That put the Chinese in silhouette. For a moment Martin thought he was getting the better of it. Then the Chinese switched over to rifles, and behind the first line of skirmishers, stalled in the firelight, the defenders could see other ranks coming on—too many to be counted. Sgt. Henry J. Shaker yelled out: "They're banzaiing us! They're banzaiing us!" and his voice could be heard far over in Third Platoon's position.

Cpl. Arnold G. Zapf and Pfc. Robert Pierce, on the left-hand machine gun, were both hit, Zapf through the left shoulder, Pierce in the stomach. A third bullet smashed the gun. Shaker called to the others: "Let's get off the hill!" The others in the platoon followed him down the backslope. Two of the ROKs, who were serving as ammunition bearers, were killed before they could clear the position.

When First Platoon broke, the left flank of Second Platoon went also; it had been hit in the same shock way. Michaely stopped most of these men as they went past his command post on the backslope; he looked them over and concluded that they were too badly shaken to be sent back in for the time being. These were his alternative actions:

A. With the aid of 1st Sgt. Edward Razer, he reorganized the position, building up a perimeter around the command post with Second Platoon on the right and First on the left.

B. He called for artillery help from the 8th Battalion and put plenty of stuff on the ridge top where First Platoon had been; also, his 60-mm mortars plastered the same target area.

The Chinese had followed Michaely's men down the slope. Grenadiers crawled forward to feel out the new position; behind them, the riflemen and tommy gunners gradually built up another fire crescent, this time on higher ground. It was a cast that could hardly miss; as the hot steel took steady toll, Michaely began to think that he would witness the total destruction of his company. His wires to Battalion had gone out, and he could not raise Murch on his SCR 300. He could hear his wounded men calling: "Medic, medic!" and each time he heard the cry, a Chinese out beyond his lines echoed it mockingly. Though a small thing, he could feel it grating on his own nerves, and he figured it must be getting to his men. At least half of the men in the shrunken perimeter were already out of the fight, either from wounds or from having their weapons hit.

A half portion of help suddenly appeared out of nowhere—about a dozen American fighters under a sergeant. He said to Michaely: "We're a platoon from Fox; we got cut off during the attack; we're trying to get back." Michaely answered: "You'll stay here and fight with us; move in on my right!" They jumped to it.

The fall-back by the left wing had not yet wholly split the company though Lieutenant Land's Third Platoon still held its ground atop the ridge. That was because the command post was downslope to the rear of Land's position, which meant that the jury-rigged perimeter was more or less in extension of Land's holding, though he was on an east-west line on the high ground and Michaely's force was faced at approximate right angles to Third Platoon, and covering a fold in the ridge.

At first, Land was in considerable doubt whether his men were to follow when the left flank broke and went down the hill. His position was built up around an LMG sited on a conspicuous knob in the center. The three rifle squads were distributed evenly on the two sides of the gun. Neither the gun nor the rifle pits drew concentrated fire at the time when the company split. From among the trees downslope, a few

Chinese rifles and tommy guns kept popping away at the sky-line. But most of this fire was going high. Land recognized that his flank was now open. Michaely sent him word that if he could do so, he should disengage and fall back. But the message, as Land received it, was not clear, and he therefore decided to hold his ground.

One other development had already given him pause. He heard an American voice crying for help from over to the left. He traced about 40 yards and found Lieut. John Merrill, leader of the Second Platoon, who had been badly wounded while helping his men clear from the hill.

Not far from Merrill, Land ran into Sergeant Razer, once again making a Trojan effort and serving as a one-man rescue team giving first-aid to three other Americans who were down. Land doubled back to his position and sent a party forth to help Razer and bring in Merrill. At Michaely's position down-slope, probing had revealed that the woods between Michaely and Land were free of Chinese interference, and so carrying parties were clearing Michaely's wounded upward to the Third Platoon position. They came in considerable numbers, and soon there were more than twenty wounded men within Land's lines, seriously encumbering his fighting power.

In other respects, events were taking a more favorable turn for Michaely and the "main body." At last, the radio operator got through to the Battalion, and Michaely reported the seeming hopelessness of his situation. Murch was given the information that George Company was "fully engaged and its left flank wholly surrounded." Major Dudley, the battalion executive, asked Michaely: "Do you think you could block them if you moved to the ridge where you wanted to dig in this evening?" Michaely said yes, and was authorized to proceed.

Third Platoon was apprised of the pending movement, told to stand steady on the high ground and fight as a rearguard while the others started southward, then come out carrying the wounded. Michaely had noted a trail running down a finger of the ridge which the Chinese had not yet blocked—

a convenient exit from his position. He led his men that way, figuring he might make it unobserved. Hardly had they started when, looking leftward, the men saw a body of about thirty Chinese marching down a parallel finger not more than 150 yards away. They froze in place and maintained silence. The Chinese column continued on, finally vanishing into the dark.

Within a few minutes, Michaely and his handful of survivors were on top the ridge to the rear. There they stayed through the night. They did not have to fight again, which was fortunate, since Third Platoon did not get back to them. But many times they heard enemy bands pushing through the brushwood at the base of the new position. That closed the experience for George's main body. Altogether, the actions of this one night cost it forty-seven men and two officers, wounded in action and killed in action.

Michaely had told Land to follow out. This was easier said than done. When the lower element began to move from the ridge, Third Platoon was hit its first hard blow. That was in part an effect from the artillery fire ordered by Michaely against the other end of the position. It drove the Chinese along the ridge and against Land. As he then stood, he was in position only to be destroyed piecemeal. So he ordered his men from their diggings and swung the line around; thereby the platoon simply straddled the hogback.

It took only one intense shower of hand grenades from the Chinese to demonstrate the untenability of that position. Land ordered his men out: "Follow me!" He led them down to the same trail via which Martin and the others had moved to the command post.

Partway down the hill, the trail forked. One path led southward across the flat; the other turned upward toward the ridgeline and the general direction of Fox Company. Land could no longer see any sign of Michaely's force.

So he decided on the instant to follow the lefthand trail toward Fox Company rather than take the chance of wandering in the darkness and missing George Company.

The platoon got to Fox Company without encountering any further fire. Gough's front was quiet for the moment. Land had time to get his wounded—thirty-five men—onto Fox's vehicles next the command post, in readiness to move back.

Land asked Gough: "Where's your weakest point? I'll fill in there." Gough directed him to a gap in his line just westward of the command post. The platoon crossed a draw and got its weapons set up again. Thirty minutes after its arrival, the Chinese hit again.

Murch had realized before the fight was one hour along that his battalion position and the further fate of the division were dangling by a thread. He called for artillery fire—continuous fires—to be put north of the ridge where Fox Company held. The 8th Field delivered all it could, within the limits of its supply. In less than three hours, 900 rounds were exploded into that ground.

Gough was in dire need of such help. At the time of the arrival of Land's platoon, he had only thirty-two men in line, and these four scattered squads were trying to hold segments of a 1,000-yard front. At midnight, coincidental with the attack on George Company, the Chinese had made an abortive thrust on Gough's left. In that mêlée, one half of First Platoon had been driven westward down the ridge, from where it wandered into Michaely's perimeter. Then sustained mortar fire came in on the position. Very shortly all of Gough's wires were out, including the platoon wires and those connecting him with Battalion. One round smashed the radio of the artillery forward observer. That left one SCR 300 as his only link with higher levels. He called Murch, told him the company was about to go under, and asked for four tanks to keep the road open to the rear.

His mind was running that way when Land's platoon appeared at the command post. To the rear of his rifle line, and rubbing shoulders with his own Third Platoon, there was a small hill hard by the road out. By putting Land there, he was in effect refusing his right flank while writing a small insurance on his line of retreat. He wanted the armor for the same reason. That Third Platoon happened to be at this stage in a retarded position, next the hill where Land stood, was only because the Chinese had again won ground with a grass fire. The blaze started in the center of Gough's line in front of Third Platoon's ground and leaped up the hill so fiercely that the men had been driven from the height and had fallen back on the command post.

One incident in that fall-back shows how quickly a good man will learn to love a weapon which has served him well. Corporal Mosier had been on the hill with the same .50 machine gun which had been captured during the day from the Chinese. He had fired five boxes of ammunition since midnight and was still firing when the grass blaze bore upward toward the platoon. He was down to his last twenty or so rounds, and was pouring fire upon a line of skirmishers following behind the flames when suddenly the gun went out from overwork. Without ammunition, and with the gun no longer useful, Mosier still threw the heavy weapon over his shoulder as he pulled away from the flames and headed for the command post, the last man to clear the position.

These were the actions preceding Land's arrival. Gough's line was already broken, and the brief quiet was due only to the circumstance that the Chinese were crowding into the gap on the ridge top and getting their weapons set. Yet such was the pressure that none of this was explained to Land; he mistakenly concluded that Fox had been unscathed and that he was but re-enforcing a relatively solvent position.

That was the more reason why Land's platoon felt particularly pleased with itself when it made a clean kill as the fire fight resumed. The Chinese mortars had swung around to Gough's right and were preparing to fire from his rear. Land saw six men, with two mortars, walk boldly into the open and begin to set up the mortars right next the road. The Chinese crews fired six rounds while Land's men watched, fascinated, only 70 yards away, scarcely realizing that while the shells were going far over their heads they must be hitting close to

Gough's left flank. Then Sergeant Kennedy got tired of the show, opened fire with the LMG, and cut them all down.

Already, the Chinese atop the main ridge had opened fire on the command post and the road with rifles, one HMG, and a bazooka. The tanks which Gough had called for arrived in the midst of this clutch; and when the Chinese turned the rocket fire against the tanks, they pulled back to the valley and took position on the far side of the road. Gough went to one tank, beat on the hatch and yelled until at last the tank unbuttoned; then Gough talked on its radio to the tank platoon commander. His message: "Tell Murch that I'm surrounded." He was still there, standing by the tank, when the message came back from Murch: "You are authorized to withdraw." At that moment a rocket from the hill went past Gough's head, missing him so narrowly that for seconds he felt stunned. Then the Chinese HMG traversed toward him, and bullets rattled off the armor. Gough climbed a tank, swung its .50 machine gun toward the hill and, in a few minutes of firing, knocked out both the machine gun and the rocket launcher.

Murch, already under small-arms fire in his own command post, and listening to a steady build-up of tommy gun fire in the vicinity, was called at 0130 by General Kean and asked about his situation. He said it wasn't promising. The division commander then asked if Murch could hold through the night until the 35th Regiment pulled back across the river. Murch said: "I'll do the best I can." He asked Kean for air support of his front line. (Until then, there had been no use of direct support by air of the tactical line during night engagement.) The general told him that he could get him some B-26s, and Murch assured him that he could control the action with his TAC party.

These things had happened at about the time that Michaely was clearing his hill and Gough's center was being breached. Murch then had the artillery mark the north and south edges of Ipsok with white phosphorus for the air attack to guide on, and he called Gough to tell him that the strike was coming.

The bombers got there within thirty minutes. Though they were carrying 500-pounders, they made no attempt to unload them, but limited the attack to strafing in front of the big ridge. That they hit at just the right spot and poured every round into the enemy country was largely sheer luck, since there were moments when the bullets were striking less than 50 yards in front of Gough's men. The surprise and the extreme accuracy of the fire had a marked effect on the Chinese, for it came right at the crisis of the fight, when it seemed most doubtful to Gough that any part of the company could survive.

At 0230 Murch was authorized by Division to break contact and move to a new position 3,000 yards to the south. That note of relief coincided with the hottest part of the air attack against the Chinese lines. Thus the word was passed to Gough in the best possible moment, when the enemy was experiencing a spasmodic moral recoil.

But Gough felt it necessary to stay by the tanks and get the column formed up on the lee side of this protecting shield. Four more tanks were to be sent from Baker Company to assist the withdrawal. He was out of contact with the platoons because of the broken wire, and some way the word had to be passed.

Lieutenant Bruce took over the mission of climbing the ridge, crawling through enemy lines to collect the separated platoons, and getting the company reassembled. Both the Second and the First had become enclosed by a circle of enemy skirmishers after the Third had been driven from the high ground. This delicate task consumed the greater part of an hour. The Chinese also acted as if they were tiring, and Bruce remarked that their shooting ardor diminished greatly after the air strike.

There was little firepower left in the outfit by the time Bruce had collected its remnants and steered them to the as-

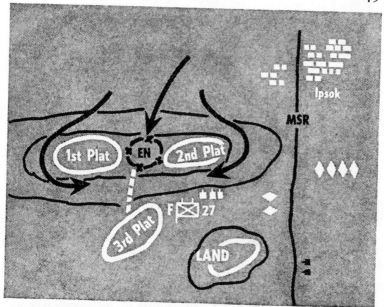

GOUGH'S FIGHT

Detail of Fox Company, 27th Regiment, night of 27-28 November.

sembly point near the road. Exclusive of Land's contingent, only twenty-three able-bodied, nonwounded men could still be counted in Fox Company. Four of the BARs had been destroyed by Chinese fire. The one light machine gun remaining was out of ammunition. Every carbine had either run dry or become inoperable.

Dawn was not far away by the time Gough concluded that the round-up was as complete as it was ever likely to be. Even so, it took an additional half hour to build up a sufficient covering fire to enable the withdrawal. The tanks were given this mission, and while they were plastering the foreground, the air and the artillery rained smoke and fire on Ipsok.

There was one delicious moment just after Gough's infantry had loaded on three of the M-438's and the tanks had started southward on the haul out. The men took a last look at the skyline of the lost ridge. What they saw almost made them rub their eyes. In great numbers the Chinese stood on the conquered ground, clearly silhouetted against the glow from the blazing shacks of Ipsok. The tanks swung their machine guns around, trained on the hill, and cut loose all together. They saw enemy soldiers fall like ripe wheat under a scythe. Then they chugged down the road. The Chinese did not follow.

This small but deadly skirmish had already achieved its main object—blocking the Chinese in the northeast while the 35th Regiment was completing a difficult withdrawal from the southwest corner of the division sector. The 35th was getting back relatively intact, and that was also partly because Colonel Fisher had continued to play it by ear.

On the preceding evening, Fisher had witnessed the beginning of an attempt to envelop his regiment. It looked innocent enough at first. Two groups of about 100 men each, dressed as Korean farmers, had sifted through his lines. On gaining the high ground to the south of his position, they unmasked and set up as a roadblock force closing the withdrawal route to Yongbyon. At the same time Fisher's First Battalion was hit by an attack from the northwest and the regimental command post became engaged by rifle and mortar fire. These things happened while the 35th was disposed along the ridges north of Yongsan-dong, a town west of the Kuryong-gang and about five miles southwest of Ipsok. The crossing by which Fisher could rejoin the division lay some distance to the east. On his own initiative, at midnight, Fisher ordered his regimental combat team to get loaded and prepare to head for the river. The units had to slug their way through Yongsan-dong before breaking loose.

It was a propitiously timed order, enabling 35th RCT to stage back across the Kuryong-gang while Murch's thin defense still kept the east bank clear of enemy forces. Fisher had arrived at Yong'O-dong and was going over the situation with General Wilson by the hour when Murch was authorized to break contact. Fisher's withdrawal took the form of an attack toward the southeast, thereby to gain time and elbowroom so that the artillery and tanks could clear the crossing. By dawn, these heavy attachments were safely on their way and by 1100 his last infantry battalion had followed.

Before midafternoon, the 35th RCT was again established in a defensive position on the high ground running northeastward from Yak-San, among the ancient ramparts of Yong-byon, the Walled City.

But there was little or no fighting on that ground. Already the main forces of the Chinese were converging on Kunuri, ten miles farther to the southeast. When the breakaway hour came for the 35th RCT, Fisher marched his column to the small ferry which strides the river halfway between Kunuri and Anju, and there crossed the Chongchon. For his outfit the end, like the beginning, was clean as a whistle.

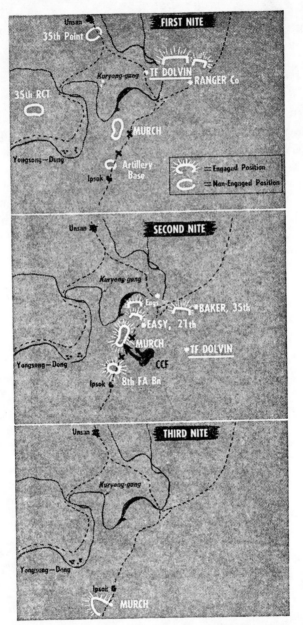

25th Division owed its successful extrication to the depth of its center.
Here is shown the contraction from three nights of battle.

# 13

# A Small Artillery Problem

NORTH AND SOUTH OF IPSOK DURING THE FIRST THREE days of the November battle, the issue had been settled pretty largely by what happened between infantry forces of the contending sides.

Even so, the form of the fight was shaped in large measure by what had developed within the artillery. Though within 25th Infantry Division the two arms were teamed in as perfect union as is possible under the abnormal handicap imposed by North Korea's formidable hill terrain, certain aspects of the artillery action must be given separate study to put their common experience in sharper focus.

It is therefore necessary to turn back to the events of 25 November when Task Force Dolvin, making its thrust north, turned eastward along the Kuryong River, leaving on its rear two ridges not yet cleared of enemy forces.

In midafternoon, Dolvin was visited by Brig. Gen. George B. Barth, the division artillery commander. Noting the wheel eastward, Barth became greatly concerned that this maneuver would uncover the 77th and 90th Field Artillery Battalions—preparing to base near Ipsok—which had the mission of supporting Dolvin.

On returning to Division, he discussed this danger with General Kean, and the division commander agreed that it was real, indeed. He therefore decided to move Murch's battalion of the 27th Infantry forward to the middle ground, where it could blunt a direct thrust against the artillery base and at the same time be in position to assist Dolvin. That decision, so quickly considered and made, became the key move in the conservation of the division's power under the surprise enemy attack.

Manifestly, the CCF attack on that first night was loosed from too far back, the dispositions of the 25th Division considered. The division was not thinly deployed on a wide front; it had more the look of an attack by parallel columns, which put the artillery base and the trains, etc., at greater depth than the Chinese had likely anticipated. So the first hard swing landed mainly in air, unlike the onfall along the Chongchon. It could not have been by design that the enemy attack that night was lacking in the circle-and-block tactics which is CCF standing procedure. Something had gone wrong with the plan; the Americans weren't following the book.

At Ipsok, the 77th Field Artillery Battalion, other than having to sweat its batteries to enable Dolvin to hold his forward ground, passed an uneventful night.

On 26 November, just after dark, the 8th Field Artillery Battalion relieved the 77th and 90th Battalions on the ground west of Ipsok and moved its guns right into the same slots. These two battalions were being rushed southward to rejoin their parent organization, 1st Cavalry Division, which from its reserve position was already in movement to the southeast to counter the turning movement against the right flank of the Eighth Army.

The 8th was expecting to fire immediately and, therefore, did not have time for a reconnaissance or survey. The battalion position was in a fairly expansive flat (by Korean standards) next the river. Immediately to the north of the guns stretched a winding valley, its mouth formed by two small ridges just forward of and a little off to the flanks of the batteries.

Eighth set up with a two-battery front, Charley on the left and Able on the right. Baker was about 300 yards to the left rear. Battalion HQ Battery was to the right front, bumping the 60-foot hill which ran down that side of the general position.

Lieut. Col. A. T. Terry and his executive, Maj. Julian B. Farley, talked it over and agreed that the chance was most remote that the battalion would be hit that night. But the batteries were told to prepare as if certain that the enemy infantry would be on them before morning. The local ground was reconnoitered in the darkness and the perimeter was then outposted to best advantage. (See sketch map.)

At 2330, Maj. Joel M. Genung, the operations officer, heard by telephone from the forward observer, Capt. Lewis Millett, that Task Force Dolvin's front and command post were being hit hard, and that the Chinese attack seemed to be drifting toward Dolvin's right rear. Capt. Robert E. Dingeman, the HQ Battery commander, got the word out to awaken all hands. Extra .30 and .50 ammunition for the machine guns was issued to all batteries, and a jeep whipped around, passing out three or four cases of grenades to each battery position. From long experience, the 8th had ceased issuing grenades to its individuals, except as an emergency arose. When pressure slackened, the men tended to discard grenades into the unit trucks. Movement shook the pins loose, and equipment had been lost because of this carelessness. The 8th thrice previously during the Korean campaign had been attacked by enemy infantry at its gun positions; it had grown wise about what things would work.

Genung was at the FDC (fire-direction center) when at 0050 a call came in from Charley Battery, reporting that the men in the gun positions had seen a "column of troops" marching toward them down the MSR. The night was overcast but the moon was bright enough that the report seemed credible. Genung asked: "Do you have an OP? If so, get them to find out if the column is friend or enemy." Charley Battery replied: "Check!" Five minutes later Charley Battery called again. It could see another column of men coming out of the hills directly to its left. "And," said Lieut. Rolly G.

Miller, "they're blowing bugles." Genung asked: "How far away?" Said Miller, "200 yards."

Able called as Miller hung up. It, too, had seen the column and was receiving small-arms fire at the gun positions. Miller came back with the same information: "I'm getting small-arms fire now: can I return it?" Genung answered: "Yes, go ahead."

While these calls were occurring, the Battalion wire to Murch failed. Sgt. Richard G. Soloway, with a detail of five men, started out in a ¾-ton to repair it. The vehicle blundered right into the colunm which was moving on Charley's position. The Chinese fired with rifles and tommy guns. All four tires were hit, and Pfc. Vigil was hit through the legs. Soloway got back to the perimeter carrying Vigil on his back. The three others had already run for it.

From the light machine-gun outpost on the right flank, Cpl. Clayton O. Humphrey called Dingeman and said: "They're blowing bugles directly in front of me, but I see only three men. Could those be our bugles?" Dingeman still doubted that the Chinese were at hand. He said to Humphrey: "If there's music in front of you, let me hear it." Humphrey held the instrument outward, and Dingeman could hear the bugles quite distinctly. So he took the hill at a run to see whence the noise was coming. Then he doubted no longer; the Chinese were in strength on the ridge just northeast of his position. But meanwhile the three men whom Humphrey had had in his sights had faded back across the rice paddies.

Charley Battery, like Genung, was still "jellying on the pivot," though having received permission to fire. At first its commander, Capt. Paul C. Kueber, had hesitated to believe his ears. Only a few seconds before the wire truck went out, a call had come from Pfc. Elmo L. Barrett who was in the OP on the right of the battery. "I see people moving in front of me and I can hear bugles," said Barrett. Kueber replied, "Bunk! That's your imagination working on you." Said the private, "Well, if you think so, just listen!" and he held the instrument out toward the sound. Kueber heard, and at last, he believed.

The outposts still had not fired because of their individual uncertainty. They had been apprised that their own infantry was having a hard time up front, and they were afraid they would shoot some of their friends.

M/S Stanley Wood was circulating with M/S Eddie R. Crocker through the gun positions just to check on things. Wood called Kueber and said: "There are unidentified people just 50 yards in front of these guns. They're talking a strange language. I'll be damned if it's Korean." Kueber replied: "Hold fire just a moment more! I've heard the same thing from our outposts. But I've got to make certain there are none of our people coming back at the same time." (This incident accents the complexity of the identification problem at an artillery location.)

Right after that, the decision was taken out of Kueber's hands. SFC James E. Holster who was on one of the lead guns near a group of Korean houses hard by the road heard a bugle blow. The call came from a group of marching men—perhaps fifty of them—not more than 100 yards away. That was enough for Holster. Without waiting for an order he put an artillery round right into them. It was the first shot. He saw the round blast half a dozen of the marching men. That shattered the silence beyond repair. All along the front of the perimeter, men opened fire with rifles, machine guns, and the howitzers.

Lieut. Roland B. Shriver, Jr., jumped to order both of Charley's outposts back into the gun positions, figuring that otherwise they'd be overrun. He got through only to the OP on the right. Cpl. E. Opperud, who had a BAR, and Barrett, who was on the LMG, were in such a hurry to comply that they left the LMG behind. Shriver ordered them to run back to the hill and get it. But M/S William Golden spoke up and said that he'd recover the gun, which he did.

But he barely made it. By the time he got back to the battery, Chinese were all over the hill, and Baker Battery was raking it with HE and WP fire.

Shriver hadn't raised Pfc. Stanley Welchel, who had the LMG in the OP on the lefthand ridge. Welchel continued to fire away, though the enemy columns cut directly between him and the battery. There were two ROK soldiers with him. Both were killed. Welchel stayed there all night defending his ground.

The BAR team on the hill to the right of HQ Battery had already pulled back, on Dingeman's order, to cover the LMG farther south along the ridge. But it was still no go, because Chinese mortar rounds were now hitting on the hill crest and getting steadily closer to the LMG. Dingeman called the whole outpost off the ridge and gave it a new position on the flat ground. He figured that the Chinese were trying to work south along the high ground and get on the battalion's rear: the one best bet seemed to be to burn the hill with as much WP as the batteries could throw that way. Baker, with its guns located 250 yards from the ridge, was in best position to do it. Able, within 150 yards of the ridge, could have shifted some of its guns to fire in that direction, but for the time being was engaged in stopping the Chinese coming via the left flank ridge; the gunners were going to it with such a will that during several minutes they fired violet smoke at the enemy before someone discovered the error and switched to lethal shell. Charley Battery was engaged full tilt with the threat to its immediate front.

Genung, stepping outside the FDC, saw a Chinese machine gun operating from the same ground from which Dingeman had just withdrawn the BAR team, and firing directly down into HQ Battery's positions. This was a switch, as the Chinese who had come in on the northeast shoulder had thus far concentrated most of their fire toward Able Battery. Accompanied by Terry, Genung went back to the fire block covering the road intersection on the battalion's rear; Terry wanted to find out if the rearward route was open in case a withdrawal became necessary. The men in that position told him that they had been drawing quite a bit of small-arms fire but that it all seemed to be coming from the forward ridges.

By the time Terry and Genung got back to the FDC, the Chinese mortars were working back and forth across the gun positions quite steadily; it was all heavy stuff, with plenty of boom-boom, but the enemy aim was not good.

Able had joined Baker in trying to knock out the Chinese on the northeast ridge with howitzer fire, but the enemy machine still clacked along at a great rate. From the FDC, Genung listened to this duel. Such was the closeness of the batteries to their target that the sounds of the guns going off and of the shells exploding on the ridge came right together.

In Charley Battery's position, Sgt. William F. Aragon was on the .50 machine gun alongside the road, which turned out to be a key piece in the battalion dispositions. The gun had been moved to that point just a few minutes before the Chinese attack started. In the beginning Aragon turned the fire of the .50 against the hill on the right, since the attack seemed to be building up mainly from that direction. But about one hour after the firing began, the Chinese who had approached the perimeter via the main road got into the houses just forward of Charley's command post and began firing from the windows with tommy guns.

Until then Kueber's gunners had been hopeful of stopping with howitzer fire the threat from that quarter. They had picked off four or five large groups maneuvering directly to their front at ranges of less than 500 yards. By the glow from WP shell, they had seen other groups moving in from the flanks and had taken them also under fire. On one occasion, Able and Charley sighted simultaneously an SP gun advancing on the perimeter via the road, and together took it under fire. Which battery killed it is still a question; the one certainty is that it was got.

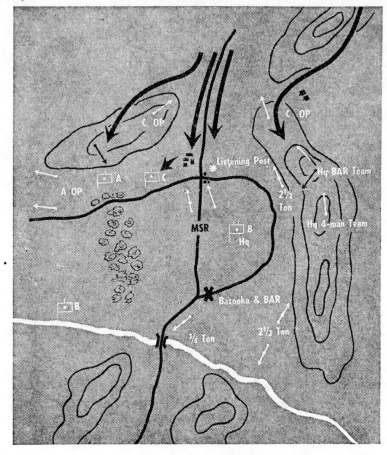

ARTILLERY AS INFANTRY

Ipsok position and action of 8th Field Artillery Battalion during the perimeter defense.

At first, the Chinese who had nested in the Korean huts reacted as if they didn't know they were looking right down Charley Battery's throat. Though they threw out automatic fire in large doses, it was all going over the command post and the gun pits, almost under the muzzles of their rifles. One small group of Chinese, trying to bound forward from the house cover, broke into the position of the No. 2 gun, which was under Holster, but were driven off before they could fire more than a few rounds. One of Holster's ROKs was wounded; one Chinese was killed.

Crocker and SFC Robert E. Gafford got a 3.5 bazooka. Standing right in the middle of the battery position (the guns were on line with the command post) they blew the main house apart at a range of 35 yards. This two-man team continued to bang away at the rest of the houses until all the walls were down. At the same time, the battery was directing its small-arms fire obliquely toward the road so as to cut across the rear of the Chinese who had moved in closest to the guns. Aragon, at the .50 machine gun, continued to fire straight down the road, using periodic bursts of twelve to twenty rounds.

Able's howitzers had knocked out the machine gun on the northeast ridge after about fifteen minutes of fire. But that served only as a temporary depressant. In blowing apart the houses, Crocker's rocket fire ignited the debris. It blazed mightily, and the flames, high-lighting the locations of the two forward batteries, attracted a rain of small-arms fire from the enemy skirmishers out beyond the glow. Genung, who was scouting out the westward-leading road to see if the two batteries would be able to extricate themselves, got only as far as the listening post and was there turned back by the patter of bullets on the forward ground. As he started his return to the command post area, he heard the cry: "Medics! Medics!" arising from Able's position. It sounded ominous, but there was more sound than fury in what was occurring. Most of the bullets threatening Able were coming from the ridge to the west where a Chinese BAR team and a score of riflemen had got on the rear of Pfc. Welchel's LMG position. The fire was consistently high, and other than a few nicks, Able weathered the night unscathed. The BAR team and a dozen other Chinese were found on the ridge next morning. They had been killed by artillery fire at ranges more appropriate to an exchange of grenades.

At about 0430, the decision was taken to withdraw the battalion. By then, the area had been under a relatively intense small-arms and mortar fire for approximately three and one half hours, but it was not a well-aimed fire. The Chinese had shown no expertness with their weapons at any stage, and the use of the howitzers against them appears to have robbed their infantry effort of all organization; the battalion got ready to retrograde on orders from higher up only because the untenability of Task Force Dolvin's position was already demonstrated, and it was evident that a general fallback was imminent.

Despite the volume of enemy fire, poured in frontally and from the high ground along the flanks, the battalion had lost only two men killed and less than a dozen from wounds. To those who had judged the fight by what they could hear from the FDC of the roar and rattle out along the perimeter, this seemed like a small miracle. The battalion had fired 333 howitzer rounds in defense of the local ground, all of it at targets between 80 and 400 yards away. Charley Battery had used up 128 rounds in breaking up enemy groups along the road directly in front of its guns; the rest had been fired against the high ground.

The perimeter front was still under mortar and small-arms fire. To displace, the two forward batteries had to wheel right, pivoting around Aragon's position to get on the main road. Colonel Terry asked Kueber if he thought the maneuver could be made O.K. and got a favorable reply. Right after that, Kueber undertook the pathfinding job, leaving for a reconnaissance of the new positions 2,000 yards to the south and taking along with him two ammo trucks, a kitchen truck, a wire truck, and a jeep.

Aragon's position was strengthened. Beside the .50 which he was firing, Pfc. Lloyd A. Perry was posted with an LMG. As the position was laid out, the guns and other vehicles had to come from the left of the two machine guns and make the turn on the outside. This meant that for a moment each vehicle making the turn masked their fire and presented an inviting target to the Chinese. It was arranged that Aragon and Perry, working both sides of the road, would fire strongly as each vehicle approached the turn. Thus synchronized, the .50 and the LMG proved an effective damper upon the enemy weapons forward, though two jeeps and three trucks were badly shot up (not destroyed) in making the turn.

Shriver was in charge of running Charley's guns through this ambuscade, but couldn't even get started with the No. 4 piece. There happened to be several large craters right in the middle of the battery position. Because the gun's prime mover was with Baker Battery, Shriver tried to get the gun out with a ¾-ton, and the truck got stuck in a crater. To struggle further in that moment seemed foolhardy. He told SFC Richard Turek to thermite the gun, and Turek pulled the pin and threw in the grenade. The enemy fire was building up again and individual Chinese skirmishers began to crowd in. Just as SFC Lester S. Stevenson was getting ready to march-order his gun, he saw a Chinese rifleman running straight for it. Stevenson pulled out his .45 pistol and plugged the Chinese in the head—range 60 yards. Then dusting off his hands as if he had been doing that kind of shooting all his life, he yelled: "Let's go, men!" That drew the only laugh during the withdrawal.

The battalion withdrew without further untoward incident. What followed suggests that the Chinese were likewise preparing to pull away at the same time, probably to re-enforce the roadblock groups which had set up to stop the southward march of Task Force Dolvin and Murch's battalion.

After daylight, Shriver sent a patrol back to the old position to see what could be saved of the vehicles and other materiel which had been abandoned. The scene was altogether quiet. Not an enemy soldier was to be found. Nothing within the camp had been looted or otherwise disturbed.

Because of an odd break, the patrol recovered Charley's No. 4 gun in good working condition. Turek's thermite bomb had failed to do the business; the material was defective and had fizzled. Higher levels got a false impression of this incident and entered it into the records that the No. 4 gun had been lost to the Chinese raiders, who had in fact hit the No. 2 gun and been driven off.

Chaplain McCluskey volunteered to accompany this patrol. Shriver asked him why. McCluskey said he wanted to look for wounded; it was on his mind that Welchel was still missing. So he was permitted to go. When the patrol came even with the old position, it met Welchel walking down the main supply route. Both of his feet were frozen. He was carrying his machine gun, tripod, and empty cases. He laughed when he met the patrol and said: "I feel happy as hell."

Like Pfc. Edsel Turner of the 38th Infantry, he had known briefly the rare experience of holding a drawn field single-handed and thereby winning a personal decision—one man against the world.

# 14

## The Web of Fate

AT DAYBREAK ON 29 NOVEMBER, A MOTOR CONVOY, manned by Turks and carrying supply intended for the Turkish armed force, drove north from Sunchon and began the descent into the valley of the Kaechon, where it expected to fold into the rear of 2nd Division.

The motorcade did not complete this prospectively uneventful run. Only a handful of survivors—some of them badly shot up—got away to tell their woeful story, which by the time it had filtered through to Division Headquarters was barren of significant detail.

Somewhere a little to the north of the village of Yangwan-ni (the G3 journal gives YD 461866 as the coordinate, though this appears to be an error) the Turkish column had moved full-length into an enemy ambush. Fire at close range had struck it from both sides of the road, destroying most of the vehicles. To those who escaped the trap, it had seemed that the enemy was present in the strength of "one company."

This was the first warning that an enemy force was on the division rear and harassing the road along which it expected to march. The alarm was heard at the command post by 0730; it did not go unheeded, though in the nature of the swiftly changing situation, it was but one of a hundred freshly acute pressures developing all around the division circle.

A score of division MPs were rounded up and dispatched toward Yangwan-ni to feel out the situation. They moved too fast and too far and got wiped out for their pains, and Division gained nothing from the reconnaissance.

Shortly before noon, a platoon of tanks from the 71st Battalion—then in IX Corps reserve—was dispatched south on the same mission. The armored column moved through Yangwan-ni without drawing as much as one rifle bullet. Continuing on toward Sunchon, with the mission of helping "Nottingham" (the British column moving north from Sunchon), the armor radioed to Division that the road was clear and the enemy gone.

That report was taken with a pinch of salt for obvious reasons. Division Reconnaissance Company was next ordered to take the same route, develop the situation at the roadblock, and destroy all opposition. Having started its move in midafternoon, the company was engaged by fire from the ridges on both sides of the road as it came upon the ruined Turkish convoy. Perhaps one hour later, it radioed Lieut. Col. Ralph Foster, the G2, that upon deploying and attacking toward the high ground, it had become pinned by enemy automatic fire. One platoon of tanks from the 72nd Battalion and Charley Company of the 38th Infantry were rushed south to re-enforce this effort. The force fought through the remaining hours of daylight but made no progress. At dark, it was ordered by Division to break contact.

Thus the day's striving came to nought, almost nothing having been added to information about the rearward situation beyond what the Turkish survivors had initially reported. At Division, it was reckoned that the Chinese were in position to menace perhaps 1,000 yards of the main supply route adjacent to Yangwan-ni. But substantial proof was lacking that these were the true limits of the threat.

One fateful omission had already occurred. In the Turks who survived there was knowledge which, had it been revealed, might have saved the division. Their column had run into an earlier ambush two miles farther south along the highway. Dead men and shattered vehicles marked the spot. This vital information they had failed to make known, either because of shock or because of the language barriers. There are sufficient penalties in any war; but there are added ones in coalition struggle.

By the irony of fate, the estimates and decisions by which the division became committed to a withdrawal via the Kunuri-Sunchon route moved almost precisely apace with the march of events which cast a shadow athwart the right-of-way.

During the five days' battle, General Keiser had several times complained to Corps that they were wasting his troops by ordering short withdrawals which did not permit breaking contact with the Chinese; instead of a four- or five-mile retrograde, he wanted lines far enough to the rear so that he would have a reasonable chance to extricate his division and get it squarely faced about again before the Chinese struck. He had argued when told to set up at Wonni that this half-step retirement cost heavily and accomplished nothing.

When at last he won his point, it was a Pyrrhic triumph. In the early morning of 29 November, at about the time the Turkish convoy was exploding within the roadblock, Corps authorized 2nd Division's withdrawal to Sunchon. The order did not specify over which routes the move should be made; that was left to Keiser.

Approximately two hours later, Keiser talked on radio to General Milburn, commander of I Corps. Milburn asked: "How are things going?" Keiser answered: "Bad, right now. We're getting hit in my CP." Milburn then said, "Well, come on out my way," which meant via Anju. However, Keiser wasn't under I Corps, and having the impression that 25th Division had not yet cleared via the westward route, he feared that by turning that way he would compromise both himself and his neighbor.

At about 1100, he jeeped to IX Corps' command post, then two and a half miles west of Kunuri on the Anju road, and talked to the G3, Col. Louis Kunzig. Army G3 had just called down and given Kunzig the boundaries governing the withdrawal of both corps. Kunzig was busy drawing lines on a map. Keiser got another map and copied what he saw. This was the only direction he ever received as to his further movements. He did not get a direct order to withdraw, and the road by which he should take the division out was not specified.

The jeep had been too slow because of the blocked traffic. So Keiser flew in an L-5 back to his own command post—a journey which helped fix his decision. From a few thousand feet up, he could look for miles across the plateau country to the south and southwest. He could see people by the thousands—seemingly refugees—choking its trails and roadways. The sight made an indelible impression on his mind. If these people were still fleeing the enemy, there was yet time to get the division out—so ran his thoughts. But long afterward, he came to wonder whether what he had witnessed that morning wasn't part of the Communist build-up flowing toward his own rear.

As the day wore along into evening and the inconclusive ending of the opening joust with the roadblock was reported to him, he still did not attach decisive importance to the failure to eliminate the enemy on his rear. All that had been proved was that the CCF who had made the sneak penetration were doggedly determined; he believed that the block they held was nonetheless relatively shallow. Before morning, he was to alter this opinion, largely because of the rise of pressure elsewhere along his right flank. But for the time being, it seemed to him that what had happened to the southeast signified a minor error rather than a portentous threat—boys had been sent forth to do men's work. The forces which had given over the fight for the night had not been heavy-barreled enough to undertake it in the first place.

While they had been attempting vainly to free the road to Sunchon, the MSR between Kunuri and the division command post was becoming choked with vehicles already ordered to the rear. Within the block were not only several of the service trains but 8076 MASH (Mobile Army Surgical Hospital) complete with patients and about thirty female nurses. Darkness was already at hand. Every time the staff glanced roadward at the stalled transport, it was reminded that if the trains did not clear southward during the night, it would be impossible to break off the battle and withdraw the fighting elements on the next day.

Lieut. Colonel Holden, Division G3, called Corps and asked if the road through Anju was open for the movement of the division trains. The answer was: "We think so." It was thereupon decided to turn the trains about on the narrow road and shoot them westward. With such of his MPs as were still available, Lieut. Col. Henry Becker set about the task. At 2200, Becker told Holden that the last of the trains had already cleared for Anju and had probably made it just in time: he (Becker) had got the word from two 25th Division MPs that the enemy had at last closed on this road also and was holding a roadblock about four miles west of Kunuri. The report was not confirmed from any other source. No party was sent forth by 2nd Division to scout the area and report back. This was a hiatus in operations, perhaps due in part to the fact that the locale was in 25th Division's sector. But its consequence was that Holden accepted the report as true and it helped dispose him to the Kunuri-Sunchon route despite the known risks which attended it.

Now on the evening of 29 November, the 23rd Regiment was north of Kunuri, while the 38th was to its east. The division was still determined to keep tied in with 25th Division where the main roads came together just outside the town, and to maintain a line at that point. Accordingly, the 23rd was ordered to move back across the Kaechon River, take up new ground to the northwest of the division command post, and protect the road junction. The 38th was then to come in line on the right in extension of 23rd's position, with its far flank curving toward the southeast. Division also directed that the Turkish remnants should build on this same line to the right of 38th. But it is to be doubted that the Turks ever received the word. Their last radio had been destroyed. The one liaison officer which they had sent to Division had been missing for twenty-four hours. They were no longer in any part a cohesive force, and while there is some doubt that they got the order, there is none whatever that they did not comply.

For Peploe's 38th Regiment, the new maneuver promised untold difficulty, after an already back-breaking day. His two forward battalions had become enveloped during the evening hours and were hit hard from all sides after dark. The 3rd ROK Regiment—still in good shape with about 1,200 men able to do duty—gave him a fairly firm left shoulder. Peploe started to swing the rightward battalion of the ROKs toward a prominent ridge (Hill 182) on the rear of his own compromised battalions, and so give them a guardrail. But before the move could be executed, his own Third Battalion had drifted back to that ridge. So he withdrew the ROKs to a semicircular hill mass about 1,000 yards beyond his command post. The Chinese had already swung around his dangling right flank and were pushing toward the command post along both sides of the Kaechon River. Ignoring momentarily this threat to his rear, Peploe extended the ROK right flank northward to cover the road along which his own battalions were attempting to withdraw.

Right in the middle of this delicate situation, he received the order from Division to withdraw across the river; that meant continuing what was already in motion, only doing it a little faster so that 38th would be ready when 23rd had completed its move. At 0100 Peploe got word that the last of Colonel Freeman's people had crossed the river except for the one company assigned to hold the gate while the 38th passed through. There had been no easing of the enemy attack; he was still driving hard out of the northeast, and his fire build-up was now strengthening steadily against Peploe's lower right flank. The perimeter built around the ROK regiment held until 0400; by then, the two forward battalions of 38th had fallen back on the main body, ready for the move across the river.

At that moment, the Chinese attack tapered off, and then died. Along the new line, 38th and 23rd were to join hands around Hill 201. Peploe's plan had two of the ROK battalions moving out first and forming a line from 201 to Chichon, serving as an anchor until the others arrived. The ROKs started, but they didn't carry out the order. They went on an aimless bivouac of their own, and Peploe next saw them after dawn near the division command post.

In the light of later events, Peploe concluded that the Chinese broke off the fight when they did and let him withdraw unharassed across the river so that they could march their own strength southeastward and re-enforce the fire gauntlet building on the division rear. But an otherwise incomprehensible action perforce signaled nothing significant to Peploe at the time; he hadn't yet heard of the Yangwan-ni roadblock.

The 38th's withdrawal and the events which had forced it had almost stripped the regiment of medical support. All of the battalion aid stations had been abandoned during the night's fighting. Second Battalion's station had been knocked out by mortar fire. The other two had been lost when the enemy roadblock which had closed on the rear of the two forward battalions made it impossible for them to withdraw their vehicles. What medical help was left from the three battalions consolidated as one regimental group in the early hours of 30 November. Of the wounded, ninety were given preliminary care and then evacuated via the Anju road. That left sixty-one who would have to ride out with the regiment. The attendants made room for these casualties by jettisoning supply and borrowing vehicles from other units. Tents were slashed, bottles broken, and kits wrecked in the darkness; nothing could be burned lest the blaze provide a target for enemy fire. The wounded had to be stacked several deep in the litter jeeps and trailers because their number soon overflowed the transport capacity.

Even so, for the time being this was a minor detail among the worries besetting the command. In handing the 3rd ROK Regiment its assignment, Peploe purposed mainly to screen his own artillery base, still north of the Kaechon River, while his own battalions were being funneled to the new defensive line south of the river. When the ROKs drifted off, apprising no one of this deviation, their departure uncovered the batteries and put the gun crews in the division front line.

Peploe was not aroused to this situation until dawn. His own lines, anchored on the hill mass around Yongchon, were drawing some automatic fire from leftward, but the pressure from the north had subsided. Then looking across the river, he saw the heavy guns of the 17th Battalion and could hear the crackle of rifle fire near the gun positions. Headquarters of the division artillery and the batteries of the 82nd Antiaircraft Battalion were also on compromised ground, forward of the infantry. To Peploe's eye, it appeared that unless something was done quickly, the artillery position would be lost. So the 38th was again formed up into companies, with orders to start back across the river.

But the move was never made. Just at that time came the order directing the 38th to load and make ready to lead the division column down the Sunchon road. It was then about 0800. Yet the artillery, left to its own devices, remained untouched, except for random fire from a few snipers. The enemy threat from the north and northeast had evaporated. The division artillery elements beyond the Kaechon were ordered to rendezvous immediately near the division command post, bringing out only their essential combat vehicles and abandoning their kitchens, maintenance trucks, etc., should the enemy pressure rise again. By noontime, the Artillery HQ (minus the fire-direction center) and the 82nd Battalion had kept the assignment. The 17th still held its ground because traffic was blocked solid along the road.

Still, as of the evening of 29 November, the rearward threat was a cloud scarce larger than a man's hand. No one believed that a crisis impended because of the interference south of Kunuri, and the majority within the division did not yet know that the road was in any way compromised.

Colonel Sloane of the 9th Infantry got the word when he proposed sending his Service Company to a village down the Sunchon road and was warned off because Chinese forces were already sitting on the village. So he rerouted the company via Anju; just after sundown, a few members of his I&R platoon, who had gone with Service Company, got back to Regiment and told Sloane that the Anju road was open and the company had got through.

The roadblock became his personal business when at 1930 he was called to Division and told that "as early in the morning as possible" he would take his regiment and destroy the enemy force on the division rear.

Holden, G3, pointed to the map and, using the end of one finger, designated the spot where Sloane's men would hit and then break into the blue.

Sloane mentioned that his men were badly worn and that his "regiment" was now two battalions, each having the strength of a company. (Second had 200 men and Third 240.) He was reassured that his force would be equal to the task. Holden and Col. Gerald G. Epley, the Chief of Staff, gave him a quick reading on what had happened at the roadblock and said that, from their size-up, he would be fighting "not more than two Chinese companies."

Sloane asked: "Who's in contact with them now?" and Holden replied: "We broke contact at dark." Sloane did not feel good about that. The commander of Charley Company, 72nd Tank Battalion, present at the conference, was ordered to meet Sloane with one platoon of tanks when the 9th passed Division HQ on its way out.

Holden then sat down and wrote the operational order which led to such vast consequence. It was done in red crayon on a piece of scratch paper by the light of a guttering candle. This was all of it: "When R/B is open, follow this priority for movement south: (1) 38th Inf (2) 2nd Recon Co, Div HQ, MP Co, 2nd Signal Co (3) Divarty (4) 2nd Eng Bn (5) Rearguard—23rd RCT (23rd Inf, 15 FA Bn, 72nd Tank Bn minus Co C, Battery B of 82nd AAA.)"

So ran the words which, with minor exceptions forced by the conditions of the fight on the following morning, determined the order of march in the division column. Holden presupposed that it would be executed as ordered after 9th Infantry had completed its job of "banging through."

Sloane gathered his own commanders together at 2330 and described the mission. The force would proceed "by marching" from its own assembly area to a line two miles to the rear of division command post, where the column would deploy and attack, Second Battalion taking the ridges west of the main supply route while Third Battalion moved along the ridges to the east of it. He figured they would be in contact by 0700 at the latest.

The moon was still high and bright when the column started. Less than one mile beyond the division command post, the march stopped briefly while Major Barberis undertook to get flanking patrols up the ridgetops on both sides of the road.

Sloane started forward to see what caused the delay. Before he could reach Barberis, Second Battalion came under rifle and machine-gun fire from the ridges, and the men jumped for temporary cover next the roadway. This had happened *more than one mile north of the point where Sloane had expected to find the Chinese roadblock.*

That sounded an alarm bell in his brain and he promptly radioed his battalion commanders to come in for a conference. Barberis told him that Easy Company was already close-engaged and was losing a few men, but that the rest of the battalion was deploying rightward toward the high ground. Third Battalion was also in motion toward the ridges east of the road. To help rig a line, HQ and M Companies had both been formed as provisional rifle companies, except for one skeletonized platoon of M, which was operating both the 81-mm mortars and a section of HMGs. The tank platoon, temporarily, was clinging to the road and serving as a reserve.

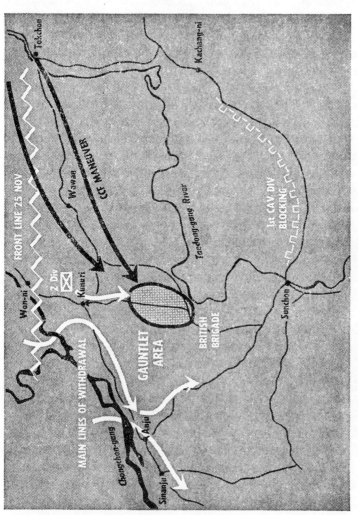

SITUATION OF 30 NOVEMBER AS EIGHTH ARMY DISENGAGED

The British Brigade was attacking north in the area shown to check the enemy pressure and 1st Cavalry Division was swinging wide to the eastward for the same object.

All that the enemy did that morning conspired either to compound the mystery of the situation or magnify the illusion that it was threatless. Sloane had his few minutes of shocked surprise from being engaged prematurely. Then when he punched, the blow landed in air, as if the first brush had been sheer accident. By 0700, his men had taken the first hill mass to the right of the road and a small hogback to the left of it. There had been fairly heavy fire from a ridge one half mile to the south, to the right of the main supply route, but this had not impeded the companies during the climb, and the resistance in the foreground had vanished.

Momentarily winded by the climb, the companies rested on the skyline. Sloane called for an air strike against the ridge whence the fire was beating upon the MSR. Trosani, his artillery liaison officer, brought him word the strike would be long delayed because of the heavy ground haze. Hardly five minutes after that, the bombers appeared and made several runs against the ridge, using rockets and napalm. In the wake of the strike, the Chinese fire dwindled.

At about 0800, one platoon of tanks moved south through Sloane via the MSR with the object of getting through to "Nottingham"—the British advance northward from Sunchon. They radioed their progress and made it to the south end of "The Pass" with no real difficulty; the way therefore seemed unbarred.

About two hours were lost in these probes; they were precious hours because the division was getting ever closer to an irrevocable decision. On getting the favorable news from the armor, Sloane told his flanks to push on, then loaded one platoon of infantry aboard tanks and started it down the road. Immediately, the men in the hills, the party on the road, and Sloane's command post began to receive mortar and machine-gun fire; it came in steadily, though not in great volume.

At 0920, Sloane was told that the ROK regiment which had been with Peploe was being attached to him. Captain Jones, the Intelligence officer, guided the ROK commander,

Colonel Chung, to a rendezvous on the right of the road. Chung said he would like to have a hand in the battle. Sloane sketched the situation and gave him his mission; he was to clear the ridges west of the MSR. As soon as the ROKs passed through Second Battalion, Sloane intended to swing Barberis' men to the east to re-enforce Third Battalion. Chung said: "I'll be ready at 1030."

Though time was racing, Sloane accepted the arrangement, feeling that his own regiment was rocking on its heels. Chung's survivors, on the other hand, were slow in getting up to the line of departure. Earlier in the morning, not far from the division command post, they had come through an Ordnance-Quartermaster dump and they now had the look of merchants going to a trade fair.

Northward of Sloane's narrow front, other developments were helping shape the fateful climax. The division was getting set for the ride out. Peploe's companies were already mounting the tanks and the regiment's own organic vehicles preparatory to making the break for Sunchon in the van of the division column. The march order had been prescribed— Second Battalion in the lead, followed by Third, and then First. There would be no difficulty about finding riding space aboard the armor and the trucks. Peploe's battalions now averaged about 200 men apiece; their rifle companies counted between twenty and thirty-five men.

Peploe had no apprehension that the experience would prove other than a road march into friendly ground. On the day previous, he had heard little or nothing about the fester on the division rear. In midmorning, at approximately 1030, he was at the artillery position when the message came through that the roadblock was practically cleared and the last of the Chinese were cornered on the ridge to the south. That was before Sloane had taken his third look at the situation. Peploe's subordinates had about this same view of what was in prospect.

They had not smelled out the possibility of a fight, and in consequence they did not load tactically so that, if engagement came about, men who knew one another would be ready to fight as units the moment they unloaded.

For example, Second Battalion was ordered to load aboard the tanks. Then it was felt that the armor should be distributed along the length of the column so that one tank would be covering a serial of about ten thin-skinned vehicles. In consequence, Second's companies were split apart, and before the move started, the battalion was scattered along the length of the column. Third Battalion loaded partly on organic vehicles while others of its groups found room in the artillery trucks. Third Battalion was supposed to go out on the vehicles of 38th Field Artillery Battalion, but in the event the men boarded any passing truck or jeep which availed them space: in this way, the "Rock of the Marne" Regiment became fractionalized before the starting signal was given, and the last chance for control passed from the hands of the men who led it.

Around the division rim, then, in this hour of midmorning crisis, when decision was being forced by the sheer march of events, the appreciations of situation by the commanders and staff members who were most directly at grips with the problem had little likeness one with the other. In the nature of the case, with the camp being struck, units moving, and installations being uprooted, the flow of information to the corners of the perimeter became a trickle, and some elements heard nothing at all.

In the upper corner where the rearguard stood, the enemy pressure from out of the north became steadily ascendant. Freeman, who commanded the 23rd RCT, worried less about what was developing in the lower corner because he worried more about whether finally he would be able to extricate his own force by any line of withdrawal.

Sloane, whose troops were under the gun next the roadblock, still believed he was coping with a localized resistance, but figured that for the time being his own force was held nonetheless.

Chung, the ROK commander, whose men were to make the assault, must have estimated that his task meant not more than the sweeping of two or three ridges, else he would not have so readily accepted responsibility.

Peploe, whose regiment was in the van of the column and would therefore bear the brunt, was preparing for a march.

Holden, G3, thought that the 9th Regiment was still "banging through," and was still riding on his estimates of the prior evening.

General Keiser's own reflections were much more somber. In his own words: "That morning my impression was that we were seriously confronted by an aggressive enemy which had moved across our rear. But the division had to be withdrawn quickly or take terrible losses where it stood. From what I saw and heard I concluded that the enemy already had built up a considerable strength *all around us.*"

In contrast to Keiser's impression that he was at the point of being encircled, the moves to "develop the situation" at the lower corner of the perimeter where Colonel Chung was readying his ROK line proceeded almost casually.

At 0900, Skeldon, who commanded Peploe's Second Battalion, reported to Division and was given a note by Holden, G3, to carry to Sloane confirming Skeldon's attachment to the 9th Regiment during the fight to clear the roadblock. Capt. Reginald J. Hinton loaded Skeldon's men on the regimental armor—twenty men riding each tank. The battalion strength was 220 as Skeldon faced toward this new mission; they had no inkling that their worst hours were ahead, and that they would total but eighty-six by the close of the day.

Yet the specific assigned task—helping 9th Infantry—had little to do with this, for Sloane was marking time while awaiting Chung's advance, and Skeldon, getting up to Sloane somewhere about 1100, also played his opening part from the sidelines, witnessing the ROK attack which was already in motion.

As Skeldon came up to Sloane's command post, located in the low ground just short of the enemy-held ridges, the road and the command post area were already under mortar fire, and machine-gun bullets from enemy country were chipping the iced surfaces of the surrounding paddy fields. Skeldon's men, tank-loaded and stretched out along the road rearward of him, drew little or none of this fire at the time. The gun was too far distant to enable the gunner to judge of its effect and he continued to spray unoccupied ground.

Skeldon went forward to a culvert where Lieut. Colonel McMains, commanding Third Battalion, 9th Infantry, had his command post. It was along the road perhaps 200 yards and provided a better look at the enemy-held ridge. The sector was being well splashed by a tumbling bullet fire coming from the heights; the culvert, therefore, provided some sanctuary. Skeldon judged that the Chinese machine gun was about 600 yards away. Chung's ROK line was already moving toward the object, its advance being roughly parallel to the road.

An air strike doused the ridge with rockets and napalm while the ROKs were crossing an intervening hill, and for a few minutes dampered the Chinese fire wholly. The ROKs continued on. They swept up the first hill in fairly good order and drove off about twenty Chinese. The ROKs continued the advance to the next ridge. Then as the two forces closed within reaching distance, and Skeldon could hear grenades exploding on the hill, he saw the ROK line waver, break, and run with fifty Chinese in pursuit, heaving grenades until the ROKs had cleared the hill. There was a second Korean assault, carried off less determinedly than the first and repulsed by the Chinese in yet stronger numbers. To his rear, Skeldon could hear the .50s on some of the American tanks join the fire fight, some firing in support of the ROKs, while others bore on the ridges leftward of the road, where the attack by Item Company, 9th Infantry, was stalled. Skeldon saw some of the running figures fall, and he concluded that the .50s were doing their part well.

Peploe, witnessing the negative consequence of this same action, decided that the wisest course was to get his regimental column ready to move, including Skeldon's people. He was under the mistaken impression that the British in "Nottingham" were only a short distance beyond the fire block. So he told Hinton, his tank commander, to pull some of the tanks off the road into open ground and maintain fire on the Chinese machine guns while the other vehicles were getting started.

Because Hinton's tanks were loaded with infantry, and the tanks of Charley Company, 72nd Battalion, were already among the paddies and squared away to blast the hill, Hinton passed on the mission to Captain Dew, their commander. One of Dew's tanks had become mechanically disabled while on the road. That blocked the lead serial, containing Dew's tanks and Skeldon's men, for another twenty minutes while a detour was built around it. Despite the delay, there was no real trouble. The Chinese, succeeding on the hill, were still not ranged in on the broad target strung along the valley.

In this somewhat hesitant and confused fashion ended the main attempt to clear the Chinese from the ridges to the right of the road, which Sloane's probing had indicated was the stronger flank in the resistance at what Division still thought of as a shallow "roadblock." Obviously, the giving over of the assault on the high ground to the right, coupled with the decision to start the road column rolling at that moment, as per the division order, was the very crisis of action, though no one yet sensed it. Had the ridge-clearing maneuver been pressed, the great depth of the Chinese position would have become gradually more apparent.

It by no means follows that the division would have then found a ready solution for its problems and extricated itself with relatively light additional loss. The division, numerically and in moral strength, was already less than half solvent. The deployed enemy already in great strength barred the Sunchon road. The Anju road might have been taken; likewise, the division might have been enveloped and annihilated had it waited longer in the Kunuri area. These were the ineluctable circumstances and the possible forfeits inherent in the situation.

Even so, the importance of the noontime moment when the action changed from attack on a wide front to an attempt at break-out by a road column cannot be missed. As in the charge of the Light Brigade, the nature of the order was inexorable and its effect was complete. Until a short time past 1200 on 30 November, 2nd Division had remained a coherent body responsive to the will of command. Once started on the road, it became inorganic and could be neither controlled nor recalled.

The precipitating events, therefore, need to be appraised in an objective light, however grim and regrettable their detail. Why had the attack failed along the high ground? To the trained eyes of Skeldon, it was because the ROKs had made a weak bid at a time when they were getting effective support from the American armor. McMains, who had been on the same spot longer, felt differently. He had witnessed in detail the ROK attack up the first ridge and said of it, "The Koreans charged determinedly, with as excellent marching fire as I ever saw in my life."

One of Skeldon's subordinates, Lieut. Charley S. Heath, was closer to the scene and played a direct hand in the fire fight which closed it. Heath was moving among the tanks which were in position to fire on the ridge under attack by the ROKs. His main interest was to try to persuade the leaders that their salvation lay in getting underway, and that they should so inform the higher levels. (Heath, too, believed that the Chinese position had no depth.) The tanks were simply squatting there with little knots of infantrymen refuged behind them. On his own authority, Heath was exhorting them to give up their long-range shooting, let the ROKs take care of the Chinese on the ridges, form up with the infantry, and march. He felt that the force was wearing down merely from waiting.

Then he heard two of the 72nd's tanks open fire with their .50 machine guns. Looking toward the ridge, he was horrified to see that the American fire was bearing directly on Chung's forward elements. Two of their lead files were knocked down by bullets. The fourth and fifth ROKs in the forward group were carrying a cerise panel. They faced toward the tanks and waved frantically. This was within a few seconds of the time that they had begun to exchange grenades with the Chinese.

Heath sprinted for the tanks, yelling as he ran and beating on the sides of the tank with his helmet as he got there. A tanker looked out. Heath yelled: "You're hitting into our troops. Fire more to the left!" and ran for the second tank. The .50s quieted, but it was already too late. The ROKs were retreating down the hill on a dead run. They had dropped the cerise panel where the fire had caught them at high tide.

Someone stopped them at the base of the hill, reformed them, and started them up again. Heath saw the line once more work its way gradually to the ridge crest. It got within a few yards of where the cerise panel blazed on the ridge. At that moment, the same two tanks opened fire on the men in the lead. This time the Koreans did not run down the hill. They turned about and walked down as if too tired even to beat a fast retreat. Heath saw some of them vent their disgust by heaving their weapons away as they fell back.

The Chinese came on promptly to re-enforce their now unpressed position. In clear sight, they walked brazenly along the skyline, not more than 350 yards from the Americans in the valley. One of the tanks which had come with Skeldon's Battalion thought the chance too good to miss and opened fire. In a jeep near the tank sat a colonel trying to use his radio. Heath heard him give the tankers holy hell for making too much noise while he was talking. The tank quit shooting, returned to the road, and tried to move forward.

From the hill, still a second Chinese machine gun clattered away, firing on a line straight toward the road. But an embankment interposed, and its merciful earth continued to collect the shower of enemy bullets while the Americans, a few yards beyond, felt neither sweat nor ricochets.

# 15

# Into the Gauntlet

Even when two thirds of its fighting power is gone, there is great weight to a division if it is formed up on the road, foot in mid-air, ready to complete its first stride toward the rear.

About noontime, General Keiser moved through his struck camp and got a feeling of this impetus as he proceeded to Sloane's position to get a personal view of the ridge-clearing maneuver. Sloane, uneasy about the situation, was casting about for some new approach to it—something halfway between a slow crawl through the hills and a full commitment via the road. He had just been on radio talking to the assistant division commander, General Bradley, about it. His suggestion was that the division operate a tank shuttle through the block, sending forth only a few thin-skinned vehicles at a time under the protection of one or two tanks. The idea was disapproved.

Keiser witnessed the ROK regiment's failure on the right flank. There was added irritation from the same direction; some of the Chinese had moved around Chung's open flank and were now firing toward the command post from the rear.

Keiser reckoned that the stalemate on the high ground made the road march something less than a calculated risk, but he still did not think that the price would be excessive. The Chinese forces in the vicinity of the command post had not shown any real fire power; they were harassing rather than hard-hitting. Besides, he believed that the linking with "Nottingham" would occur not far along the road. That was assumption only, as he had no information about the British location or strength. The two forces were not in radio contact; none had been attempted. Nor had Division received any indication of what wavelength to use in trying to raise its next neighbor down the road.

Two companies of Turks—remnant of the defeat in the north—got to Sloane's lines about the time that Keiser was striking his final balance. Sloane's ground was drawing increased fire from the ridges east of the road, where Item Company's attack had stalled earlier in the day. The Turks were directed to advance on this line and destroy the CCF positions; the 72nd's tanks would give them supporting fire.

Then Keiser personally gave Peploe the order to get his vehicles in motion. It was an oral message, the two men being together at the time. As Sloane put it, "The order changed the nature of the operation." The 9th had failed with a sweeper; the 38th would try with a bulldozer.

It also changed things diametrically for such men as still remained in Sloane's command. They were already deployed in the lower hills, flanking the road. The regimental Service Company and trains had gone out the day before; practically no organic transportation remained to lift the 9th. When the demarch through the center got underway, these men had to come down out of the hills and then, as individuals, find whatever space they could aboard the passing transport. So there is no 9th Regiment organizational experience to be recorded in the passage through the fire block. The regiment dissolved into its individuals, and they were as scattered as birdshot dropped from a hand.

During the last half hour of waiting, Heath, the young lieutenant who had been so anxious to see the armor hit the road, had suited his action to his words and, walking forward, had loaded on the lead tank of Skeldon's battalion.

Aboard it were Lieut. John Knight, Lieut. R. M. Rhotenberry, and eighteen enlisted men of George Company. Lieut.

James Mace, the tank commander, was on the .50 machine gun when the order was passed by Captain Hinton, after the relay from Peploe, for the tank to "How Able!" Mace did not leave the gun thereafter and he kept pumping lead forward whenever the tank came to a curve and flankward against every hillside which commanded the road.

The Turks assembled for their foray against the leftward ridges at just about the time the first tank got up speed.

There rode with this pathfinder all of the advantages which attend surprise and all of the moral handicaps which attend going first into an unknown situation. Due largely to officer steadiness, and particularly to Mace's handling of the machine-group problem, its performance was a total justification of the risk. Alone among all of the larger vehicles of the column, this tank got through to "Nottingham" with every member of its company aboard. They were badly scared and bruised, but otherwise unhurt.

Knight told his riflemen on the right of the tank to fire whenever they saw anything on their side which looked threatening, and the men on the left to do the same. They followed orders. Each man with an M1 was carrying full belt and an extra bandolier. The carbine men were low on magazines, but four full boxes were carried atop the hull. By the end of the run, all of this stuff had been used.

For perhaps 2,500 yards, Mace's tank raced along, knowing no real trouble. Five times during this first leg bullets spattered against the hull, coming at such intervals and in such numbers as to mark the presence of that many enemy machine guns, well spread out along the route. Knight and Rhotenberry sat next each other, inches apart. One burst of bullets ripped the paint from the hull in the space between them, where their legs dangled over the side.

Mace gave a yell, and from a 15-mile pace, the tank ground to a sudden stop. Directly ahead the road was fully blocked. In its center was an unmanned M39 utility carrier, and on the nigh side of it, partly off the road, an M4 tank and 2½-ton truck. *These stalled vehicles were pointed north.*

Machine-gun fire was now pouring in on the tank from both sides of the road. Knight shouted to his men to deploy in the ditches and take up fire immediately, which they did. Mace was working the machine gun and at the same time yelling orders to his driver.

In the matter of a minute or two the tank and the truck had been shunted off the shoulder. The carrier was something else; it was set square and wouldn't budge. The enemy guns kept pouring it in; they were at almost right angles to the line on which the tank had been moving, and from their positions on the gently sloped flanking ridges had about a 30-degree angle of fire against the tank and the thin-skinned vehicles now blocking on its rear.

Heath jumped out to see what could be done about the carrier. It was in perfect condition, fully loaded and mounting four guns. Just then he heard a moan from the ditch off to his right. It was a Turkish soldier. He lay on his back, and in one hand he feebly waved an empty canteen, while he whispered over and over, "Me Turk, me Turk, me Turk." Heath shouted for water; there was none in the party. So Heath shook his head and pointed rearward in an attempt to indicate help was coming. A bullet had gone through the man's belly, another through his shoulder. The clotted blood on his jacket had turned black, which meant he had been there many hours. That discovery hit Heath like a kick in the groin. He saw in a flash that it signified the Chinese had held the ridges to a depth of three miles *or more* for at least thirty-six hours and the division was walking into a giant trap. But the column was already committed; there could no longer be thought of turning back.

As he climbed aboard the carrier, a bullet knocked his rifle from his hand and carried it under the tank. He lowered himself into the driver's compartment and looked for any kind of lever which might release the laterals, finally locating two levers right next his head. He thrust them forward, then jumped out, and the tank pushed the carrier into the ditch.

Despite a bullet storm, Mace waited there, standing in his turret until Knight had gathered all of his infantrymen aboard; in no other tank in the column was this same care exercised, which failure accounted for much of the division's loss.

The tank started. At the moment of take-off an F-51 came in so close to it with strafing fire that it must have hit next the Turkish soldier in the ditch. One rocket exploded right next the tank. The concussion lifted one rifleman bodily from the hull and he was airborne when his companions grabbed him and pulled him back. It also blinded Heath in one eye, though several days later his sight came back. The tank was passing other ruined vehicles along the road. They wore the markings of the Turkish Army.

Perhaps six minutes had sped by while Heath had performed his act of courage and the column waited. They are among the most costly six minutes in the fighting experience of Americans. By design or accident, one carrier forming a roadblock had transformed the situation. With the enemy gauntlet firmly established, the column's one chance for successful survival was that it could barrel on through, losing a vehicle now and then, but never giving the enemy a broadside standing target which would enable him to perfect his adjustment on the road. One wait killed that possibility, and all of the other waits, and hurts, misery, and death which followed came partly of it. In one serial after another, the jeeps and trucks, kitchens and ambulances, which were spliced in between the tanks, like chicks following a hen, had braked to a stop. There was nothing to spare them from the fire, save the inaccuracy of the Chinese gunners off the flanks. When any of the work vehicles were wrecked by bullets or mortar bursts, it became a block to the column, and its riders became castaways, trying to hitchhike out of Hades. When a tank halted because the traffic had blocked, its infantry riders took to the ditches, to survive if possible and to fight back as best they could. But when the way opened again, the tank

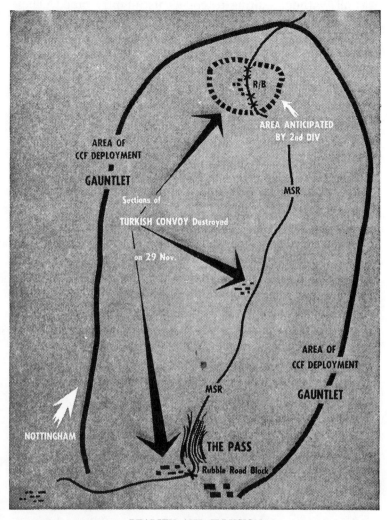

**REALITY AND ILLUSION**

On 30 November, 2nd Division's column expected to break through a shallow enemy position. Instead, it was enveloped full length by a Chinese division already holding the ridges commanding its line of march.

was off, without waiting to collect its infantry brood. These were among the things which doubly scrambled a command lacking tactical unity at the outset. Of the contingent which traveled on the third tank in column, only ten of twenty-two men got through. From the second tank, not one infantryman survived. These were typical of the day's score.

Mace's tank ran on southward, drawing fire and giving it back. Approximately 6,000 yards airline beyond the departure line, it came at last to the highest point on the Kunuri-Sunchon road. This was "The Pass," a defile about one quarter mile long where the road ran through a cut with steep embankments of dirt and loose rock rising 50 feet above the right-of-way.

Heath could feel that Mace's men had gone suddenly jittery. He yelled to the infantry: "Look out for bazookas!" and they responded by firing toward the hill caps as fast as they could pull trigger. Just as they entered the slot, they saw a few Chinese running off to the left, range 75 yards. Knight shouted: "Give 'em hell!" but they were lost to sight behind the hill before the Americans could get a clear sight. A spattering of rifle fire swept over the tank as it ran through the cut. At the end, it passed a group of six Chinese squatting at meal; they had disappeared behind the rocks before anyone could sight on them. To the right were more wrecked Turkish vehicles pointed northward.

Then came the final scare—an artillery shell burst on the hill just above the tank. Heath thought this was the enemy coup de grâce—an artillery enfilade pointed right on "The Pass," and he yelled to Mace: "Give it everything!" Five hundred yards farther down the hill they came to another roadblock, three vehicles formed into a barricade and topped with trunks, spare tires, mattresses, and other weights. The tank rammed it at full speed and rode over and on; the jeeps which followed had less fortune.

Around the next bend in the road, all hands tensed as they saw a tank coming at them. It was friendly. Nottingham's outposts were just beyond it. The British brigade, heavily engaged to the south of "The Pass" throughout the morning, had fired the artillery round which exploded on the hill as Mace's tank came through, in an effort to keep this final door from banging shut.

So closing to within friendly lines, Knight's party at last knew the worst of it—or at least thought so. Instead of dealing with a shallow enemy roadblock, the division was moving into a fire gauntlet more than six miles via the road. But the intervening ridges prevented Mace's sending back along the column a radio description of what had been learned. It would have done little good in any case since the column was already in the middle of its ordeal, and what Knight's party had seen and felt was only a fraction of the tactical reality. Mace's tank had simply breezed through. Its bout with the fire could have signified the presence of not more than one thinly deployed battalion of the enemy.

The speed of the run had been deceptive. Somewhere between thirty and forty machine guns and about ten mortars were either already bearing on the road or about to go into position as the Chinese build-up continued. At least one Chinese division was engaged in tightening the noose. All of these estimates are based upon numbers seen, and fire experienced, by men within the serials farther back in the American column. The pin-pointing of that many weapons could be done with reasonable accuracy since the pattern of their use was quite consistent throughout the day. Nowhere did the Chinese set up a gun to fire head-on at the column and enfilade it, though the frequent road turnings were favorable to that employment. They chose only sites from which they could broadside it, which gave the gunners more immunity, but, by reducing the angle of fire, probably lessened its over-all effectiveness.

But it is a small point, for their weapons were efficient enough. By the time Mace had reached Nottingham, the division had been dealt such punishment that all along its length men knew they had risked a shower and drawn the lightning. Whether by accident or design, the Chinese attack was timed and regulated so as to serve first as a lure and then a bludgeon. Before the column jumped off, the enemy fire was so irregular as to create an illusion of general weakness; but as promptly as division's forward serials were committed to the road, this changed with the speed of light and the fire build-up in the command post area became intense in volume, and spread steadily over a greater radius.

Small-arms and machine-gun fire ranged in on the flat ground from the ridges on both sides of the road compelling the infantry already loaded on the tanks and waiting for the "go" signal to jump down and head for the ditches. Then salvoed mortar fire began to shake the earth around the command post and the idling tanks. It did not come in clusters but was obviously fired from one battery of four tubes, since there were simultaneous hits in that number at various points. Between thirty and forty rounds were fired in this shoot. The chief victims were among the ROK soldiers and among several hundred civilian refugees who were gathered in a compact mass waiting for the road to clear. The 72nd's tanks, which had been readying to hit the road with some of Peploe's troops, had to return to fire positions to shell the ridges. That delayed the departure of Fox Company and put increased stress on its leader, M/S Owen McGregor. Lieut. Joseph F. Roiux, who had joined Fox only the day before, was with the company, but in the night action he had been hit by fragments from a rocket, and was still dazed and almost speechless. So McGregor had taken over. When the mortar fire felled several score of the Koreans, not having already enough to do, McGregor helped rig a first-aid station and clear the wounded. This was the easiest hour that he was to know during the day.

As to the column, the details of how it became broken up and disorganized toward the total scrambling of its personnel, which in turn produced greater losses and the evaporation of all tactical unity, are illuminated by what happened among the vehicles which immediately followed Mace's tank. Their experience was recurrent in other parts of the train through-

out the afternoon and night, only as more vehicles became
knocked out along the route, thereby requiring a greater number of ditching operations under fire, and more frequent stalls
or turnouts by the vehicles which were still mobile, the fragmentation of the groups steadily accelerated, more men were
hit by the Chinese fire, and the drain upon nerve and body
proceeded ever closer to the point of total exhaustion.

When the first tank stopped to clear the M39, the men on
the second tank bailed out to the roadside. Capt. Jason E.
Forney was two vehicles behind them, riding a jeep. The machine-gun fire was beating against the thin-skinned vehicles;
their occupants deployed to the ditches. Forney worked up
the ditch to a group of eight men from Skeldon's A&P platoon, who had been riding the tank under Lieut. Dallas
Clayton. They were acting like soldiers and concentrating
their rifle fire against one machine gun on the left of the
road. As the block opened, suddenly the second tank whisked
away, leaving all of its riders stranded. A machine gun from
the right now joined the fire. Forney started walking up the
road with the eight men. Two of them were struck and killed.
Other lighter vehicles in the wake of the tank also made a
dash for it, stranding their riders. Forney saw some of the
firers take out after them as hard as they could run, until
they fell in the roadway or realized the hopelessness of the
chase.

Forney yelled to the men to get down in the ditches; he
saw an air strike coming in and figured as an off chance that
if it singed the hills commanding this strip of road, there
would be a lull in the enemy fire. That was how it happened. For about eight minutes no vehicles came by; the
column had blocked again farther back. Then the planes
strafed both ridges. A tank running empty, having already
shaken its riders, appeared around the bend. Forney stopped
it and got the stranded infantrymen aboard. He jumped
aboard the trailer of a jeep which was following the tank.
There were already seven men aboard; all were actively firing
toward the ridges, except one man who lay flat on his back

reading a prayer book. Forney said: "Give me a piece of that."

The incident was typical. Still, the scrambling and break-down of the infantry units was not due primarily to irreso-lution on the part of the tankers. They were at grips with an unprecedented situation. Having been told to keep mov-ing, they were forced at intervals, by the blocking of the column, to stand and fight. When the road opened again, each commander had to make the snap decision whether to wait for the regrouping of his riders, and thus further stall the vehicles to his rear, or take off and desert one small group for the benefit of the majority. In the nature of the case, some made the wrong decision. The true fault was that nowhere in the column was there any unity of command. Each small-unit leader was trying to manage his own group, but none was given authority over both his men and the elements which moved them. Control had also slipped from the hands of the senior leaders. Battalion commanders had no radio contact with their companies. At exceptional risk, they could double along the column to see how the men were faring, but when they did that, they ran the chance of throwing another block against it. So whenever the pinch came, the tankers had to act in the dark.

Lieutenant Hollingsworth, and the men of George Com-pany who had come along in the third tank, saw how these things worked out. Just before the second tank had deserted its infantry group, they had seen one rifleman break from the ditch and try to board it. The fire from the enemy gun cut into the road just like a scythe as it reached for him and finally struck him down. Hollingsworth's men were already in the ditch, strung out rearward of their tank for about 30 yards. They had noted that the armor was attracting most of the Chinese fire. One rifleman—he had joined the com-pany only the day before and Hollingsworth didn't know his name—sang out: "Hey, lieutenant, I seen where they're shoot-ing from." The kid was firing his M1 like mad at a spot on the ridge not more than 300 yards away. The other riflemen joined him. Hollingsworth ran to the tank and got the gunner to swing his .50 against the same target. They knocked the gun out; within perhaps ten minutes the Chinese had another machine gun firing from the same spot. Hollingsworth had no chance to check the ditches for casualties. But when they loaded again, he found he was seven men short, though he was never to learn how they became lost. The others went on. (This is the same apple-cheeked youngster who had fought so bravely when the battle opened; he was later KIA.)

It was not greatly different from the ride of Mace's group, except that the enemy guns, having had their warm-up shoot, now knew the level and were pounding their slugs home. As the tank passed the wrecked convoy, the rifleman sitting to the right of Cpl. Jacob Schnabel got a bullet through his chest. Schnabel put an arm around him and held him on. A few minutes later, the man to his left got hit through the groin. Schnabel, age 44, grabbed for him also. The man was wholly inert and the weight was too much; together, the three men slipped closer to the edge of the hull. The man screamed: "Let me go, let me go," and at last, having no choice, Schnabel released his hold, and the man pitched face forward from the speeding tank onto the side of the road. Almost at the same instant the man on Schnabel's right got a second bullet in the back, coming from the other direction, and it tore him loose from Schnabel's grasp and spilled him on the roadway. Pfc. Allen H. Hix took one bullet through the arm and another through his leg; he continued firing, not saying a word to the others, and they didn't know he had been hit until the ride was over. Two of the ROKs were struck by bullets as the tank sped uphill toward "The Pass." Then Schnabel was hit, and the new kid who had spotted the CCF machine gun took one in the shoulder. Though the deck was getting slippery with blood, the survivors, to Hollingsworth's amazement, were still chins up. On making the sharp right turn at "The Pass," they were on top of the second tank (still running empty) and had struck it before their own mount could stop. No real damage was done to the metal. Hollingsworth enjoyed hearing his men yell, "Get out of our way, you lousy sons-of-bitches!" and other endearing greetings. They rode on toward the British lines with a score for the run which could be told in neat round figures—five whole-bodied men among the ten who survived of the twenty who had started.

The trucks and jeeps between the second and third tanks had varying fortunes. Some were destroyed when the M39 forced the first halt. A few bullets through a radiator, gas tank, or the rubber usually meant a car down, a group of infantrymen stranded, and the need for another ditching operation if the column was to get by. Those who were left and could not flag a passing vehicle came gradually together as they drifted by instinct away from the fire-beaten zones toward the most convenient defilade. But they were all strangers to each other, and though they had the strength of numbers, they lacked the common bond of understanding which might have enabled them to organize and proceed by fire and movement to neutralize the nearest Chinese gun positions.

What happened to vehicles and men on that day provides an interesting spot check of machine-gun effectiveness at the varying ranges, and many of the findings are at odds with the field manuals. The killing guns—those which destroyed both motors and men—were invariably sited at anywhere between 200 and 500 yards from the roadway. There were others which fired at 600 to 800 yards' range. They had little or no effect. The bursts did not even disconcert the passengers or those who were moving afoot. The fire from these more distant guns was invariably high or short, and it usually stayed that way. Much of it was plunging fire, but the drop from weapon to target cannot wholly account for the high degree of inaccuracy. Nor could the dust cloud which enveloped the column explain it. The distances were simply too great for the eye of the gunner to see where his stuff was striking; hence the capability of the weapon in itself mattered little.

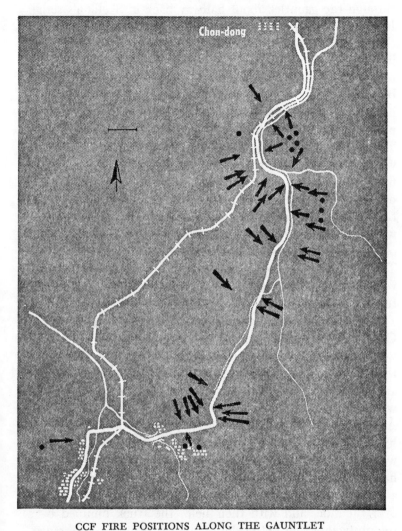

CCF FIRE POSITIONS ALONG THE GAUNTLET

Only the machine guns and mortars which were definitely located are shown on the chart. The black dots denote mortars.

Capt. George W. Isenberg and Capt. James J. Casey jeeped through the gauntlet about halfway back in Skeldon's serial. Isenberg had started out in a jeep with Skeldon. But when they passed a group of wounded men, Skeldon loaded them in his vehicle and took off afoot. Isenberg then hitched a ride with Casey. When the head of the column was stopped by the M39 carrier, their jeep was around the bend, several hundred yards to rear of it. That part of the column was promptly brought under fire by a machine gun to the east. This was a different gun from any thus far mentioned. It was sited on a ridge about 600 yards away, and though its fire continued to traverse along the line of the road, no real damage was done. Immediately the column resumed motion, these same vehicles made their run through the ambuscade where the three (and later four) enemy guns had set up overlooking the M39 and other wrecked Turkish vehicles. These were much closer—300 to 400 yards. A number of the vehicles in Isenberg's sight were hit and wrecked while going full speed ahead. His own escaped unscathed.

When the jeep raced through "The Pass," Isenberg and Casey fired their M1s as fast as they could pull trigger; such was the steepness of the embankments that it seemed to them they were aiming straight upward. As they moved downhill and approached the half-down barrier of wrecked vehicles where Mace had bulled his way through, the traffic blocked. Ahead of them a ¾-ton had been towing a jeep which had had its radiator and gas tank riddled by bullets. The barrier was high in the center and was flat only where the tank treads had hit it. The truck made a run for it, hit hard, stalled for a moment—then the towline snapped. Its passengers swarmed over the side, and with their help, the truck bumped over the obstacle. From both sides of the road, and at close range, rifle fire was coming in on the stalled cars. Several men in the wrecked jeep were hit and the others sprang from it and ran down the road. Isenberg's jeep made a fast run at the barrier and cleared it after a terrific bump. But in the split second spent on the passage, Isenberg noticed that the barrier was composed partly of cases of ammunition. They made the hairpin turn near the bottom of the hill, just prior to reaching the British lines. Machine-gun fire from the direct rear ripped through the body of the jeep as it rounded the curve.

The hour was approximately 1430. The fire by this gun marked the beginning of the effort by the Chinese to ring "The Pass" with machine guns and thereby seal the bottle at its neck. Whether they had previously overlooked the importance of this terrain feature or had timed their move with the object of squeezing hardest after the artillery was on the road can only be conjectured. But the build-up now starting around "The Pass" was to reach its climax in the late hours of the day.

As hard as were the conditions, individual Americans met the crisis with their accustomed fortitude, bulwarked by a sense of humor which is often the salvation of our troops in any hour of pressure. Sgt. Johnny Lewis of HQ Company, Third Battalion, was trying to run a jeep on one flat when his group got into their second batch of machine-gun fire. A rifleman in the back seat got a bullet through his leg; Lewis stopped the jeep and got into the ditch to give the wounded man first aid. He wouldn't take it. He said: "No, you guys keep moving; I'll fix myself up and catch another vehicle after a while." By then, several more bullets had finished Lewis' jeep. The group did a snake-crawl down the ditch for about one mile, and finally hitched a ride in a 2½-ton truck. A short distance further along, the convoy again came under machine-gun fire, and bullets hit into the road next the truck. A mail clerk aboard the truck turned to one of the riflemen saying, "I almost forgot—here's a letter I been holding for you. Take it while there's still time to read." The kid replied: "Kiss me! But you picked you a helluva time to play post office."

Pfc. James H. Sefton was also riding a 2½-ton. A machine gun had been firing against the convoy steadily on one given line. The fire switched suddenly, came right down on the truck, and split the beam on the sideboard. Part of it fell on the head of the man next Sefton. He said: "That seems to be the signal to get out." Then he jumped from the truck, and they never saw him again.

But while the front runners had their difficulties, they ran in luck compared to the vehicles which pushed off in their wake. Only the first section of Hinton's tanks, trying to shepherd the forward elements in Skeldon's battalion, got away to a running start. As happened to Fox Company under Sergeant McGregor, the men of Easy Company, under Capt. John B. Yount, became engaged and stalled by the Chinese mortar fire which beat upon their vehicles while still at the line of departure. The men unloaded and took to the ditches so that the tanks could shell the ridges and damper the fire. They were still engaged in this long-range effort when the two companies of Turks advanced against the ridges to the left of the road. The Turk line attacked boldly up the first hill, losing a few men as it moved, but still going strongly as it passed over the skyline. Already the mortar fire against the vehicles assembled on the low ground had stopped, and there was a marked diminution in the small-arms fire from the ridges.

The tankers yelled to the infantry to load, and quickly Easy and Fox started on their way through the gauntlet. They got perhaps 600 yards before they were stopped by a block somewhere ahead in the column. But even as they rolled forward to that point, they saw the Turks streaming back in great disorder across the hill which they had previously taken. Come to the second ridge, the Turks had withered under the fire of two well-placed machine guns. These weapons were not bearing directly against the vehicle train carrying Easy and Fox. Yount had already told his men that when the tanks stopped they were to deploy to the roadside ditches and start shooting, to forestall any Chinese attempt to close on the column. They were thus engaged when of a sudden their tanks took off at full speed.

This was done without warning to the men. Seeing the way become open, the tanks ran for it. Only two of Easy's men managed to board the first tank; the second one ran empty. Their flight dissolved the company. Some men started legging it toward "The Pass." Others stayed fast and waited for any vehicle that might give them space. But from that moment on, they neither functioned as a group nor fared well as individuals. Of the forty-two men who started, only seventeen got through to Sunchon. One of them was SFC Virgil L. Leggett, who hitched a ride on a jeep. By the time Leggett's party had crossed "The Pass" and begun the descent toward Nottingham, the Chinese fire from the ridges against the roadway where the enemy had built the rubble roadblock was very intense, though their skirmishers had not yet fastened on the heights above the cut. Ten vehicles were blocked back of the rubble pile because the driver and riders of a ¾-ton truck had abandoned their vehicle there in the face of the fire. While one machine gun from near the ridge top and enemy riflemen from the foreground continued to bang away at the stalled trucks and jeeps, Leggett's party took to the ditches. They were there for about ten minutes. Leggett could see twenty or thirty Chinese in foxholes up the ridge slope not more than 60 yards away; one man, apparently an officer, was walking among them shouting orders.

The informal skirmish line in the roadside ditch got busy with rifles and carbines. The men on Leggett's immediate right and left were struck by bullets, as were several others. But the Chinese began to back away as the fire exchange took toll of their number. A Negro MP climbed into the ¾-ton, put it in reverse and ditched it, so that the other vehicles could clear. But several others had been ruined during the stall and had to be ditched also. There were now five men in Leggett's jeep and five in the trailer. Two of its casings had been blown out by bullets. Though it almost overturned in mounting the rubble heap, it finished the run in a slow crawl and delivered the party into friendly lines.

Follow along again with M/S McGregor, still trying to hold together his handful of survivors from Fox Company, aboard the careening tank. His vehicle once more halted as it came to the bend in the road where the two other tanks had stopped to engage the ridges with fire, blocking the passage. McGregor's tank engaged, and so to save his men, McGregor wearily led them to the roadside ditch, deployed them, and told them to fire. Lacking visible targets, they aimed at brush patches and rock outcroppings, just on the chance that their bullets might find flesh. For perhaps ten minutes this seemingly useless exercise continued. Someone yelled: "Let's go!" The men loaded, and the armor churned along, the tankers continuing to fire the .50s at the ridgetops as they moved.

Conditions could hardly have been worse. The dust cloud raised by the tanks seared the lungs and inflamed the tear ducts, so that men were half blinded. In the fierce cold, the tank's metal numbed the fingers, and it became ever more difficult to hold on. Even so, the Americans who still held rifles rode mittenless through the ten above zero weather, and the trigger fingers, thus kept ready, pulled against any likely target. Not so the ROK fighters in the group. McGregor noted that they rode heads down, hands holding on as if in mortal terror of being thrown loose.

At about midafternoon, the tank passed the stalled M39 carrier and started across a flat stretch. This was the deadfall. A steep, elongated hogback ran parallel to the road 200 yards to east of it. Two machine guns partway up the slope were zeroed in at just the right height to singe the riders. The earlier vehicles had felt fire at this point in the run; it is therefore a reasonable presumption that these were the same guns which had menaced Mace, the deadliest links in an ever-tightening circle.

McGregor heard bullets hitting the tank's side, with a buzz as from a bee swarm. Three of the ROKs riding in the lower portion at the rear were struck and fell onto the road. The tank stopped. Its commander yelled to McGregor: "Get the men off and walk alongside; we'll screen you." McGregor took a hasty glance at the three ROKs. He guessed they were dead. So he left them and moved with the tank, as it did the first fifteen yards slowly. Suddenly it speeded up. McGregor yelled, "We can't keep up." The commander shouted back: "I've got to get to hell out of here." McGregor's men ran, some few managing to scramble aboard, others missing the lunge and falling flat in the roadside, still others just trying to keep abreast it and so escape the fire.

This wretched race lasted perhaps 70 yards. Then the tank sideswiped a jeep abandoned by the roadside. The collision hurled the jeep directly into the path of the running men, and they went down like tenpins. Others who were trailing the tank piled up violently against its hull. Some lay flat and did not move again; others picked themselves up, tried to limp away, and were cut down by the machine-gun fire. Mc-Gregor was knocked out momentarily as he struck the jeep and fell, under a pile of his own ROK soldiers. When he came to, the tank was lost to sight in the dust cloud up the road, but he could still see two or three of his men shagging along in its wake. His own legs were spent.

He ducked behind the jeep and trailer to escape the machine guns, which had continued tracing up and down the road. As he flopped down, he found himself between a dead GI and two who were wounded. One had taken a bullet through the stomach; he died within five minutes while Mc-Gregor patted his hand. The other man had been hit in the leg. He said to McGregor: "I think in a few minutes I'll be able to get up and run for a vehicle." McGregor looked at the leg; someone had slapped a bandage on it. But the bone was broken and part of it stuck out through the flesh. McGregor said: "We'd better take it easy for a while." Now more vehicles came whizzing by them; it seemed to McGregor that hundreds of them passed him. He called and called, attempting to stop them, but it did no good, and at last his throat became so sore from the strain and the dust that he could call no more. The machine guns were still blazing away at the road and their close-in fire had turned the flat into· a speedway.

McGregor said to his companion: "I think our best chance is to lay flat and play dead." They stayed there motionless for somewhat more than an hour. Another tank came by at full speed, and just as it passed, a GI was shot from its hull and pitched outward toward the jeep. His boot caught in the track as he fell and the machine wrenched part of the leg away. He landed in a pool of gasoline which had flowed from the bullet-riddled jeep, and his head struck violently against the rear wheel. McGregor reached out and pulled him in. He had time to note that the man had been shot through the stomach. The man uttered two low moans and died in McGregor's arms.

As if in a dream, McGregor saw Skeldon walking straight toward him down the road. He tried to yell to Skeldon to get down, but his voice was gone. The machine guns suddenly opened fire again; they missed Skeldon, but he hit the ditch promptly. McGregor said nothing as he went past, keeping low on the far side of the road.

McGregor felt that he couldn't take it any more. He said to the wounded man: "I'm going to try and rejoin the company." The answer came: "Go ahead! You can do nothing more for me." Another tank came along. It was moving moderately slow. McGregor moved along in its shadow for about 50 yards, unable to summon the strength to climb aboard.

The tank speeded up. As it passed beyond him, McGregor found new cover off to the right of the road. This was a grader ditch about 300 yards long, perhaps three feet deep, and wide enough for the body of a man, if he lay parallel to its course.

From end to end, this sanctuary was already filled with bodies, the living and the dead, wounded men who could no longer move, the exhausted who were trying to rest, the able-bodied driven to earth by the fire. It was the sump pit of all who, like McGregor, had become detached from their vehicles and abandoned to each other. There were perhaps 200 men in the ditch so that the bodies overlapped. Americans, Turks, and ROKs, their identities had become for the hour almost indistinguishable, and many who still lived lay almost as motionless as the corpses.

Yet McGregor at last saw that there was cooperative motion and human response even in this shattered mass. The men who were still partly mobile crawled forward along the chain of bodies toward the upper end of the ditch. As they moved, those who were down and hurt cried: "Water! Water!" or "First aid! First aid!" Long since, nearly all canteens had been drained dry. But McGregor witnessed how the able-bodied checked long enough to do what bandaging they could as they made the upward climb; there were some who stripped to the waist in the bitter cold and tore up their undershirts to use them for dressings. He saw others stop their crawl long enough to give their last drop of water to the man under them. And with a boost from a leg or an arm, the wounded who were bound to the ditch tried to assist the passage of the able-bodied seeking mainly to get out. It was like human cargo making slow progress on a moving belt of its own kind. In his dark hour McGregor saw more of the decency of men than he had ever expected to find.

McGregor, like the others, looked for water. He took a canteen from a dead ROK. It was bone dry, as if its owner had sucked the last sweet drop before death took him. He tried it with a second dead man, but had no better success. Vehicles continued to race by and dust settled on the ditch in such showers that all faces and all uniforms looked alike. As a truck or tank passed alongside the ditch, a few men would break from it and reach for a handhold. A few made it. Others were mangled in the attempt. Sometimes they tried to board carriers already so fully loaded that the riders kicked or pushed them away and they fell violently back into the ditch.

Here was a grandstand view of the ruin of part of the column. The machine guns on the enemy ridge still held the road in a vise. Some of the cars attempting to race past did not make it. Their tires were blown apart, their radiators destroyed by the rain of bullets, as they came abreast of their foundered comrades. Having pulled off to the roadside, the occupants were sometimes cut down by another burst of fire before they could make it to the ditch. There was a gradual pile-up of vehicles the length of the ditch which served it as an added revetment.

McGregor saw a six-by-six driving hard along the slot. He stood and waved. It slowed down for him because the center man in the front seat was his battalion surgeon, Captain Benton. The surgeon and the man on his right were firing M1s as the truck moved. McGregor was so spent that when he hit the running board he fell over in their laps and remained there. They rested their rifles on his body and continued fire as the truck raced on. For a few minutes McGregor slept.

For the rest of the afternoon the grader ditch continued to draw men like a magnet, some going there to lie down and die from wounds, and others to rally strength briefly before continuing the struggle for life.

Sgt. John Furst of Headquarters Company, Third Battalion, 38th, had started out on a kitchen truck. It was shot from under him by a machine gun concealed in a cornfield. He started hiking, then hitched aboard a jeep trailer. When the trailer neared the stalled M39, the jeep began zigzagging all over the road. Furst realized that the driver had been struck, and he jumped off just before the vehicle ran off the shoulder and overturned. Machine-gun fire was raking the embankment on that side—prohibitively. Furst was tired; he sat down on the opposite embankment, where the enemy gun had no chance to reach him. Out in the center of a rice paddy, 75 yards away, Furst saw one of his own company cooks, sitting on the ice and talking to three other GIs. Furst joined them. At that moment, automatic fire swept in on them from another gun on the same side of the road. Furst had no time to duck. He heard two piercing screams right next him. The other three men had slumped over. He knew they were hit; he didn't wait to see if they were dead. On a dead run, he started for the road, and a hundred yards up the line he saw the grader ditch and jumped for it. The machine-gun fire had followed him all the way. As he went headlong into the ditch, one bullet landed under him, kicked up a rock, and cut his face. He stayed in the ditch for perhaps an hour, slowly working his way to the far end. At last he felt a little better. He returned to the road and kept putting one foot in front of the other until he heard a friendly voice and knew he had arrived at Nottingham.

Having started with Skeldon's rear element, Captain Hinton, who commanded the 38th's tanks, rode a jeep through the gauntlet. As with most of the other vehicles which remained mobile, it was a leapfrogging journey. When blocking occurred, the carriers which were in position to do so pushed out and around the cars which had been either knocked out or were idling while their riders sought cover. Thus the scrambling of the convoy, not only as to men but as to motors, was continuous.

Hinton was back of Fox Company when the first block occurred. He hit the ditch along with McGregor's men. There was little choice in the matter; according to Hinton, there were three machine guns beating a crossfire on the road, two from about 300 yards' distance and the third at longer range. CCF riflemen were firing from the same positions, a point proved to Hinton's satisfaction when one bullet buried itself in his wristwatch, numbing his arm. He worked the bullet loose; it was about .28 caliber, an explosive round with a detonating point sticking out the end.

At least four times the column stalled again before Hinton's jeep got half through the gauntlet. He had worked some distance forward and was running just to the rear of two of his own riderless tanks. There occurred another block, this time in a defile, just short of "The Pass." Suddenly the roadway swarmed with Chinese; they had appeared right out of the rolling ground and were making for the vehicles at a dead run. Three jumped aboard the forward tank. Two were shot off it by riflemen before they could do any damage. The third man, grenade in hand, reached for the hatch. From within the tank someone yanked the hatch shut. It sheared off the grenadier's fingers as it closed, and just then he got a bullet through his head and pitched onto the road. From just off the side of the road a 2.36 bazooka let go at the second tank, and the round missed it by inches. Skeldon had walked right into the middle of this mêlée. He saw forty to fifty of the enemy in one skirmish line coming straight toward him, firing rifles and tommy guns as they bobbed along over the uneven ground. Nearer still, not more than thirty yards away, one Chinese stood in his foxhole, firing a rifle. Skeldon drew a bead on him, and he went down. But the others kept coming, still pumping lead. Such was the noise from the fire fight that Hinton couldn't hear his radio, though at the moment the tank commanders were all trying to get him for instructions. From the ditches, scratch groups of infantrymen were in full action, trying to save the day with rifle and carbine fire. But they were outnumbered ten to one; Hinton had seen at least 200 Chinese charging the position. The tanks were all but powerless to help. Their pieces were fouled by the sides of the ravine, and with only about 20 degrees of traverse on each side of the center line, they couldn't bear on the Chinese until they were practically atop the American skirmishers.

At that moment the American air came over and went straight for the mark. Their rocket fire was put so close to the road that one round stunned Lieut. Tom Turner, Hinton's executive officer, and put him unconscious in the ditch, where he lay for the next hour or so. But other rounds landed right amid the advancing Chinese. Their line wavered and then turned. The tanks backed out of the defile and got both their artillery pieces and the .50s into action within a few seconds. While they blasted away at the Chinese backs, the air was laying it on from overhead with rockets and napalm. Those who participated in this one brief open fight of the day said of it: "None of the enemy had a chance to get away." Skeldon hitched a ride the rest of the way, urged on by the feeling that he could best help the division pull through by getting things organized at the far end.

But the ride seemed almost endless, and there was seldom a respite in the Chinese fire which beat upon the road. Skeldon noted that toward the end of the run, his own riders were beaten down and listless, making no attempt to return the fire. On his own ¾-ton, space became so cramped as more and more men tried to climb aboard that the party kept checking on every man who had been hit; if they could feel no heartbeat, the body was removed to the roadside to make room for someone still living. Skeldon said: "We passed many American casualties but there was no point in stopping to check whether they were dead or only wounded. Both behind and in front of me, I saw vehicles in which none but the driver was in a normal position; on some of the trailers, even, the prone men were stacked three deep."

When he reached Nottingham, Skeldon's first act was to get his own tanks turned around and moving toward the south end of the gauntlet from where they could shell the heights above "The Pass," thereby assisting the passage of the remainder of the column. The artillery got into the act not a moment too soon, as the Chinese were now concentrating strength toward this natural cul-de-sac.

Some of Skeldon's wounded who had preceded him through the gauntlet had been too exhausted to leave the armor and look for medical help. Skeldon got them loaded on a truck and accompanied them to Nottingham's field hospital.

A British surgeon asked: "How many wounded have already come through?"

Said Skeldon: "At least 100 from my Regiment alone, and that's only the down payment."

That was a conservative estimate, but the news was bad enough for a hospital staff which was already out of bandages, plasma, and most medicines, because of the excessive expenditures of the past few hours. Nottingham also had been hit in a bit of a bloody mess.

Lieut. Col. Harold V. Maixner's Third Battalion—numbering sixty-three men—started the run on eleven jeeps and one ¾-ton truck. This convoy got one and one-half miles along the road before it was halted. Two machine guns on a ridge 600 yards to the eastward and a line of Chinese skirmishers not more than 150 yards to the westward had caught the column in a crossfire, and several tanks ahead of the battalion had stopped to fight it out. Maixner's men deployed to the ditches to gain cover. For perhaps thirty minutes this static situation continued. Peploe, overhauling Maixner, broke it up. He jeeped on forward, after telling Maixner that it was imperative to get in motion again as quickly as possible. Under his spurring, the tanks were soon doubling back along the column. Maixner halted them, pointed out the ridge where the Chinese machine guns were operating, and told them to fire away. As the tanks worked it over, an air strike came in and hit the same ridge with rockets and napalm.

Then Maixner got one tank pointed southward again and told the commander to get going and move around any vehicles which were in the way. He yelled to his men that he was starting, and they were to load and come along. But five of his jeeps had been knocked out during the wait, and eight or nine of his men were wounded. Those with lesser wounds were piled on the trailers of the vehicles still mobile; a few had been hit so bad that they had to be left in the ditch. The convoy started again with riders on every jeep hood.

From there on the fire from the flanks built up steadily in intensity, the worst of it coming when the convoy entered "The Pass." A machine gun on the west side of the cut was boring straight down the slot, its bullets chipping off slabs of slate from the cliffside and showering them on the riders. At closer range, from the clifftop, the Chinese snipers took toll. Three of the men riding with Maixner were hit. He stayed at the wheel and kept pounding forward until suddenly the pilot tank stopped. Maixner jumped out to see what was wrong. Ahead of the tank, a jeep had been hit by fire and knocked out just as it came abreast an already immobilized 2½-ton truck, thus blocking the road.

The tank started forward toward the jeep, with the object of running it down and crushing it. At that moment, Maixner saw a human foot projecting from under the jeep's trailer. Maixner yelled at the top of his voice. By some miracle the tank driver heard him and braked. But it was a split second late. The tank track had squashed the foot flat. Its owner, a colored soldier, already hit by a bullet through the abdomen, had crawled under the trailer to escape the fire. He lay there screaming: "Kill me! I can't stand the pain." The tank backed away and freed the leg. There was no room in the convoy for the wounded man. They laid him down under the dubious cover of the stalled truck, and turned to other things.

There was fresh fire from a machine gun forward along the left embankment. Maixner had the tank fan this slope with its .50 for about ten minutes before continuing on. The tank rammed the jeep and left it crumpled in the roadway. The lighter cars skirted around it. The convoy rolled on toward Nottingham.

In this small incident were all of the elements of the greater drama at "The Pass" which shortly followed. The Chinese had at last clamped on the heights in their bid to seal the gauntlet at its end by concentrated automatic fire. Within "The Pass" itself, the column was becoming ever more slowed and choked by the weight of its own ruined metal and human debris.

Maixner's battalion was the last large group to make this part of the run in relative freedom of action. The door banged shut after them at about the time they got to friendly lines. They had started as a "battalion" of sixty-three men; they were now forty-five.

## *16*

# Trouble in "The Pass"

Just as in classical Greek tragedy events move toward their predestined course, so the actors in this drama,
however courageous and selfless, were powerless to change
the result.

Once troops entered the gauntlet, they had to keep strain-
ing forward. The alternative was to abandon hope and for-
sake any useful part in the salvage operation. Merely to keep
moving required greater resolution than to take cover and
await what developed. The strong made that choice; some of
the weak rejected it, waited overlong for help which did not
come, and paid the price of death or capture. The reader
must judge whether, in what was done, American honor was
sustained by the action of the majority.

In the memories of those who made the journey, there are
many vivid pictures, instinct with courage. They recall seeing
Colonel Chung and his Korean staff officers jogging past the
blocked vehicles toward "The Pass," running as calmly as
their own countrymen in a Boston Marathon. They remember that their own division staff walked the route heads up,
and that the G4, Lieut. Col. Frank C. Sinsel—a man with a
gimpy leg—hobbled along on a cane. Their own generals
came out in open jeeps so that their closed vans could be
used for ambulances.

The giving of praise or blame is always easy but the understanding of anything is difficult; it is a truth which applies to
this story. Under the most normal conditions, there are limits
to what the mind may perceive and require of the will. The

stress imposed on 2nd Division during the withdrawal was abnormal even by the standards of the battlefield. Its numbing effect upon action and reaction cannot be ignored by those who would judge fairly of the event.

In the anxieties which attended the urge to stay mobile, other values were slighted. The leader of a small group or the driver of a vehicle was absorbed in his task of getting just a few people through to safety. The column became a train of small rescue parties, each operating in relative detachment from all others. The local problem blanked out everything on the horizon. There wasn't time for any man to think acutely of what possibly might happen to the people who came along later, or to govern his action according to their need.

Of these things came in part the extra ordeal in "The Pass" above the village of Karhyon during the late afternoon. The potential threat in this manmade terrain feature was clear from the beginning. Mace's tankers, on their trail-blazing run, had recognized it as a trap which might be baited and sealed against them, though it had not so proved.

Still, there had been no action to prevent the door's swinging shut. The Division Command, not yet on the road, had no knowledge of its menace. The junior commanders, though sensing the danger as they rode through "The Pass," were weighted with other burdens. On reaching sanctuary, they had to find and regroup their shattered units.

Furthermore, doubling back was for them out of the question. The British brigade, driving north along the Sunchon road, had fought hard through the day, attempting to gain "The Pass" from the south end, and had been stopped by strong mortar and machine-gun fire from the ridges directly west of it. Out of the division's first serial, which came at it from the north, a scratch force might have been organized to scale the slope and outpost the heights. But to stop there before the run was completed, form into squads men who did not know one another, and then assault the ridge would have been an act of initiative calling for gods rather than mortals. So no chance was really lost, though the commanding embankments might have been had for a song during the early afternoon.

For much the same reasons, the village of Karhyon, which lay beyond "The Pass" in the low ground to the left, remained unoccupied by both sides, though it contained a threat as a build-up point.

There were no engineers and no heavy machinery to keep the passage clear of rubble and wrecked transport. Whatever was dropped there by any part of the column further constricted "The Pass" against the elements which followed. A jeep crushed at the wrong point or a truck deserted and not ditched were like self-inflicted wounds in the side of the division.

In midafternoon, the Chinese coil of automatic fire tightened around this situation. All along, the enemy had been doing a little random skirmishing with small arms around the exits. Now a circle of machine guns closed around the ramparts.

In the next sequence, a few vehicles left standing at the wrong point became the cork in the bottle. This was the day's most savage irony—that by making too much haste, the Americans built a better roadblock against themselves at the top of "The Pass" in late afternoon through sheer accident than the enemy had been able to engineer at its southern foot in early morning with malice aforethought.

So the enemy worked his design, abetted by the errors of those whom he sought to entoil. But of their mistakes—if that be a fair word—it needs be said that they were not mean or craven, and whether they could have been avoided is a great question. Men rushed not because they were thoughtless of the distant comrade back along the road, but because they were conscious of the anguish of the comrade right at hand. Not all judgments were clear, nor could they be. For this was a host which had for five days survived massacre without sleep and, unrested, unfed, and freezing, was now being extended to the limit of human endurance.

Yet it is wonderful what just a little rest will do for a man. Consider again the strange case of Sergeant McGregor of Fox Company. He was completely spent when, following his ordeal with death under the jeep and in the grader ditch, he fell across Captain Benton's lap and started his truck ride to "The Pass." McGregor slept a few minutes—the sleep of total exhaustion—and when he awakened while still in the gauntlet, he was already rebounding.

Benton's truck must have been right on the heels of Maixner's convoy, for "The Pass" was almost empty of moving vehicles when the truck entered the cut, and the Chinese had at last completed their fire encirclement of its heights. Along the cap of both embankments and at both ends of the slot, enemy machine guns were firing down onto the roadway. There were perhaps twenty to thirty knocked-out vehicles cluttering its surface; one of them—the truck which had almost stopped Maixner—now prevented Benton's passage. Dodging or hiding among these wrecked vehicles were about a score of American riflemen and a few ROKs. They had tried several times, they told McGregor, to break out of "The Pass," and, at both ends of it, had been turned back by a sheet of machine-gun fire, losing several of their number. But there was no refuge within it. Chinese snipers were working down the slate slopes. The wrecked trucks were being subjected to a well-aimed bullet fire. Hand grenades were exploding in the alley.

With McGregor in the truck were Benton, Captain Miller, First Battalion's surgeon, Captain Caley, regimental dental officer, and M/S Holt from Item Company. They held a council of war and decided the best course was to round up the men and try to break out by climbing the right-hand embankment. The start was good. Twenty-three men started. McGregor found a brush-covered slot in the face of the cliff which shielded them from easy view and, climbing hand over foot, they made it to the top of the wall without a shot being fired on them. That put them on a lower fold of a quite formidable ridge. McGregor decided to keep climbing. The party had progressed perhaps another 200 yards when Mc-Gregor spied a knob ringed with empty foxholes. He yelled "Let's get in there and hold them off!"

The Chinese must have heard that cry. Immediately, from somewhere upslope, a machine gun cracked down on them. In the duck-away, the party split into three or four groups. McGregor now had only seven followers. He led them downhill along the south slope of the ridge, doing no fighting whatever and going to ground whenever they sighted any enemy skirmishers. At last they found themselves moving through a maze of quite low hills. A platoon of Chinese came toward them. McGregor countermarched his group for about 600 yards; this time he was stopped by a Chinese company coming from the opposite direction.

He took a third tack. Experience had taught him caution. This time, after proceeding for only a short distance, he called for a volunteer to go to the next rise and see what lay ahead. A Negro private responded but he was weaponless. McGregor gave him his own carbine and field glasses. He made it to the ridge top, and the others saw him train the glasses forward. At that moment a strafing A-26 let go at the hill with several rockets, and one of them missed the boy by a whisper. He tore back through McGregor's party like a man gone mad. They heard him shriek something about "Chinks" and "strafing" as he went past. He was still carrying McGregor's gun and glasses when they saw him for the last time bounding over the hill toward the point where they had seen the Chinese company. For another hour, McGregor kept steering this little band through the wilderness. At last they closed into Nottingham.

Starting out with twenty-six men of Item Company, M/S Carl L. Stevens had had a hard run before getting to "The Pass." It was a typical experience. Twice he had lost a jeep to the Chinese fire; finally he hitched a ride in a ¾-ton. By then the company had fragmented, and he had with him only two or three known comrades.

As the truck drew abreast the grader ditch, the driver was hit by a bullet through both cheeks, just below the eyes. They put him in the ditch to give him first aid. Looking down its entire length, Stevens saw an unbroken line of wounded Americans, Turks, and ROKs. Only then he noticed that a fully loaded ammunition trailer was hitched to the truck on which he had been riding. A score of wounded men had huddled next it, seeking its cover while waiting for a ride. Every minute or so a mortar round was exploding in the vicinity. Stevens told the men to get back but they would not heed him. He then suggested to his friend, Sergeant Allen, that the trailer should be ditched somewhere farther along the road. When no one would take that responsibility, Stevens and Allen decided to quit the truck and go afoot. The premonition was quite sound. Sometime later a shell hit the trailer and the load exploded, with terrible loss to the men in the ditch.

They hiked to "The Pass" and got there after it jammed. As Stevens saw it, the ruin left by the tank which had bulldozed a way through for Maixner's battalion became the key piece in the trouble. "The Pass" was physically blocked by a wrecked jeep alongside a 2½-ton truck. From the embankment the Chinese machine gunners and riflemen concentrated fire toward this point. A ¾-ton and a second jeep had then piled up behind the two wrecked vehicles. This had occurred right at the summit in an hour when there was no power present for the clearing of the wreckage, even had the enemy fire permitted it.

Stevens saw only twelve wounded men in the vicinity of the wreckage, two being Americans and the rest ROKs and Turks. The log-jamming of human material, which marked the worst stage of this trial, was then only incipient. It came as the convoy was stopped by the physical block and the men riding it, finding themselves wide open to enemy fire from the heights, left their vehicles and pressed up into "The Pass," only to come under a worse fire. It came also of the paralyzing fear which this incessant bullet stream induced, a fear which drained their emotions and made the majority incapable of any positive reaction. Mind and nerve were already at the breaking point, such had been the strain of the journey. In "The Pass" there was no place to hide.

Stevens and Allen started working down the left side of the road, using the wrecked vehicles as cover—so they thought. But a machine-gun burst caught them before they had taken more than a few steps. Allen was hit in the leg, and a GI just in front of him was killed. Sergeant Hof, of Item, and an artillery sergeant who had been serving Item as a forward observer (name unknown) jumped for cover in a ditch which was well revetted with loose rock. Twenty yards beyond them, Stevens rolled in behind an embankment. There they stayed for one and a half hours, while the pile-up of men in "The Pass" thickened around them. But of what happened to all others, each man, hugging earth, saw very little.

Stevens could remember a group of Turks—perhaps twelve of them—running by and trying to make a break through the far end. A machine gun ripped into them, felling several, and the others jumped for the roadside ditch. He saw a ¾-ton truck drive hard toward the block. Just as it approached the rise, an enemy bullet found the driver, and the truck, loaded with men, careened off the road and was lost to sight as it pitched over the side of a draw with a 40-foot drop. Above the tumult of the fighting, Stevens could hear no sound from this company as it ditched. He thought the effects had proved fatal, but it was not so. Cpl. Clarence L. Vanhoose was a passenger in that truck. Just over the lip of the ravine, it struck a boulder which braked the descent. The men scrambled out in that instant, with nothing worse than skinned knees and elbows, and the truck was empty when it dropped into the hole.

Sergeant Hof had started firing with his M1. He gathered four or five riflemen around him and told them to start firing. He yelled over to Stevens: "We can see gooks up there. When we fire, they pull back from it. Start firing and you'll feel better." This was the personal stuff of which the recovery was finally made. The mass had become numbed beyond possibility of reorganization. Action came of a relatively few men doing the thing that lay closest to hand.

By some special grace, the train of litter jeeps carrying the 38th's wounded from the Kunuri fighting had ridden through the gauntlet with fewer scars than any of the fighting serials. Nor was that because Lieut. Paul A. Maxson, the assistant surgeon who rode the lead jeep, was able at all times to keep them moving. Their main troubles were of a different order and are best described in Maxson's own words: "We stopped numerous times because the vehicles ahead of us had become engaged and we had no choice. But when this happened, we searched the ditches alongside for our wounded, and as we found them, we stacked them in the trailers of the jeeps until they were three and four deep. There was no way to keep these men warm; we had no blankets for them. Those who were evacuated in the first place were well blanketed, but were in terrible condition. The men in the top litters urinated on the men below them. On passing the division artillery, we had filled all canteens, and so there was no water shortage. Fortunately, we had not eaten for twenty-four hours, and so elimination was low, despite the tensions produced by fire and fear. The road was worse than corduroy. Much of the time, the vehicles were jolting as badly as in a swing across open country. The pain must have been terrible. But I did not hear one man complain. I could not attend them; there was not time. But when I talked to them they acted as if they were glad to be aboard."

On getting to "The Pass," Maxson's convoy was stopped by the stalled traffic in the fire block. As it stood there, machine-gun fire from the right embankment cut right along its length. In one trailer, three of the wounded were killed; in another, two met death. The more lightly wounded men jumped from the trailers and out to the side of the road, where there was a deep ditch. Maxson's driver, Sgt. Robert Gilstrap, was shot through the knee. The radio at Maxson's back was shattered by bullets. Maxson lay flat on the road to escape the fire; still, one burst covered him with rocks and dirt.

He then worked up to the side of the embankment. Looking along it, he saw nearly a squad of men make separate attempts to regain the vehicles and get them going. He watched what happened at the lead jeep. Three men tried for it, one after the other. Each was killed as he reached for the wheel, and one by one, he saw them fall and lie quiet in the roadway.

Looking down "The Pass," Maxson noticed an American tank which was circling toward the village of Karhyon. To him, that meant that the village must be in friendly hands. He got his aid kit and started that way. There was a fairly deep ravine leading out from "The Pass" which wound toward the village. He found eight or ten wounded men resting in the ravine. Most of them had leg wounds. He dressed the wounds, and afterward, as he continued on his way, the men hobbled or crawled along with him. Not being a combat soldier, he did not try to organize them.

Farther along, he came upon Cpl. Donald Mortweet of the Medical Company. Mortweet had a compound fracture of the left arm and a bullet through his groin. Gilstrap, with a bullet through his knee, was down only a few yards from Mortweet. Maxson gave Mortweet morphine, then asked Gilstrap: "What shall we do with him?" Gilstrap said: "We'll take turns carrying him." So they started, crawling along on hands and knees, with the free man helping to steady the burden while the other carried Mortweet on his back. For the wounded Gilstrap, it must have meant untold agony. For Mortweet, it was worse. After 600 yards of this tandem pickaback travel, he became violently ill, vomiting and defecating all over Maxson. So they stopped, and Maxson took Mortweet's pants down to see if he could stop the bleeding in the groin.

When he looked up, a Chinese soldier was standing right over him. He was pointing to his neck, from which the blood was spurting. Maxson tried to wave him on his way but the man wouldn't move. He continued to gesture, as if wanting the wound dressed. A wounded lieutenant lying in a ditch a few yards from Maxson took out his .45 pistol and waved it at the Chinese; he took off on a run. Then a ROK soldier came by and offered to help.

There was a hut not far away and Maxson pointed toward it and in sign language told the boy to go there, tear off a door and bring it back. By the time the ROK had returned with his improvised stretcher, Maxson and Gilstrap had ceased to care whether they were hit or not, and so they arose and walked boldly in the open. To their surprise, there was no fire. The tank had withdrawn a few hundred yards to the westward and was now machine-gunning the heights above "The Pass." There were about twenty huts in Karhyon; so far, the village had not been seized and organized by either side, and it stood there, still reasonably intact, a possible prize in the no-man's land between the forces.

Maxson found that about two score of the allied wounded had, like himself, followed the drainage line to the hutment and were resting under its roofs. Six of them were litter cases who had been carried to the village by other soldiers, mainly ROKs and Negro fighters. He sent a messenger to the tank asking that it evacuate these men, but the commander returned word that he couldn't quit his fire mission. A jeep came driving along the road from Nottingham, looking for wounded. Maxson put the door across the back seat and placed three of the men on it; two others were stretched out on the hood; the sixth man was laid across the lap of the driver. Maxson started walking out leading the rest of the wounded. Then another vehicle came by and insisted that he board. Someone said: "A man wounded as you are should not be walking." That puzzled him for a moment. Then he realized he was bloody all over. But it was the blood of Mortweet.

During Maxson's prolonged struggle to save Mortweet, and while Stevens and Hof were resting in their holes preparatory to resuming fire, "The Pass" was filling with humanity, and many men were meeting death in the shadow of its slate cliffs or along the uneven ground which flanked the road on the northern approach. At that end the CCF machine guns and mortars, in sealing "The Pass," also delivered frontal fire against the stalled vehicles and against the troops as they quit the convoy and sought ground cover to both sides of the road. Mainly, these men were the remnants of the 9th Infantry, the lead serial of Division Headquarters, and scattered groups of ROKs and Turks. But of how the many fared, and of the confusions which attended their personal trials, men placed like Stevens and Hof knew and felt very little. They scarcely realized that the situation in "The Pass" had wholly changed and that the life of the division was in balance right at their elbow. In such an operation, men do not actually observe the battlefield. They see the world as a rabbit sees it, crouching to earth, with an eye on one little patch. On broken ground, like that of Korea, men under fire may witness nothing except possibly the lip of a bank 10 feet away, with the dust kicking up all around it as the bullets hit.

There were exceptions. Sometimes a man walks upright because he must. It happened to one individual on this day. General Keiser had been phenomenally lucky in his jeep run through the greater part of the gauntlet. After leaving his command post in the bivouac area at about 1330, he doubled along the stalled parts of the column almost without stopping and got to the final ridge at about 1515. This placed him in "The Pass" approximately twenty minutes after the column had wedged there. He personally witnessed the atrophy of the troops who had closed in just prior to his arrival. The dead lay in the ditches and sprawled across the roadway. Most of the living—even those still unwounded—were in such a state of shock that they responded to nothing, saw nothing, and seemingly heard nothing. The Chinese fire beat like hail among the rocks and next the vehicles where they stood or reclined. But they neither cried out nor sought better cover. Their facial expressions remained set, appearing almost masklike because of the heavy coating of dust and the distortion from the dropping of the jaw. An occasional one whispered, "Water! Water!" as if he had been saying it over and over and could not stop, but there was little else which was intelligible. They were saying nothing and doing nothing except that a few shuffled about aimlessly, seeming to reel in their tracks. The division commander walked among them, moving from group to group to group, barking questions, trying to startle them back to consciousness. "Who's in command here?" "Who *are* you?" "Can any of you do anything?" He got not a single response. The Americans remained as mute as did the ROKs and Turks, who probably didn't understand his words.

Keiser decided to walk to the south end of "The Pass." He wanted to see if the Chinese had effectively blocked the exit with fire, and he was still looking for men who might be rallied. It was an incredible reconnaissance for the top man. The Air Force was now working back and forth along the embankments on both sides, and the bullet stream was chipping the rocks less than 75 yards above the floor of the cut. Napalm spilled down onto the road, as it bounced off the cliffs, and set several of the vehicles afire. Clips from the .50 caliber guns were flying about everywhere. The din was terrific.

One thing made his heart leap up. A sergeant from the 9th Infantry had taken an 81-mm mortar from a ¾-ton truck, set it up in the middle of the roadway, and was now single-handedly firing the piece on line of sight against the Chinese positions atop the south exit. It was the only fire Keiser saw being delivered by an American. But he noted a few other self-possessed individuals, most of whom were trying to help the wounded. One man sat on the hood of a jeep trying to bandage the wound of a second man braced up against the windshield. Keiser saw that the man's foot had been shot away clean at the ankle. He passed another badly wounded man who was lying in a ditch. A second soldier, himself wounded, was trying to drag him to a better cover behind a jeep, but was having a hard tussle. So he was helping with his voice. Keiser heard him say: "Now get your Goddamned leg around the corner of that jeep. Do it, I say! That's the way. Goddamn it, I knew you could make it." Keiser wanted to stay and help but couldn't. There were too many wounded for any one man to be able to do much. He was looking for officers; he felt if he could find just one or two officers, he could start a recovery. So he continued on to the south exit, and when he got there, he found that the Chinese guns were bearing on the road from both embankments.

The pile-up of American, Turk, and ROK dead in the ditches and along the roadside was mute proof that the enemy gunners were on their mark. Keiser started back toward the top of "The Pass," convinced that until the air strikes, coupled with infantry parties attacking up the embankment, succeeded in neutralizing the Chinese machine guns, the clearing away of the wrecked vehicles still would not free the column.

As he trudged uphill, he found that his feet were leaden. His journey along this terrible ambush was sapping his physical energy at an excessive rate, even as it drained the last reserve of the private soldier. Never had his shoe pacs weighed so heavy! Directly in his path, crosswise of the road, lay the body of one of his men. He tried to step across it, but failing to lift his foot high enough, struck his toe against the figure's midriff. Thereupon the supposed corpse sat bolt upright and said: "You damned son-of-a-bitch." Keiser was so astonished that he replied only: "My friend, I'm sorry," and continued on his way.

In this situation, courage was needed, even the brand of it which is sometimes called "false courage" because it is drained from a bottle. The man who could supply it, though not yet in "The Pass," was legging it to the scene, despite his bruises and concussions, and with the authority of an occasional slug from a bottle of I. W. Harper.

It is necessary at this point to break the continuity of the story of the crisis in "The Pass" and return to the personal narrative of Lieut. Tom Turner, Hinton's assistant, who had been stunned by a rocket which came in too close. When he regained consciousness, he quit the ditch and started up the road again. For more than a mile he walked alongside a solid block of vehicles; no one knew why the column was stopped, but because of the sweep of fire against the train from numerous points, the riders had all taken to the ditches and roadside cover, and no one seemed to be interested in freeing the block. Just as Turner came within sight of "The Pass," he found an idling ¾-ton truck, standing empty and with a clear stretch of road forward of it. Its party had deployed to the right of the road to answer an enemy machine gun which was bearing from that direction, and the driver was so intent on working his rifle that he was unaware his truck had stalled the whole column. Turner booted him on his way. When the truck took off, two or three other vehicles followed. But that was all. Turner realized that he would have to double back along the column, routing other men out of the ditches and back to the trucks; the condition which had immobilized the lead vehicle was common to the whole train. Once men went to ground and began to exchange bullets with the enemy on a personal basis, they forgot the road and the main mission until someone prodded them back.

Turner zigzagged along the line, going at a run, sweeping the ditches clear of men, and getting the column going again in takes of three or four vehicles at a time. A rifleman yelled to him: "For God's sake get down!" Turner jumped for the ditch. An enemy machine gun, zeroed-in on the spot where he had been standing, showered him with dirt as he gained cover. Turner worked down the ditch a few yards to the rifleman. He already had the gun located and pointed it out to Turner; it was only half-concealed behind a grass screen on a ridge lying 400 yards to the eastward. At that moment an American tank was drawing abreast of Turner. He jumped to his feet, and the tank commander, seeing the white stripe on Turner's helmet, came to a stop. Turner pointed out the enemy position. The tank fired two 76-mm rounds and the second one hit the gun dead on.

Looking north along the road, Turner now saw that most of the vehicles were in motion. He jumped on the running board of a 2½-ton, intending to ride it to "The Pass." Two hundred yards farther on, another machine gun fired directly across the body of the truck. Turner ducked low to shield himself behind the truck's metal. A bullet shattered the bar to which he was holding, and he pitched backward onto the road so violently that he somersaulted into the ditch, losing consciousness for a second time. The blackout lasted for perhaps twenty minutes. When he emerged, the road was temporarily clear of traffic to the north, but about 1,000 yards to the south he could see a jam of vehicles and men. Something prodded him in the back; it was a Chinese, holding a rifle and motioning for him to get to his feet. Twenty feet away, a group of six Chinese were working over an infantryman who had been shot in the chest. Turner arose, walked a couple of steps, then fell flat, less from weakness than from the pain of an ankle which had been sprained in the tumble from the truck. One Chinese, obviously the leader, said: "Sit down if you wish." The other enemy soldiers moved back and forth along the ditch and road, giving first aid to the American wounded.

Finally, the leader got back to Turner and asked: "Where are you hurt?" speaking in perfect English. Turner said: "It's my ankle," and made a grimace of pain. The Chinese said: "Stand up!" Turner complied. Then he added, "Walk about on it; do you think it's good enough to get you back to your lines?" Turner took a few steps and said, "I think so."

The Chinese asked: "Do you object to being searched?" Turner's face expressed his astonishment. His captor said: "You don't have to submit unless you wish." Turner told him to go ahead. From his wallet, they extracted two unopened letters from Turner's wife, leaving his personal notes and money untouched. While they were fumbling through his clothing Turner suddenly remembered he had a fifth of whisky in his jacket. He hoped they would miss it; they did.

The Chinese said: "Now I want you to move down the

road, collecting your walking wounded as you go." Turner stepped off, expecting to be shot in the back. When he nerved himself to glance back over his shoulder, the Chinese had vanished. Turner collected three walking wounded in the first 100 yards, and passed the bottle around. While still about one furlong short of "The Pass," they were fired on by a machine gun. The four men hit the ditch and again the bottle was passed around. The area was crawling with allied soldiers, many of whom were wounded. On hands and knees they were pushing forward along the ditches. There was also a great deal of heavy equipment pulled off to the side of the road, though Turner did not bother to note its character. After a third shot of the whisky he got up and *ran* forward about 200 yards; the pain was gone from his ankle. He came to a detour where the road swung right through a ravine, with off to his left a ruined bridge. His mind seemed foggy, and he knew he was not seeing things too clearly. But it seemed to him there were at least 150 men, some wounded, others able-bodied, in the ravine and the ditches near it.

More vehicles were approaching from the north. Beyond the ravine he saw seven or eight bodies lying flat in the road; no one moved to clear them so that the traffic could pass. Turner started across the ravine, intending to drag the bodies to the roadside. A rifleman yelled, "Hold it, lieutenant! Nobody's made it across there in ten minutes. They have a machine gun directly above us on the right. They'll cut you down if you try it."

Turner wiggled up the opposite embankment. He could see the gun not more than 25 yards away; it was in easy hand-grenade range. He called out for grenades, but there was none among the company in the ravine. Then he asked: "Who'll join me in rushing the gun?" One GI said: "If you want it, you take it, lieutenant." Another said, "Take it, and shove up." The others didn't answer.

Figuring that the Americans were spent, Turner doubled back down the road, yelling for a ROK or Turk who could speak English. One South Korean responded. Turner ex-

plained what he wanted. In a few minutes, the man was back
with thirty-six ROKs, all of whom were willing to make the
attack. At Turner's suggestion, the interpreter selected fifteen
who looked the most able. Turner led them to the ravine and
explained the tactics. In the defilade, they could stand momentarily shoulder high without great danger of being hit.
He wanted two teams of four men each to fire alternately
jack-in-the-box fashion from the ravine, while with the other
three he moved about 30 yards to the right and rushed the
gun from the flank. He thought he had everything lined up,
and was ready to make the pinch-out. Then looking around,
he found that all fifteen ROKs were at his back; misunder-
standing what he wanted, his base-of-fire crews had followed
along. He thought: "What the hell!" and then on sudden
impulse, he yelled: "Banzai! Banzai!" vaulted over the embankment and started for the gun. The ROKs came right
after him; the mob was almost atop the position before the
Chinese crew saw them. Too late, they tried to turn the gun
around; the one burst they got off went wild. Then they tried
to run; the ROKs shot them down. This was the first gun
knocked out by direct infantry action at "The Pass."

Small as was the taste of success, it fired Turner's new
teammates. They wanted to carry on, and get another machine gun. Turner explained through the interpreter that to
hold together, they would need to get better organized. They
moved back to the road as he explained to the Koreans what
he wanted.

Two airplanes came over. The first was strafing with its
machine gun. The fire hit among the ROKs and struck down
several of them. The second plane was right behind it. There
was a heavy explosion (from a rocket) and for the third time
during the afternoon, Turner was blown unconscious into the
ditch.

Still far back in the column, a tall, spare man of about forty
was carrying along with the main rescue mission. Capt. William O. Burla, photo intelligence officer of the Division G2
Section, had been told that morning that, on the move south,

it would be his task to collect the wounded. There were no doctors to help him; he was given a staff of four drivers and two first-aid men. Together they organized a train which included the three generals' vans, two ambulances from the Engineer Battalion, two 2½-ton trucks from the 38th Infantry, and one small truck from the Division Aviation Section.

There was hard common sense in Burla. Before ever hitting the road or lifting a casualty, he had his men load the trucks with all the bedrolls and blankets which were to be found in the command post area. The convoy started forward in midafternoon. By then the ambulances were already filled, as were the vans, with litter cases, and at least twenty more lightly wounded were riding on the trucks.

They proceeded very slowly along the road, checking the ditches and scanning the nearby paddies in search for any American, ROK, or Turk who still moved. It was not a perfect job; frequently the fields aflank were hidden by ruined portions of the column or vehicles temporarily stalled. Also, before the party was far along, it became obvious that the train would be overloaded long before the run was done. So Burla gave his helpers a rule of thumb: If a body lay perfectly still, they should not check it for a heartbeat, but to save time and help those with the best chance to live, would regard it as dead. In clearing wounded to the vehicles, the sweep also cleared the dead from the road to the ditches. Burla continued to collect bedding wherever it had been abandoned.

The side gates of the trailers on the 2½s were laid across the frames of the trucks, in this way making double deckers of them. Even so, the wounded had to be stacked before Burla was within sight of "The Pass." His eight vehicles were already carrying 140 wounded men.

When the shock cases whimpered from the cold, they were tucked in with bedrolls and blankets. There were enough ampules of morphine at hand to take care of the chest- and belly-wound patients. This was about all the care that could be given. Perhaps it was enough. Burla said in his matter-of-fact way, "They asked only for water, and of that we were not short."

But two men of the 140 died on the ride out, both from stomach wounds. Only twice did the train come under Chinese fire, and luck was with it each time. One of the ambulances had its radiator shot away by a machine-gun burst; a 2½ took it in tow immediately. One wounded man lying in the bed of a truck was hit by a second bullet; he managed to survive.

Burla's convoy, moving toward "The Pass," was behind the forward serial of the division artillery and the last serial of the 38th Regiment, the First Battalion, under Lieut. Col. William Kelleher, which for lack of other transport was making the ride mainly on artillery vehicles.

When the column became wedged in "The Pass," just after General Keiser's arrival, these elements became long stalled in the median ground one to two miles short of the final ridge. There they were taken under mortar and machine-gun fire from the flanking high ground. The road became littered with knocked-out vehicles. Quad-50s and 155-mm howitzers were deployed to the paddy fields to provide protective fires. As the day wore on toward sunset, with still no sign of a break-up ahead, anticipating that they might be held for the night, he began to consider how they would defend if this was to be the final stand.

Meantime, the lavishing of rockets, napalm, and .50 machine-gun fire in repeated air strikes against the embankment tops and the ridge extensions was the only consistent counter against the Chinese effort to keep the trap closed at "The Pass." For the planes which participated, it was a race not less with the setting sun than with the enemy reserves boring down from the hills to keep possession of the heights, despite the knocking out of gun after gun. To win it, the pilots risked to the limit, coming in so low against the ridges that it many times seemed to the men in "The Pass" that a crash was certain.

General Bradley, the ADC, got into "The Pass" not far behind General Keiser. Such was the lack of junior officers at the scene that, having no option, the two generals found themselves directly commanding individuals and a few scratch squads of skirmishers.

On getting back to his jeep after reconnoitering the south exit, Keiser tried to raise "Robin 10" on his radio. That was Freeman, commanding the 23rd Regiment, which at the extreme north extension of the division was still fighting as rearguard against the Chinese crowding down past Kunuri.

Keiser thought Freeman might send help. His plan was that a task force of one infantry company riding on tanks might go out the westward road, circle, and come at "The Pass" from the south end, using its artillery to break the enemy clamp on the heights. Considering the time, the distance, and the strength, this concept was hardly realistic.

In any case, he couldn't get Freeman on his radio, though he did raise Sloane's command post, just at a time when Sloane was in contact with Freeman. The message was put, and the conversations were relayed by Sloane, with the interlocutor putting the questions and passing along the answers and the orders. Freeman at this same time was pressing upon Keiser another matter; it concerned the method of his own withdrawal from the Kunuri area. In some manner, with the two men thinking and talking about totally different things, purposes became crossed and the authority for action proportionately clouded. It is not possible to say exactly how it happened, though in the main, what came of these conversations is relatively clear.

To put this episode into its proper time setting, it is now necessary to interrupt the continuity of the narrative as it relates to the crisis in "The Pass" and view the situation where the division still faced north.

At their position on the far side of the Kaechon, Freeman, who led the rearguard, and Lieut. Col. John W. Keith, Jr., who commanded the artillery, talked over their situation. They agreed that this was the final hour; either they would move to withdraw, or they would never get out. The swell of Chinese fire and music from their front rose steadily higher.

That was what Freeman wanted to say, if he could get through to Keiser on radio. Keith had already given the same message to the division artillery commander and had asked permission to put some of his gunners into the line as riflemen. To Freeman's eye, a withdrawal via the road which the division had taken was wholly impractical. He sought authority to go out westward via the Anju road. This was what he put to Sloane and, so he thought, through Sloane to Keiser. That was the question which Sloane himself understood he was putting to the division commander. To Freeman he relayed Keiser's words, "Go ahead—and good luck." In the aftermath, there was some question about whether Freeman's withdrawal via Anju had been done on proper authority. Memories had become hazed by the terrible pressures of the hour. Keiser could not recall that he had approved Freeman's diversionary march. Freeman thought Bradley had given it the O.K. Bradley said no. But Sloane and two witnesses who were in his command post at the time, Colonel Messinger and Lieut. Colonel Gerot, agreed that this was how it happened. In any event, Keiser took the all's-well-that-ends-well view. Later, he simply said: "Thank God, Paul, that it worked out for the best." He was content that the regiment had been saved.

But it was still far from salvation as sundown neared on 30 November. Freeman and Keith discussed whether it would be better to attempt to take out the howitzers or destroy them. They concluded that there were too many sharp turns on the road out; one piece might overturn in a defile, block the road, and hold up the whole column. Mutually, the two men took the decision to fire off all ammunition, destroy the guns, then send the artillery vehicles to the T in the road near Songhangni where they could pick up Freeman's infantrymen as they fell back from the ridges. With the rearguard also was the remnant of Sloane's First Battalion under Major

Hinkley, who had taken command the night before after Major Hill had become missing in action.

Two of Keith's forward observers had just completed adjustment on two main targets—one a group of about 400 Chinese moving toward the perimeter from the far side of the Chongchon at about 3,800 yards' range, and the other a column of about 500 Chinese advancing parallel to the other body, at about 4,000 yards' range.

One other prime target was in the background—the village of Pugwon, which was a focal point in the draw leading from the west, whence had come the main enemy attack of the night before. Pugwon, on the main road from Kujang-dong, was 11,400 yards in front of Charley Battery. Able and Baker were assigned the more close-up human targets.

The batteries got all of their cooks, clerks, and handymen into an assembly line to feed the guns. The gunners and crews did their assigned work, but every other artilleryman present was put into the daisy chain. It had to be fast and also accurate, as the 23rd's men were quitting the high ground and any shorts would have worked havoc.

From the moment Freeman issued the order until the last round was fired was just twenty-two minutes. In that brief interval, the battalion fired 3,206 rounds—a rate of eight-plus rounds per gun per minute—one of the most phenomenal shoots on record. The paint peeled off the guns. Breechblocks turned black. Such was the overheating from this fire that the tubes were doubtless ruined by the strain, even if the gunners had not thereafter thermited them.

And the Sunday punch did its work; such metal as was sacrificed was paid for tenfold in the salvaging of men. There was a prolonged lull in the Chinese fire. The forward observers reported that the enemy advance had stopped cold, and his men were furiously digging all along the line; they reacted as if convinced that they were about to be strongly counterattacked.

Just one gun and a little ammunition had been husbanded. Keith had his men remove firing locks and sights from the others prior to leaving, as experience in the Korean fighting, had taught him that a thermite grenade will not always effectively destroy a 105 howitzer.

First Battalion of the 23rd—with one company of the 72nd Battalion's tanks—had been maneuvering as the ultimate rearguard of the division's withdrawal from the Chongchon area. Charley Battery of the 15th was pulled out while the others were still completing the big shoot; its mission was to outhaul the first infantry elements as they came back from the hills. The one live gun remaining in Baker Battery was put to work firing one round every fifteen seconds against the road junction in Kujang-dong. The battery commander, Capt. Robert W. Smithson, remained with the gun and continued the fire until the last of the artillery vehicles was on the road.

Dark was falling when Freeman and Keith at last quit their command post, 2,500 yards forward of where the batteries were forming in column. Freeman's First Battalion had wholly broken contact with the Chinese, and most of the infantry had already loaded, some on trucks and others on tanks. By the time the two commanders had come even with the old artillery position, the traffic was solidly blocked on the road, almost as far north as the edge of Pugwon. It remained so wedged for about one and one half hours, putting the tail-end vehicles in the strange position of providing physical cover to the howitzer Smithson was firing, which was supposed to be protecting them.

A few Chinese riflemen worked around the sides of the column and into the ground where rested the 15th's ruined howitzers. For some minutes there persisted a sporadic sniper fire against the stalled vehicles. A dead silence followed. A rocket exploded as if in signal. Then from the high ground, four or five enemy machine guns cut loose on the tail-enders.

Almost coincidentally, the column got in motion and kept going for about three miles. A few vehicles were shot up, but the rest pulled out without serious damage. The enemy continued the pursuit across country but had little effect.

Hinkley and his few survivors from the 9th's First did not join the withdrawal. The order was given him; he would not comply. The great part of this battalion is carried missing in action.

Ten miles and more from this scene, Tom Turner again regained consciousness. He had been out for perhaps forty minutes. The whole scene was in shadow; in another twenty minutes it would be dark. He could see a few ROKs and Turks moving forward into "The Pass"; the automatic fire from its north end had quieted. But the choke of vehicles remained. He met Lieutenant Rucksberry, Second Battalion's motor officer, who told him that at least four CCF machine guns still dominated the south exit.

As he moved among the men, he heard the word passed around: "Don't fire! Friendly troops are attacking up the ridge on the left." In the center of the road, a sergeant was working a .50 machine gun mounted on a truck. From atop the fender another man was peppering the slope with a Thompson. A lieutenant came toward them on the run shouting, "You dumb bastards, those people are trying to surrender." The boy with the Thompson replied, "If that's surrender, it doesn't suit me; they were all carrying arms. Anyway, we got them—ten Chinese, and they're all dead."

Not far away Keiser was coping with this same problem. The stalled vehicles were still drawing rifle and tommy gun fire from the heights. But the cry was going up from many parts of the column: "Cease fire! Cease fire! Cease fire!" Keiser is an old China hand and he sensed a trick. He moved down the line shouting: "Stop this 'cease fire' talk! These Commies know English. They're yelling that from the ridges and you're echoing it. We're just beginning to get them on the run."

Two light tanks from the Reconnaissance Company had just pulled up to within a few hundred yards of the north exit and were shelling the ridges. Bradley went to Keiser with the suggestion that they might be more useful within the cut. A captain from the 38th Infantry said to Keiser, "If I can have the tanks, I can use them to bulldoze the wrecked vehicles aside and open up the way again." Keiser told him to collect the tanks and go at the job. This was soon done, with Bradley and the unnamed captain directing the operation. Coupled with the final air strikes, the restoration of movement within "The Pass" was what mainly shook loose the Chinese still trying to hold the south exit.

But Turner had already gone on his way, trying to break out of "The Pass" by moving along the right-hand ditch and into a draw which angled from it toward the southwest. From the higher ground, the passage looked to be in defilade. But on entering, he found that the Chinese fire from the ridges was on direct line to the bed. It was necessary to hug the embankments. The draw was peopled with wounded, many of them lying there impassive and paying no heed to the GIs, ROKs, and Turks who passed Turner as he limped on his way. Suddenly this traffic stopped and backed as if the passage had been blocked. Turner took another swig from his bottle and climbed from the ditch to go forward and see what caused the block.

At last he found it—two riflemen were half-carrying, half-dragging a third who was shot through both legs. Such was their weariness and the weight of the burden that they barely inched along, while behind them about 200 other men were denied a chance to escape the fire zone.

Forward of the men a few yards, a narrow but sheltered bay gave off from the side of the ditch. Turner told the riflemen to step aside at that point and let the column pass. One man raised his rifle, saying: "You son-of-a-bitch, I'm helping a wounded man. You get out of my way or I'll shoot you."

Turner already had his pistol in his hand. He raised it and said this: "I gave you an order. Move that man as I said or I'll shoot you both." The wounded man was crying to the others, "He's right about it. Do what he says!"

They pulled aside into the bay. Turner went with them and stayed until the last of the men who had been stalled to the rear passed by. Turner yelled as they went by: "Double time! Double time if possible." They picked up speed as they went downhill, and in a minute or two the Chinese fire stopped.

One of the riflemen said to Turner: "Lieutenant, I was wrong. I beg your pardon and I wish you would shake hands." Then they shook hands all around and the wounded man said, "I feel better already."

Turner showed them how to make a hitch with crossed arms, then lifted the wounded man into them. They walked down the ditch with Turner following along, carrying the rifles, ready to give a protective fire if it was needed.

Where the draw ended, they climbed a small hill. At its base on the far side, they saw four of the 72nd's tanks and knew they had reached home base.

A couple of British officers came toward them. One said: "Now everything is going to be O.K."

There must be one brief flashback to Kunuri to recount the closing scene during the breakaway. It was well past midnight before the last of Freeman's people had cleared the town, heading for the hill mass to the west along the Anju road. But these were not the last Americans to get out. 25th Division's rear columns had still to cross the river.

All along during the Chongchon battle, Colonel Blair's Third Battalion of the 24th Regiment had held to its advanced ground unscathed, though right under the enemy gun. The beating given 9th Infantry during the last stage of the fight north of Kujang-dong had further isolated its position. Colonel Corley personally had hastened to the spot with a few tanks to give the battalion comfort. But the rampant enemy, on the loose elsewhere through the countryside, continued to ignore this small enclave.

While the other forces of the rearguard were funneling back through Kunuri, the 27th Regiment coming at it from the west and the 23rd Regiment from the north, Blair's battalion, though it had withdrawn a distance, was still a protrusion deep in enemy country. Blair held to his command post inside Kunuri after Freeman had retreated. At 0200 on

1 December he was still there and talking to Colonel Corley by field telephone. Corley, with the body of the regiment, was still west of the river. Their conversation was broken midway as Chinese soldiers entered Blair's command post. He got out with his skin.

Corley felt that Third Battalion's luck had at last run out. He tried to swing his First Battalion over to cover Third Battalion's rear; but it was down to two light companies and was holding tight to 27th Regiment's shoulder for protection. Corley ordered Third Battalion to withdraw southwestward to high ground nearer the main body. By then first light was breaking. The Chinese saw the movement and converged against Blair's men from north, northeast and east. Six air strikes were ordered up in a vain endeavor to hold back this tide. The surge continued unabated. The formation simply fell apart, and it became every man for himself. Some of the Americans ran until they collapsed from exhaustion. Others held their ground and fought back. Those who stayed were butchered. The others who had run themselves into the ground were picked up bodily by the Chinese, supported until their legs were again working, and then pushed on their way back to the American lines.

This war is a succession of enigmas. None is less scrutable than the nature of the Chinese enemy.

## 17

# Trial of an Artillery

W HEN THE SUN SET, NOT ONE HOWITZER HAD GONE through "The Pass." Most of the infantry had either cleared the barrier or had moved to within seeing distance of it. But the artillery column was strung out all the way from the approach to the final ridge back to the jump-off area, where some of its elements had not yet formed in procession for lack of road space.

Thus, in the unforeseen situation, the artillery became the division rearguard, having to repel infantry boarders and doing it in the dark.

The long presunset wait behind "The Pass" cast its shadow the length of these battalions and filled the command with a premonition of the coming night's crisis. There was still little or nothing to be done which might ease it, though no possible source of help was left untried.

Brig. Gen. Loyal M. Haynes, his staff, and HQ personnel were with the forward artillery elements during the long wait. This put them in a narrow belt of low ground next the villages of Sahyoncham and Sinchangcham. To the south, the blazing of tracer fire above "The Pass" intensified steadily as did the pounding from the American Air, the planes rushing their final strikes before the dark closed down. To the distant listener, it sounded as if the fight was being lost at that point.

To the west of the column, from a hill south of Sahyoncham, a machine gun opened fire on the artillery vehicles at about 400 yards' range. In the thickening gloom, the tracers showed all hands that the gun was ranged in neatly on the target. Haynes ordered up a Quad-50; it went promptly into action, spraying the hills to the westward. Several 155-mm howitzers were deployed into the paddies east of the road, whence they shelled the westward ridges.

Colonel Kelleher and his depleted First Battalion of the 38th were in column about 1,000 yards to the rear of Haynes. Kelleher was called up, and with him came Colonel Norum, the regimental executive. Haynes wanted them to look over the high ground commanding the road in his immediate neighborhood to see where an infantry screen might be set which could break down the Chinese rush toward the guns. The two infantrymen agreed that Hill 122 and the ridge opposite it might serve that purpose; they would be ready, if Haynes directed it, to take all men off the vehicles and do the outposting.

Haynes then called a conference. Attending it were Norum, Colonel Buys, Colonel Goodrich, and Lieut. Colonel Hector. He said approximately this: "The last air strike has taken place. The column is still motionless. The question we now have to decide is whether to stay on the road on the chance that there will be a break-up forward, or form a perimeter of the artillery in this vicinity and the remaining battalion of the 38th, and try to last the night. I will wait fifteen minutes before making my decision." During the interval, the others talked it over. They informally agreed that, in view of the shortage of riflemen, if they had to go into perimeter defense the main chance lay in pulling the vehicles off the road, forming a wagon laager and firing the guns from within the closed circle.

In that critical fifteen minutes, the break-through in "The Pass" at last induced movement to the elements which had blocked just forward of the artillery. When the conference resumed Haynes said: "Gentlemen, I see trucks moving up ahead. The decision has been made for me. We will follow along."

The dark was now complete, save at the point where a blazing vehicle threw its glare across the roadway, illuminating the column as it moved past from out of the shadows. On leaving the conference, the commanders collected their men, got underway with the vehicles that could still roll, and started for "The Pass." For just these few minutes the enemy force in the vicinity of Sahyoncham made no effort to hasten their going, and the whole scene became strangely quiet.

Only a few hundred yards to the rear of Kelleher's battalion the survivors of the Division Military Police (on the preceding day an MP force had made the initial assault against the roadblock and had been wiped out) were having a quite different experience. Lieut. Col. Henry C. Becker and his men had ridden the gauntlet that far without losing one of the thirty-four vehicles in which they had started. When the column stalled because of the block in "The Pass," a machine gun from the right of the road ranged in on Becker's vehicles. Becker called several of his officers together and said they would have to make a quick choice between trying to manhandle the wreckage out of the way, so as to free the mobile vehicles, or marching the men the rest of the distance to Nottingham.

Quite suddenly, there were six heavy explosions, landing like a broadside against Becker's vehicle line. Becker heard cries of "Help me! Help me!" mingled with a yell along the ditches: "Mortar! Mortar! Mortar!" But Becker knew it wasn't mortar—the sound told him that it was friendly artillery. (These were overs from the 503rd Battalion, which, several bends to the rear, was firing against Chinese positions atop one of the ridges.)

Becker made a quick run-down of the damage. Twenty-one of his men had been wounded by this salvo; none killed. Five vehicles had been hit dead on. One jeep was burning. In another, a wire had been shorted and the siren was wailing. That eerie noise over the battlefield was more unnerving than the shellfire and the plight of the wounded. From many points came cries of: "Turn off that Goddamned horn!" Several men had already sprung from the ditches and were pulling at the hood.

About one third of Becker's men were now afoot because of the vehicle loss resulting, in one way or other, from the fire. Becker's jeep was still running, but he had already loaded it down with seven wounded Turks, succored from the roadside ditches. His own wounded, therefore, had to be monitored aboard passing vehicles belonging to other units. Gradually collecting his mobile parts, he got them forward perhaps another 200 yards. Again, machine-gun fire from the right flank—at least three guns—drove the men to the ditches. A draw on this side of the road led to the village of Sahyoncham; the guns were on the high ground which commanded it. Becker saw a line of riflemen quit the stalled column farther ahead and start for the ridges; some of his men picked up their rifles and followed. He yelled: "Who are you?" The answer came back: "We're engineers; we're going to clean out this flank."

Back along the column 100 yards were two medium tanks. Becker ran for them and told them how to help: one tank was to get busy bulldozing wrecked vehicles off the road, and the other was to put supporting fire on the ridge tops to the right. But the moment he turned his back, they raced toward "The Pass" with never a backward look. His heart sank, for the CCF fire was building up stronger than ever, with rifles now supporting the machine guns. A Quad-50 came along; with Sexton's help, he got it positioned in the draw and ready to fire. Just then Colonel Epley, the Chief of Staff, arrived on the scene; he had come from "The Pass" to see what was delaying the rearward serials. With him was a medium tank. Epley said to Becker: "What in hell is stopping you?" As it happened, the mere appearance of the tank and the Quad-50 had discouraged the Chinese; they were quitting their ground and all firing had ceased. So Becker had no ready answer. In the lull, the column got going again.

Kelleher's run of the last mile to "The Pass" was relatively free of enemy fire or unusual interference from that quarter. He, therefore, retained a better-than-average recollection of the experience. In that distance, he passed twenty-two burning American vehicles and perhaps another hundred that were either wrecked in the ditch or abandoned in the roadway. The passage was littered with such equipment as bedrolls, packs, tentage, air mattresses, and barracks bags. Almost continuously, the vehicles were bumping over "soft lumps in the road." But the train could but roll on, disregarding them. The road shoulder was also littered with the bodies of dead Americans, ROKs, and Turks, and, interspersed among them, the forms of wounded men who had possessed just enough strength to crawl from the ditch, but lacked the power to get on their feet.

There was no moon that night. The jeeps had to crawl along and their riders took turns toeing the objects in the roadway, so that the body of a fallen soldier would not be mistaken for a bit of abandoned equipment. It was not always easy to do. When Kelleher reached the top of "The Pass," the road was again blocked by a crushed jeep and trailer. Such was the general weariness that it took more than a score of men to manhandle the obstacle to the roadside.

The ride down the south slope is described in Kelleher's words: "For the next 500 yards the road was temporarily impassable because of the numerous burning vehicles and the pile-up of dead men, coupled with the rush of the wounded from the ditches, struggling to get aboard anything that rolled. When we checked to make a turnout, away from a blazing wreck, either there would be bodies in our way, or we would be almost borne down by wounded men who literally threw themselves upon us.

"At one point, I got out of the quarter-ton to remove a body from the road. Then I saw that the man was still moving. He was a wounded ROK soldier. I squeezed him into our trailer. But as I put him aboard, other wounded men piled on the trailer in such numbers that the jeep couldn't pull ahead. It was necessary to beat them off.

"We got underway. Then I heard a scream behind me and stopped. The press of bodies had pushed a wounded Turk to between the jeep and the trailer and we were about to tear him apart. Again I had to get out and wrestle off a dozen wounded who were trying to board us. There wasn't space for even one of them and I couldn't give them my place because I had to keep my battalion moving."

There was no firing during the descent from "The Pass." The village of Karhyon was still quiet, and for the time being, it looked as if the Chinese had departed that vicinity. At the bottom of the ridge, the train passed through a ford, and a thousand yards beyond, an outpost stopped the lead vehicle and said it would be safe to turn on headlights. First Battalion had come through the gauntlet in better luck than most, having lost only two killed, twenty-eight wounded and thirty-eight missing in action—just a little more than a quarter of the strength with which it started.

Within a few minutes after Kelleher cleared "The Pass," however, the Chinese, having forsaken the heights, poured into Karhyon and used its cover as a fire base against the column's flank. Becker's men followed through shortly behind Kelleher. Riding not far behind them in the column were the heavy mortar vehicles of the 38th, aboard them four men from King Company and a mixture of riflemen and artillerymen who had loaded from other units. When this group passed into the glare from the burning MP vehicles, an enemy machine gun opened fire. The driver of the lead truck stopped. M/S Olin L. Hawkins of King Company yelled: "Keep going! Keep going!" and in a minute or so they pulled out of it. Their experience in riding through "The Pass" was not unlike what had happened to Kelleher's men.

But as they rode into the ford, machine guns and mortars from Karhyon bracketed the vehicles with their fire. From this same flank, three red flares brightened the night above the column and then winked out. Behind Hawkins' truck, a 2½-ton loaded with GIs missed the turnout toward the ford and ran on toward the gaping hole in the main road where the bridge had been knocked out. Hawkins and his group yelled their loudest, but their voices were drowned in the noise of the fire. The truck ran on. Then another flare went off—just in time. The truck braked as the light revealed the black hole ahead and came to a stop with its wheels next the edge. The gulch below was already half-filled with vehicles which had taken the dive in the darkness.

King Company had been treated much as an orphan of the storm. Its thirty men had remained back in the jump-off area among the last artillery units, for lack of vehicles on which to move when the rest of the regiment rode through. Most of the thirty had managed to attach themselves to one battery or another in the 503rd Artillery. The 503rd was alerted for the start, then was redeployed to fire positions to shell the most northern ridges, where late in the day the enemy steadily increased his mortar and machine-gun volume.

Lieut. Blair Price continued to look for outgoing vehicles with room for the last few of his men. There was a wrecker alongside the road; he told SFC Henry Seeman and four others to board it. Because the wrecker belonged to the 17th Field and that battalion hit the trail while 503rd was still shooting, Seeman's part of the column was not far behind Hawkins' in the beginning. By dusk the 17th had moved about two miles; it was then stopped by the blocking of the traffic up ahead.

Looking westward, the Americans saw a line of South Korean soldiers falling back down the ridge slope—one of Chung's groups which had been cut off earlier in the day. Lurching on another 500 yards, the big guns passed onto a flat well swept by machine-gun fire. It did little damage to the train, however. All of the fire was coming from the right, and along that side, trucks, jeeps, and kitchens, previously abandoned, afforded an almost continuous shield covering the column.

When the train stopped, the artillerymen dismounted and sought ground from which, with small arms, they could cover the crests of the hills on the right. It was a well-intended precaution, but as proved in the event, slightly misaimed. From the left there was sudden tumult. The ROKs, last seen in retreat down the ridge on the right, had crossed the road rearward of the 17th and then tried to move south across the paddy fields, parallel to the column. The Chinese had closed in on them from both flanks. As the artillerymen ran to that side of the road, they saw the ROKs streaming toward them at a run, while a line of Chinese skirmishers, formed like a rough crescent, moved pincers-fashion to close upon them. Someone near Seeman yelled: "Hold fire!" and someone else answered: "No! Fire like hell! Give it to them over the heads of the ROKs!" That was what they did. Some of the Koreans were shot down as they raced across the paddies; others gained sanctuary with the 17th.

But as the last man closed on the road, there was a crackling sound along the length of the train as fire from two machine guns on the ridges to the left (range 600 yards) ripped into the sides of the vehicles. The Chinese skirmish line went flat and supported the machine guns with close-in rifle and tommy gun fire. For the Americans, there was no going to the ditches. The 8-inch gun movers mounted both a .50 and a .30 machine gun. The gunners stood to their weapons and kept pumping lead. The small-arms firers also stood as they worked their weapons, using the movers or the body of a truck for a rampart. Such was the roar and rattle of the fire that all other noise was drowned out. In a few minutes it was pitch dark; the Chinese had had enough and the 17th had suffered its heaviest losses of the day. No man could see very much of how it had happened or what it had cost. But SFC Seeman made note that of the four men closest to him, two were shot through the leg, one through the chest, and the other in the shoulder.

Again the guns moved forward. On the wrecker, Seeman and the others began to worry as they felt the heavy wheels ride up and over "the soft bumps in the road." It was a terrifying sensation. They could have been sleeping bags; they might have been bodies. Seeman whispered to an aid man, Cpl. "Doc" Hall: "What do you think?" Hall replied: "I'm thinking what you're thinking."

But if their fears were sound, there was still no help for it. The machines of this heavy gun outfit were all terribly weighty. When they moved they raised a dust cloud which would have made seeing difficult, even if the night had not closed down. The 17th had just beaten off one direct assault. As it continued down the gauntlet, it had to stay collected, against the likelihood that the Chinese would try the same thing again. The drivers could see almost nothing of the roadway. But they could follow the loom of the vehicle directly ahead. They moved along with their great chariots riding almost bumper to bumper. It would have been all but impossible for runners to operate between them, scanning the road surface.

Their fortune upgraded after the one stiff fire fight. Going through "The Pass," they encountered several bursts of automatic fire, but were not hurt. When they started the descent, they concluded that they had about reached home base reasonably intact, and the men lit up smokes. Off to the left, several houses in Karhyon were afire. As the column turned sharply just before getting to the ford an 8-inch gun went off balance and careened into a 40-foot gulley. Then a Boffers Twin-40 * went dead in the center of the column and had to be shunted over the embankment so that other vehicles could clear. Someone went into the gulley to thermite the big gun; lights were turned on to help him. Promptly two mortars in Karhyon opened fire upon the road; WP grenades came sailing in against several of the vehicles. Nothing more was needed to urge the column on its way. The lead guns rolled on and the men quit worrying about what had been lost by the roadside.

Yet what can be said in a few words, still required hours in the doing. The ford was almost an impasse, its south bank being about 10 feet high, with the track steeply graded and curved. Only one vehicle could be risked in the dip at one time, lest the whole column become boxed. Lieut. Col. Walter Killilae of the ack-ack was with Lieut. Col. Elmer

* See Glossary of Main Weapons.

Harrelson of the 17th when the heavy guns came to this obstacle. By his account, it was 2100 when the first of 17th's train went through the ford and 2400 when the last vehicle had cleared it. Hence there was no swift dash through the fire from Karhyon for this outfit. The two officers crossed the ford and walked forward toward Nottingham till they found a medium tank and one of Killilae's own M19s. These chariots were moving north with the object of serving as tow cars to help the heavy stuff pull out of the stream bed and up the south embankment. Instead, they were diverted to shell Karhyon and so take the heat off the column during its struggle to clear the ford. In that mission they were effective. The Chinese fire ceased and the enemy seemed to have quit the village.

But the strain was still mountainous. The creek was about 30 yards across and 3 feet at its deepest. All of the lighter vehicles drowned out. They had to be manhandled out of the stream and up the grade beyond it. When the heavier stuff stalled in the water, the hauling was done by medium tanks.

Up to the passage of the 17th Battalion, the enemy had repeatedly charged toward the road, but had not once succeeded in overrunning any fraction of the division during the march-out. On the heels of the 17th's passing, this condition changed. Whereas at the southern end of the gauntlet the Chinese appear to have become exhausted by their efforts of the afternoon, loosening their grip when the night fell, in the north the fury of the attack built up rapidly under the cover of dark.

A miscellany of vehicles, mainly from the 503rd Battalion, followed in column behind the 17th. Cpl. Robert H. Weatherford, of the 38th's King Company, for example, started the ride on a 2½-ton kitchen truck belonging to Baker Battery. His group got about two miles along the road, beyond the battery's last position, before the column blocked. Forward of Weatherford was a 503rd ammunition truck, fully loaded with powder charges. Mortar shells began to fall on the column. One round hit directly on the ammo truck. The kitchen truck was 300 yards rearward when the blast went off, but Weatherford could still feel some of the impact. The explosion killed men in the three vehicles forward of the truck, and the resulting fire illuminated the landscape for half a mile around.

Within five minutes, bugles blew in the ridges to the west; immediately thereafter, Chinese moved into the circle of light from the hills. At first, they appeared only in small groups.

With Weatherford were three men from King and ten colored soldiers of the 503rd. They took to a ditch beside the road; then because they were still in the glare, they withdrew northward about 400 yards. Even at that distance they could hear the enemy leaders shouting commands and hear the men jabbering excitedly. They jumped into the trucks and jeeps and started throwing all of their contents onto the roadway. Whether their object was looting, sheer vandalism, or a further impeding of the column was beyond saying. They acted like men in a frenzy, bent on destructiveness for its own sake. More Chinese kept coming into the circle of light until at last there were about 300 of them; they continued to extend toward Weatherford's group.

During the fifteen minutes in which they pillaged, Weatherford's group had held fire at the order of a sergeant who said: "There are just too many of them." The restraint finally palled on one colored artilleryman. He took careful aim from the ditch and let them have about five rounds from his M1. To the stupefaction of everyone, that did the trick. The 300 Chinese ran back to the hills, disappearing more suddenly than they had arrived. Weatherford and the others could hear them noisily digging in on the high ground. But they were ducking in a few minutes as a machine gun on the hill began to bear directly on their ditch.

From the hill, a few snipers worked toward the ditch across the paddy fields. They could not be seen, but the men knew they were coming, because they called, "GI, GI, GI," to draw the American fire. One Chinese got into the line of vehicles, made a sneak approach along it, and was right on top of the group and had his arm back for a grenade throw when the sergeant winged him. At that point the sergeant said: "Either we get out of here now or we will all be slaughtered before daylight."

He led them across the road and into a ravine which wound toward the hills. There they stayed for some little while, doing nothing, but hoping hard.

Reviewing these several incidents, it becomes plain that the artillery still to come would meet a special hazard beyond what the lead parts of the column had experienced. The vehicles destroyed in such episodes as the 503rd's ammunition truck explosion and the shelling of the MP train had been set ablaze in the middle of the road. There was no chance to ditch them. In skirting these fiery blocks, the artillery had to make a swing-out, in the darkness, beyond the shoulder of a one-lane dirt highway with ditches on both sides. Every swerve so made by a truck or gun helped additionally to break down the thin supporting crust, increasing the likelihood that the vehicles which came later would slip, go off balance, and either overturn or become wedged sideways in the ditch. Of this came the great part of the loss which followed. Artillerymen have a love for their guns which is perhaps stronger than the feeling of any other soldier for his weapon or any part of his equipment. That guns will never be deserted simply because danger threatens is a point of honor around which the artillery has largely built the solid discipline of its corps. These batteries were not less lacking in awareness of professional obligation than were others. But as at Omaha Beachhead one battalion lost its guns because they were beaten down into the sea, it happened this night that faithful gun crews suffered the same loss because their guns were beaten into earth beyond extrication, snared behind the funeral pyre of some other outfit, or forfeited because the mover was riddled, and there was no other source of power at hand. Perhaps not every man kept the trust and did his utmost; under battle's pressure, men are not found equal. But that which needs be remembered is that hundreds died or became missing in the effort to save machined metal which in the nature of the situation was beyond salvation.

In the record there is at least one index as to whether the artillery attrition was due to mortal terror more than to insuperable physical obstacles. Gun losses by the several battalions were in almost exact relation to the place of the battalion in the artillery column. Irrespective of weight, those which hit the trail earliest, when the road was least clogged by burning blocks and stalled heavy machinery, won through with the highest percentage of pieces. Those which trailed last found all doors closed to them. The road was no longer a road but a serpentine of rubble, wreckage, and ruin.

The 37th Battalion, which followed behind the 17th, moving out at the same time as the few front runners from the 503rd, a part of whose adventure has already been described, lost ten guns during the journey. Some were hit and ruined by enemy fire. Others got hung up behind a block of debris in such way that they could not turn out and around. A few, perhaps, were lost in the dark when crews were killed and there was none to see and report.

The 38th Battalion, at the far end, last to get the call in the entire division, lost every gun and vehicle. It could not even get on the track, such was the chaos extending out over seven miles. There is no record of the retreat of this unit as a unit. Some of its men got back to allied lines by traveling cross-country under the cover of dark. Many did not. The 105s were left in enemy country. For this, it was said in parts of the American press that their action was discreditable, the consequence of bug-out fever. They could have escaped this charge had they been able to put wings on the tubes and fly with them beyond the encircling ridges.

Between the 37th and 38th was the main body of the 503rd. The melancholy, yet triumphant story of that battalion's effort to save its 155s is as filled with the travail of that night as anything which happened on the road to Sunchon.

When darkness fell, the battalion was still in position on both sides of the road firing at the same ridges near the village of Chongnyongcham which Sloane's troops and Chung's ROKs had assaulted during the morning. In return, nothing was coming against the gun positions except an occasional mortar round. When the tail of the 37th's column passed by, the battalion march-ordered and followed them in column. There was still a little flock of infantrymen nesting with the artillery. Twenty-one men of Love Company, 38th, had been told that morning that they would ride out on the vehicles of Baker Battery, and had stayed put. Love Company having lost all of its officers and senior NCOs, Lieut. Douglas D. Grinnell of Item Company took charge.

And that was fortunate. With the artillery there rode a young S3, Maj. John C. Fralish. These two men got together in the worst crisis of the ordeal and struck fire in each other, like steel to flint. The decisive impact of just a few willing hands upon a disordered situation has seldom been more dramatically demonstrated than in what they did as a team.

The column had got not more than one mile from its start and had just pulled even with the ridges which Chung had attacked that morning when it was hit head-on by a large force of Chinese. From the ridges on the left and to the rear, there was a prolonged blowing of bugles. From directly in front, and close beside the road, several machine guns opened fire. Love Company was about midway in the serial. Grinnell ran forward to look over the situation. It was then that he met Fralish and was told that the column was confronted by a well-set roadblock which embraced at least two machine guns and a considerable support in rifles. One wave of Chinese had rushed from the roadside directly upon the forward vehicles and guns. All the shock of a violent local surprise had attended the action. The men in the forward battery had met the rush as best they could. For a few minutes there had been a wild mêlée. A train of Korean refugees had been trudging beside the vehicles. In the darkness and confusion it had been impossible to distinguish friend from foe. Clubbing their rifles and carbines, the gun crews and others had jumped down and swung toward anyone who came at them. One refugee had knocked a rifle from the hands of Lieut. John E. McCord just as he was firing at a Chinese a few yards away.

But the odds were all one way. The Chinese had come boring in with rifles, tommy guns, and grenades. They were on the target; Baker Battery couldn't even see it. In the first flash seconds, the leading tractor and the rear tractor had been knocked out by explosive charges. The guns were then beset until every man of Baker was either killed, wounded, captured, or driven off. (This was accurate: only two officers and twenty enlisted men of Baker ultimately survived.) Boarding the vehicles, the enemy had looted the battery from end to end and pitched its belongings to the roadway.

Fralish was in the middle of HQ Battery when Baker got hit, and he walked to the sound of the fighting. The enemy had already pulled back before he reached the scene. Capt. Darwin C. Dunn and 1st Sgt. Albert Dahrensbourg of HQ Battery had got there ahead of him. They told him that 2nd Lieut. Peter T. Golden, Baker's trail officer, had gone forward to reconnoiter, taken a bullet through both legs, and couldn't make it back.

Several Korean houses, hard beside Baker's column, had been set afire and an ammunition truck in the middle of the battery was burning. The countryside was lighted for far around.

This was the situation when Grinnell got forward. He discussed it with Fralish; they concluded that unless they got prompt action and bucked through, the column would be totally destroyed.

Grinnell walked back toward his men. As he walked he could see shells exploding along the rear of the serial and automatic fire pressing in against its sides. He already had a plan in mind. He had mentioned to Fralish that there were a number of ack-ack wagons to their rear, and he thought if they could be brought forward, they might blast a way through for the battalion. But neither he nor Fralish carried the weight of rank and both had an hour of sweat to go through before they realized this really didn't matter.

Fralish still didn't know whether the Chinese, on leaving Baker Battery, had pulled back to the ridges or moved down the road to rig another ambush. His alternatives depended on being sure of the answer. So he took this question to his commander, Maj. Geoffrey Lavell. But Lavell just shook his head in perplexity and said they'd better talk it over with Lieut. Colonel O'Donnell and Maj. Carl Kopischke.

To these three, Fralish put a direct question: "Shall we set everything in the column bumper-to-bumper, pour gasoline over all, torch it, and go out fighting afoot, or shall we fight in place on a defensive perimeter?" The conference got nowhere. Both battalion commanders shrugged off the question. No one would take responsibility for decision. The conversasion died.

A few minutes later mortar fire began falling on the center of the column. Kopischke told his men to drop trail and start firing on the ridge to the left whence the mortar was coming. They went into action right from the road. The artillery fire touched off four or five enemy machine guns along the high ground; there was a vast increase of noise, though the aim was wild and the fire went well overhead.

Fralish made another try, requesting O'Donnell and Lavell to go to the head of the column with him, look the scene over, and decide on the spot whether to attempt to crash through, and what guns to use. They walked forward together.

As they reached the wreckage of Baker Battery and scanned forward, Fralish stood at the left of the second vehicle in the battalion column. O'Donnell stayed in the shadow to the right of it. Lavell hugged the far side of a wrecked hulk which had been shunted over toward the right-hand ditch.

From directly forward of them, not more than 40 yards away, an enemy machine gun opened fire. The burst was dead on. O'Donnell went down with four bullets in his abdomen and one in his shoulder. Lavell and Fralish went flat behind the vehicles nearest them. Fralish had missed disaster by an inch; one bullet trimmed his mustache without breaking the skin of his lip, though it left a red welt on his face which remained for several days. Lavell crawled past O'Donnell and on to Fralish. He said: "I looked him over— he's dead."

Fralish asked permission to wheel one or two of the 155s into position and open fire. He could hear the sounds of digging out beyond and it sounded not more than 50 feet away. Still doubtful that he was dealing with Chinese rather than with Baker men, he three times called: "Are you GIs?" The only effect of the challenge was to quiet the noise momentarily.

Lavell said it would be all right for him to put a howitzer into action against the machine gun, if he wished. Further than that, he would not go. Fralish kept questioning him about whether he wanted to stand and fight or try a breakthrough. He merely shook his head as if greatly puzzled and said over and over: "I don't know." Shortly after that, Lavell wandered off, somewhere into the darkness, and his troops never saw him again.

His departure took place while Fralish was getting the first section of Charley Battery deployed into a rice paddy 50 yards off the road.

Grinnell had got back to his men. There were at least two other stalwart spirits in this small party, M/S Leo G. Kelly and Cpl. Roland W. Clatterbuck. Whatever Grinnell wanted done, they were ready to carry out. What encouraged the three of them was that while there was steady fire from the flanking ridges, it was not biting deeply into the sides of the column. Unlike the Chinese which had borne down Baker Battery, the people opposing the Americans farther to the rear weren't nerved for a pinfall. But the volume of fire was building steadily, and within recent minutes rifles from the low ground had joined the four mortars and four to five ma-

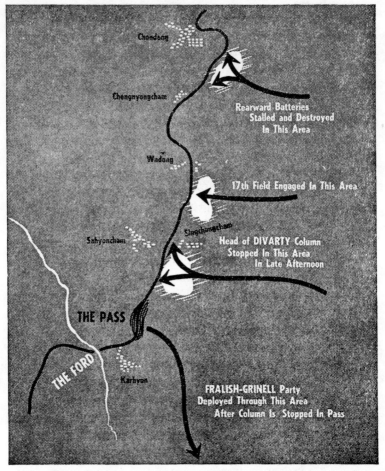

Chondong

Chongnyongcham

Rearward Batteries
Stalled and Destroyed
In This Area

Wadong

17th Field Engaged In This Area

Sahyoncham

Singchangcham

Head of DIVARTY Column
Stopped In This Area
In Late Afternoon

THE PASS

THE FORD

Karhyon

FRALISH-GRINELL Party
Deployed Through This Area
After Column Is Stopped In Pass

ARTILLERY MOVEMENT THROUGH GAUNTLET

chine guns which were shooting at the road from the more distant hills.

Grinnell was still reflecting on his big idea; lacking authority, he still decided to go ahead with it, using persuasion. He sought out Capt. Simon J. Stevens of Able Battery, 82nd AA Battalion, and in him found a kindred spirit. Stevens had taken a swing along the column to see how it was enduring the Chinese fire; he had counted twenty vehicles already set ablaze. Grinnell told him he believed the only way to save the column was to get the flak wagons forward and start shooting. Stevens needed no urging. He was looking only for a way to help. He picked out three Quad-50s and two Twin-40s and led them out. Grinnell rode along. On passing Love Company, Grinnell told Kelly to round up the men and jump aboard the AA vehicles. He didn't want to lose track of them, and he reflected that a few riflemen might be needed up front later. Though it was a tight squeeze, they managed to double past the stalled vehicles.

Before placing the 155s in the paddy field, Fralish had had the same flash inspiration as Grinnell. While the pieces were going into position, he sent Lieut. Oleg V. Warneke to find Stevens and bring the flak wagons forward. Warneke met the Stevens-Grinnell task force not far back; it was under full steam and proceeding toward the fire.

In the paddy field, Fralish was ready next the No. 1 gun. Charley Battery had some LMGs and he had put one on either side of the piece, besides deploying to his right eight men armed with carbines. Fralish personally bore-sighted the 155 toward the enemy machine gun, which he judged to be about 70 yards away. The No. 1 man stood with him between the trails as the big howitzer opened fire.

They got off three rounds. As the third shell emitted, Fralish saw the No. 1 man fall, and thought he had been knocked down by the recoil. He reached down to give him a hand. Only then he realized that the figure on the ground had no head. He saw a clean hole in the shield of the gun; suddenly everything was explained. At the exact instant of the flash, an enemy rocket round had struck, disabled the gun, pierced the shield and decapitated the man holding the lanyard.

There was no time for shock from this experience for just then Stevens and Grinnell arrived with the AA battery. In five minutes the lead M19 was at the head of the column. Fralish showed the gunner where he thought the machine gun was nesting which had felled O'Donnell. The multiple-barreled weapon cut loose, searing the foreground. After an interval, fire stopped and Fralish walked forward; he found a ruined gun and six dead Chinese beside it. Then he led the M19 past the gun, through a deep ditch, and back onto the road, with the other four flak wagons grouped close behind it. He, Warneke, and Grinnell then instructed the gun crews; they were to keep moving, firing forward and to the flanks as they moved, with the lead vehicle aiming ahead and the others alternately searing the flanks. They need not have worried; Stevens already had the idea and his crews were well in hand.

But one particular thought oppressed Fralish. If Lavell was so off balance about other things, he might have been wrong in saying that O'Donnell was dead. Fralish ran back to see. O'Donnell was conscious, though terribly wounded and in great pain. He was taking it gallantly and made light of his condition as Fralish talked to him. Fralish wanted to find a medic; but he was also under the urge to prod the other vehicles forward to where they could form behind the flak wagons. He started rearward on this dual mission. Meantime, Warneke came back, wrapped O'Donnell in a blanket, carried him forward, and lashed him with ropes to the front of the lead M19. That was how O'Donnell rode through the gauntlet and by some miracle survived.

By beating the bushes, these three musketeers, Grinnell, Fralish, and Warneke, got about thirty-five vehicles lined up behind the AA guns ready to make the break. Their hope was that when the elements rearward saw that the road was being opened and traffic was moving, they would fall in behind the battering ram and follow along. But it was a dim hope.

Looking north, Fralish saw vehicles burning far into the distance. He heard grenades exploding and knew that the Chinese had at last closed directly on the road. There was a wild blowing of bugles which continued on and on. Mortar rounds of white phosphorus were exploding frequently onto the roadway. The rattle of small-arms fire had become incessant.

He felt he could not prolong the round-up indefinitely with any hope of saving his own contingent and the guns protecting them. The task had been hard enough. Already he had shaken loose several jeeps and trucks wherein the driver was sitting dead at the wheel and the other riders were too weary or shocked to note or to replace him. He had carried the bodies to the roadside and then manhandled some other individual to behind the steering wheel. To all others, he had kept shouting, "You will keep moving and keep firing," until his voice was about gone. It was time to start.

Grinnell spread Love Company—twenty men—as skirmishers on both sides of the road, and with the ack-ack leading, the convoy started at a walking pace. Above the rattle of the guns, Grinnell found that it was impossible to make the gunners hear him as he shouted directions while moving with his own line across the paddy fields. So he hopped aboard one of the M19s and, when the convoy drew fire from the ridges, he told the flak gunners where to return it. But it was all too slow. By the time the column had advanced 600 yards in this manner, the leaders knew that the pace itself was compounding the danger from the flank fire. They decided to mount up and barrel down the road as fast as the run could be made. They still expected that the right-of-way would be fairly clear of any impediment or block, as they knew nothing about the struggle of the earlier serials.

For perhaps another thousand yards they made good speed. Then they slowed as they came to the first wrecked convoy. They saw the smoldering and ditched vehicles and the debris littering the roadway. The flak wagons blistered the ridges on both sides of the road. Grinnell walked forward to take a close look at the scene of the pillage. He saw that the Chinese had systematically laid sleeping bags spaced out and crosswise of the road. But in the interstices of this corduroy there were also American wounded, lying flat across the road. It looked as if the enemy had dragged bags and men to this position, either to force a column halt or compel the American vehicles to bray their own wounded. Each ack-ack unit had a one-ton trailer behind it; the wounded were loaded thereon. The convoy had to inch forward while the clearing was done, but the guns continued to pound the hills, and the enemy made little reply.

That was a break for one group. Corporal Weatherford and the score of men with him who had escaped the ambush at this spot were still holed up in the ravine to the left of the road, waiting for help to arrive. They had just decided to take off cross-country when they saw the flak wagons come toward them sweeping the ridges. Said Weatherford: "It was a wonderful sight. Until then, the Chinese on the ridges opposite us were riding high and seemed to be increasing in number. When the ack-ack hit them, they subsided completely." The party ran back to the road and jumped aboard the convoy.

At least thirty minutes were spent in clearing the wounded from this one block, Sergeant Kelly taking the lead in the work. He had no blankets or other material in which to wrap them, but stacked deep as they were, body heat possibly helped. It was about 2230 when the convoy got rolling again.

After a time they passed that part of the column which had been wrecked in late afternoon, several miles short of "The Pass." The signs of pillage were as before, but here there were no American wounded. One thing made Grinnell's heart sink. The convoy passed successively the ruined MP vehicles, two abandoned tanks, several radio jeeps, and about ten Division HQ trucks and jeeps; the farther they went, the higher the echelon which had been hit. It came to these men, like a punch on the button, that the whole division must have been destroyed and they were the only remaining contingent with a chance of escape.

When they came to a vehicle, or series of hulks, which barred the road, all hands unloaded to join in the ditching so that no time would be lost. As they weaved in and out through the wreckage, sometimes careening against parts of it, almost no fire came against the front of the column. The ack-ack was doing its stuff; during the entire run to "The

Pass," the lead vehicles felt nothing except a sprinkling of rifle fire and three 3.5 bazooka rounds which hit nothing vital. The CCF reaction was as if they had concluded by this time that what remained of the division was blocked solid and nothing else would come via the road. For their forces still held the hills. The fire of the ack-ack alerted them, and they cut loose with rifles and machine guns in double doses against the tail of the column. But they had taken to the ridge tops and most of the fire was high.

As they topped the divide within "The Pass" (it was then in the early hours of morning) Grinnell stopped the column. "The Pass" itself was relatively quiet, though one mortar and a few rifles were popping away from somewhere upslope. It was the scene beyond which gave Grinnell pause. Karhyon was burning from end to end and the glare lighted the whole east facing of the ridge; there the countryside seemed to be swarming with Chinese, moving out in all directions like ants teeming from a bed. From east of the village a 76-mm gun was firing toward the south exit.

Captain Stevens came forward; he had been jeeping along in the rear to keep the convoy closed up over the greater part of the distance. A council of war was held. Capt. Charles S. Barbour, S2 of the 503rd, had a map of the area. Fralish had a compass. They got down under a blanket and by the glow of a cigarette lighter studied the course which should be taken to get to Sunchon by cutting across the ridges. Since the wounded couldn't walk in any case, it was decided to send them in the vehicles past the village, leaving only the driver and a couple of guards aboard each unit. The able-bodied would strike off cross-country, thereby lightening the vehicles and giving the wounded a better chance. Stevens would take over the flak wagons, run them out first, and plaster Karhyon as he passed. There were about 100 men in the column which formed to go afoot.

At that point Fralish said: "I'm only a field artilleryman; it's time for the infantry to do some leading." Grinnell answered: "I guess that means me." He moved up the embankment on the left of the road with the men following him single file.

Stevens had a relatively simple yet dangerous job to do, and he went to it as promptly as he could get his column organized. The conflagration in Karhyon lit up the country far beyond the ford and put a spotlight on everything moving via the road, once "The Pass" was left behind. There was no option but to trust once again in the dampering effect of the ack-ack. On emerging into the open the flak wagons turned their full power against the village and the ridge beyond it. The barrage was sustained for perhaps ten minutes, but the results were not entirely happy. Stevens was personally directing the work of the lead wagon. Bullet fire came against it from both sides of the road. He headed for the ford and splashed through it and up the south embankment without excessive difficulty. But behind him, his train was already two fighting vehicles less. One M16 driver missed the turnout to the ford and the vehicle did a dive into the black hole where once the bridge had stood. But it only dropped eight feet, its fall being cushioned by the wreckage of other vehicles which had made the same error. A second M16 was knocked out by enemy fire. Stevens went on a thousand yards and came to a friendly roadblock. He then doubled back to the ford and helped the final contingent of about forty wounded to clear through it. These were the last vehicles to get through "The Pass."

Grinnell and his rifle column had climbed the embankment to the ridge saddle while Stevens was forming his column and getting underway. When they gained the crest the party became unaccountably noisy; some of the men wanted to talk; others moved carelessly, making quite a clatter. Grinnell cautioned them but the racket continued. So he stopped the march and said that the group would stay on that spot until dawn came. But he didn't confide in them his other reason—in traversing the ridge folds he had already lost his bearings.

The decision promptly exploded in his hands. By a fluke, Stevens, in turning the guns of the Quad-50 against the ridge top after plastering the village, put his fire directly on Grinnell's men. They scattered like quail before a shotgun; whether any were killed by the fire is not known; the group dissolved as men ran pell-mell for cover. Individuals got out as best they could.

Corporal Clatterbuck was soon walking alone along one of the ridge trails. For perhaps an hour he wandered aimlessly. Then his senses told him that he was "being trailed stealthily by four or five guys." He sank down behind a rock, waited for them to come up, and then pointing his rifle, challenged: "GIs or Chinks?" One man identified himself as a captain from 503rd. He said to Clatterbuck: "You say you're lost; well, what do you think I am?" They kept on walking, still with no idea in which direction they were moving. At last Clatterbuck heard a tank moving off in the distance and decided to guide on the sound. Some miles farther along his ear caught another—the noise of a truck being double-clutched. He said to the Captain: "We must be right; no Chink could do that." As dawn broke, they came to a highway, pocked with tank tracks. They studied the dust pattern, figured which way the tanks had been moving, and followed them until they met an American outpost.

Grinnell and Fralish got headed in the same direction when the ack-ack stampeded the party, and they picked up a few men as they moved along. Stevens' barrage had served one good purpose; they became reoriented on his line of fire. So they made a wide circle around Karhyon and, getting well to the east of it, started south for Sunchon. At 0500 the party had to stop and sleep for an hour; the men were completely spent. At dawn, from a high ridge, they looked back on Karhyon through field glasses and saw that it was now the site of a large enemy encampment, with many Chinese bivouacked in the nearby flat, and picket lines of Mongol ponies. To the east of the ridge where they observed, they saw another village, near it a road, and on the road a column of about seventy men moving northwest. Grinnell guessed they were Chinese. A flight of F-80s moved on the column as if to attack; but after circling several times, they flew away. For another hour Grinnell's party marched southeast. Again looking eastward they saw a body of men, this time heading south. A spotter plane was circling them and the men were waving. The truth gradually dawned that this was the same column seen earlier, and that they had been mistaken for Chinese only because, having lost direction, they were marching toward enemy country. With the addition of this column and other small groups, Grinnell shortly had 250 men.

They waded the Taedong River; it was waist-deep and crusted with ice. Soon afterward, a liaison plane landed next them on a sand bar, bringing a map, four cases of "C" rations, five gallons of water, and first-aid supplies. The men had worked for half an hour clearing the sand bar of boulders so that the plane could put down. When it took off, the two worst cases among the wounded were aboard. That left about forty wounded still with the column. But one touch from a friendly hand made all the difference; they took off with lightened step on the trail to Sunchon.

In this way, the first group of so-called "stragglers" returned to the division. It was but one incident among hundreds, each having its own special torment. Those who traveled the fastest probably had the best fortune. Many who came out late could recall almost nothing of what had happened to them.

As to men and guns, the statistics of loss in the gauntlet fight have no place in this narrative. In any case, they cannot be stated with precision. At Valley Forge, in the birth struggle of a nation, but 3,000 of 7,000 Continentals died or faded from the force in one terrible winter. In round figures, the wasting away of the 2nd Division and its attachments is roughly comparable. But it all happened in one day.

The hospitals in the forward zone overflowed with its wounded. Captain Burla, who had collected many of them from the road, found on arriving at the 5th Cavalry Collecting Station south of Sunchon that there was no room for his charges. Already, there were 250 cases lying on the ground in the winter cold, waiting for their turn on the table. He continued on with his caravan to the 15th Medical Battalion, just north of Pyongyang. There, too, the patients were lying in queue, waiting for the doctor's hand. He was told to take his vans on to the city, where there was another hospital. Lieutenant Maxson, the assistant battalion surgeon, who had also salvaged men from the roadside ditches, witnessed the streaming of the wounded into Sunchon. Of the British aid station and the 5th Cavalry Station he said: "I have never seen doctors work more heroically." More than 400 cases had been attended by morning. The waiting line still had not grown less.

That was on December 1. By Christmas Day, 2nd Division was again a going concern, en route to a new battlefield. Its swift flight upward from its own ashes, even more than this story of struggle, bespeaks the character, courage, and faith of those who survived and the others still missing.

## Map Symbols

|  |  |
|---|---|
| → | Browning Automatic Rifle |
| •→ | Machinegun .30 caliber |
| •—•→ | Machinegun .50 caliber |
| < | Pair of machineguns |
| ←→ | Two machineguns, covering opposite slopes |
| •••→ | Recoilless Rifle |
| ◆ | Tank |
| ■▬ | Mortar |
| ⇌ | Artillery |
| ⌒▥▥ | Entrenched Artillery Battery |
| ✖ | Roadblock |
| • • • • • | Fox holes |
| ⊠ | Command Post |
| ⊓⊓⊓⊓ | Defensive Perimeter |
| ⌐⌐⌐⌐⌐ | Contracted Perimeter |

# Glossary of Main Weapons

1. *The M1, also called the Garand.* The basic arm of the infantry company. A semiautomatic rifle, it fires as long as the trigger is pressed back. The rifle is gas-operated, loads an eight-round .30-caliber clip, and weighs 9½ pounds. The full-strength company (211 men) carries 132 M1 rifles.

2. *The carbine.* Fires a lighter .30-caliber bullet than the M1, with far less range and stopping power. It is a full automatic weapon and weighs 6 pounds. Its 30-round clip feeds cartridges into the chamber much like a machine gun. There are 37 carbines in the full-strength rifle company.

3. *The Browning automatic rifle* (BAR). A sixteen-pound weapon which may be fired from the hip or shoulder, or from a bipod. It can be operated one shot at a time. When fired full automatic, it will put out upwards of 500 .30-caliber rounds per minute. Each infantry division has 412 BARs. There is one or more in each rifle squad, and group fire develops largely around BAR action.

4. *The light .30-caliber Browning machine gun* (LMG). Air-cooled, the LMG can fire up to 500 rounds per minute. With its metal shoulder stock, pistol grip, and bipod, it is a load slightly more than 32 pounds, exclusive of ammunition. The LMG is an infantry platoon weapon and its relatively light weight makes it invaluable in hill country fighting.

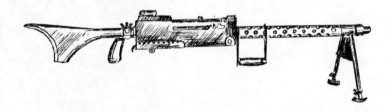

5. *The heavy .30-caliber Browning machine gun* (HMG). This weapon is fought from a tripod. It can outshoot the LMG by about 100 rounds per minute and because of its water-cooling system can sustain action for much longer periods. Also, the effective range of the HMG triples that of the LMG. The heavy gun is part of the equipment of the weapons company within the infantry battalion. There are 500 machine guns of the two .30-caliber types within the infantry division.

6. *The .50-caliber Browning machine gun.* Has a heavy barrel which enables it to fire long bursts even though it is air-cooled. Because of its weight (82 pounds) the .50-caliber gun is usually mounted on one of the larger transport vehicles and rarely figures in ridge-top perimeter defense. The gun fires up to 575 rounds per minute. There are 350 of them in the infantry division.

7. *The 3.5 bazooka.* (Inside diameter of the launcher is 3.5 inches.) Fires an 8½-pound rocket which contains a hollow-shaped charge in its warhead. The shaped charge is an explosive so arranged that its blast can be concentrated against a very small area. The aluminum 3.5 launcher weighs 15 pounds, but for efficient use is customarily handled by a two-man team. The big launcher has largely replaced the 2.36-inch bazooka, possessing double its armor-piercing power. There are now about 600 launchers within the infantry division, 80 per cent of which are 3.5s. The large rocket has a maximum range of several hundred yards. But to be sure of killing medium tanks, the team has to move to within 70 yards or less of the target.

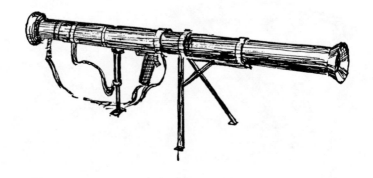

8. *The 57- and 75-mm recoilless rifles.* Along with their big brother, the 105-mm, these are a new family of infantry-carried artillery. They fire conventional shells on a flat trajectory over ranges far in excess of the reach of bazooka fire. In the recoilless rifles, the propellent gases escape via a breech device in the rear which creates a danger area from back blast behind the rifle, but eliminates recoil. That factor enables the 57-mm to be fired from the shoulder. Because of its weight (105 pounds) the 75-mm rifle is fired from a tripod. Within the infantry division are 120 of the two lighter types. The 105-mm—a new development—did not figure in the Battle of the Chongchon. Both lighter rifles have proved invaluable in Korea in the elimination of enemy hilltop bunkers.

9. *The infantry mortars.* These come in three sizes, 60-mm, 81-mm, and 4.2-inch. The mortar is a simple sealed-breech tube supported by a base plate. It is uniquely useful for lobbing shells at a high angle against targets which cannot be reached by direct fire because of intervening terrain or some other obstacle. Its main purpose is the killing of enemy personnel. The projectile is dropped in the muzzle of the mortar. It carries its own propelling charge in powder bags around its fins as well as the primer charge, which fires on striking the pin in the base of the tube. The lightest of the mortar family, the 60-mm, is an integral weapon invariably going into position with the rifle company. The 81-mm, which fires a 7½-pound shell up to 4,000 yards, weighs 107 pounds and is, therefore, not manageable on long foot marches through hill country. The 4.2 batteries are handled by a mortar company within the infantry regiment.

10. *The Quad-50.* A wheeled vehicle mounting four .50-caliber Browning machine guns which may be either fired as a unit or operated singly. Initially, it was developed to shoot down planes, but in Korean operations it has come to the fore as one of the main supports of the infantry line. Its battery fire, bracketing the target and seemingly permitting of no escape, is the No. 1 demoralizer of enemy infantry. In one day's operation, one Quad may fire in excess of 100,000 rounds.

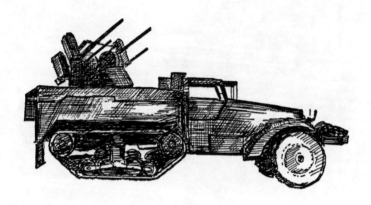

11. *The (Boffers) twin 40-mm.* Another antiaircraft weapon, this is frequently used in Korean operations to provide additional support directly to the infantry line. It is a highly mobile (35 mph) self-propelled dual mount and from the distance looks not unlike a tank.

## SIGNAL CORPS RADIOS

12. *SCR536.* A short range front-line platoon-to-company radio set, amplitude modulated (AM), weighing about ten pounds. It has fifty channels and a range of about one mile. It is being replaced by the AN/PRC-6.

13. *SCR300.* A short range front-line company-to-battalion packset. Its range is one to three miles. It is frequency modulated (FM), has forty channels and weighs about forty pounds. It is being replaced by the AN/PRC-10.

14. *SCR609/610.* A short range radio used for artillery battery fire direction from observation posts or liaison planes and for general communication between vehicles. Man-transported, it operates from a battery pack, weighs 56 pounds and is designated the SCR609. In vehicles, it operates from a power pack, weighs 120 pounds, and is the SCR610. It is an FM radio, has 120 channels, with two preset, and has a range of about five miles. It was replaced by the SCR619, which is being replaced, in turn, by the AN/PRC-9.

15. *SCR619.* Same use as the SCR609/610. The range is about five miles and it is an FM set. It weighs 52 pounds operated as a manpack set or 165 as a vehicular set and has 120 channels, two preset.

16. *SCR608.* A vehicular command set for short range use, primarily by artillery. An FM set, its range is ten miles moving or fifteen miles stationary. It has 120 channels and weighs 181 pounds. It is being replaced by the AN/GRC-5.

# Index